New Hebrews

The literature on Zionism as a political ideology is extensive, but this book takes a different approach by focusing on the cultural dimensions of the movement and their profound impact on the history of Israel and the Jewish people. *New Hebrews* explores the cultural history of Zionism, starting from the meeting of the First Zionist Congress in Basel in 1897, and culminating with the establishment of the state of Israel fifty-one years later, in 1948. Yaron Peleg explores how innovative approaches in language, literature, architecture, art, music, and body culture transformed modern Jewish culture. His study delves into the contentious facets of early Zionist culture, such as colonialism, social engineering, minority discourse, and Jewish–Arab relations. *New Hebrews* presents an interdisciplinary examination of nationalism, drawing from a diverse array of primary sources to uncover the psychology of modern Israel. This title is also available as open access on Cambridge Core.

YARON PELEG is Kennedy-Leigh Professor in Modern Hebrew Studies at the University of Cambridge. His monographs include *Directed by God: Jewishness in Contemporary Israeli Film and Television* (2016) and *Israeli Culture between the Two Intifadas* (2008). He is co-editor of numerous scholarly anthologies, including *New Directions in Israeli Media, Film, Television & Digital Content* (2025), with Eran Kaplan and Ido Rosen.

New Hebrews

Making National Culture in Zion

YARON PELEG
University of Cambridge

CAMBRIDGE
UNIVERSITY PRESS

Shaftesbury Road, Cambridge CB2 8EA, United Kingdom

One Liberty Plaza, 20th Floor, New York, NY 10006, USA

477 Williamstown Road, Port Melbourne, VIC 3207, Australia

314–321, 3rd Floor, Plot 3, Splendor Forum, Jasola District Centre, New Delhi – 110025, India

103 Penang Road, #05–06/07, Visioncrest Commercial, Singapore 238467

Cambridge University Press is part of Cambridge University Press & Assessment, a department of the University of Cambridge.

We share the University's mission to contribute to society through the pursuit of education, learning and research at the highest international levels of excellence.

www.cambridge.org
Information on this title: www.cambridge.org/9781009591478

DOI: 10.1017/9781009591430

© Yaron Peleg 2025

This publication is in copyright. Subject to statutory exception and to the provisions of relevant collective licensing agreements, with the exception of the Creative Commons version the link for which is provided below, no reproduction of any part may take place without the written permission of Cambridge University Press & Assessment.

An online version of this work is published at doi.org/10.1017/9781009591430 under a Creative Commons Open Access license CC-BY-NC 4.0 which permits re-use, distribution and reproduction in any medium for non-commercial purposes providing appropriate credit to the original work is given and any changes made are indicated. To view a copy of this license visit https://creativecommons.org/licenses/by-nc/4.0

When citing this work, please include a reference to the DOI 10.1017/9781009591430

First published 2025

Front cover illustration of Judah Maccabee by Tzvi Livni (Malevanchik) from a collection of stories for children, *The Chain of Heroism* (שלשלת הגבורה). Israel Museum, Illustration Library, courtesy of Ilana Gil.

Printed in the United Kingdom by CPI Group Ltd, Croydon CR0 4YY

A catalogue record for this publication is available from the British Library

Library of Congress Cataloging-in-Publication Data
Names: Peleg, Yaron author
Title: New Hebrews : making national culture in Zion / Yaron Peleg.
Description: New York : Cambridge University Press, 2025. | Includes bibliographical references and index.
Identifiers: LCCN 2025004089 | ISBN 9781009591478 hardback | ISBN 9781009591423 paperback | ISBN 9781009591430 ebook
Subjects: LCSH: Zionism | Zionism in literature | Zionism in art
Classification: LCC DS149 .P4225 2025 | DDC 956.94–dc23/eng/20250305
LC record available at https://lccn.loc.gov/2025004089

ISBN 978-1-009-59147-8 Hardback

Cambridge University Press & Assessment has no responsibility for the persistence or accuracy of URLs for external or third-party internet websites referred to in this publication and does not guarantee that any content on such websites is, or will remain, accurate or appropriate.

Contents

List of Figures	*page*	vi
Acknowledgments		viii
Introduction		1
1 Modern Hebrew Language and Literature		7
2 Hebrew Space and Architecture		33
3 A New Hebrew Body		69
4 A New Hebrew Festival Calendar		99
5 New Hebrew Aesthetics		127
6 New Hebrew Sounds		161
Afterword		190
Bibliography		197
Index		204

Figures

2.1	The first Templer colony in Haifa, before 1874.	*page* 38
2.2	Rosh Pina, around 1896.	40
2.3	Kibbutz Bet Alfa, around 1950.	41
2.4	The restored yard in Merchavia, 1937.	45
2.5	Hatzar Kinneret, 1912.	46
2.6	Degania, 1918.	47
2.7	Kibbutz Nir David, 1946.	50
2.8	Rothschild Boulevard, Tel Aviv, 1911.	65
2.9	Rothschild Boulevard, Tel Aviv, 1930s.	67
2.10	Rothschild Boulevard, Tel Aviv, late 1930s.	67
3.1	A Zionist pioneer, 1937.	76
3.2	Hamizrahi rabbis, Poland, 1919.	77
3.3	Zionist pioneers, 1920.	77
3.4	Pioneers, Kibbutz Gal-On, 1946.	78
3.5	Female pioneers, Merchavia, 1917.	82
3.6	Female pioneers, 1930s.	82
3.7	A Yemeni Jewish family, near the Sea of Galilee, 1910s.	84
3.8	Cossacks, 1855–1860.	88
3.9	Armed Bedouin, nineteenth century.	88
3.10	Members of Hashomer, Merchavia, 1913.	88
3.11	Zipora Zaïd, late 1920s/early 1930s.	91
3.12	Baruch Agadati performs a dance based on Hasidic motifs, ca. 1924.	95
3.13	Baruch Agadati performs a dance based on Arab motifs, late 1920s.	95
3.14	Agriculture students dancing the Hora, 1946.	96
4.1	Judah Maccabee, by Tzvi Livni, 1946	104
4.2	Lyla Tchertkov, Tel Aviv Purim beauty pageant queen, 1926.	108
4.3	Rekieta Chelouch, Tel Aviv Purim beauty pageant queen, 1927.	109

List of Figures vii

4.4 Zipora Tzabari, Tel Aviv Purim beauty pageant queen, 1928. 109
4.5 Hannah Meyuhas-Polani, Tel Aviv Purim beauty pageant queen, 1929. 110
4.6 Omer festival, Kibbutz Ramat Yohanan, 1940s. 123
4.7 Agriculture students with Tu Bishvat produce, Haifa, 1932. 124
5.1 Second Zionist Congress, Basel, 1898. 128
5.2 Drawing by Ephraim Moses Lilien, 1902. 129
5.3 Hanukkah menorah, Bezalel, 1920s. 132
5.4 Ze'ev Raban, poster, 1929. 135
5.5 Nahum Gutman, *Tiberias*, 1926. 136
5.6 Reuven Rubin, *Jerusalem*, 1925. 138
5.7 Itzhak Danziger, *Nimrod*, 1939. 140
5.8 Ruschkewitz, illustration for *To Children's Land*, 1939. 145
5.9 Ruschkewitz, depiction of Tel Aviv in *To Children's Land*, 1939. 145
5.10 Nahum Gutman, *The Beginning of Tel Aviv*, 1959. 147
5.11 Zoltan Kluger, *Workers Coming Home after Work in the Fields*, 1940s 150
5.12 German Youth Aliyah members dancing the Hora, Kibbutz Ein Harod, 1936. 151
5.13 Helmar Lerski, *Jemenit*, 1930s. 152
5.14 Shamir Bros, cigarette advertisement, 1948–1949. 154
5.15 Frank-Ruhl font, 1924. 156
5.16 Haim font, designed by Pesach Ir-Shay. 157
5.17 Elly Gross, book jacket, 1944. 158
5.18 Haruvi, sage plant, from *The Botanist's Brush*, 1923. 159
6.1 Idelsohn's rendition of the first notes of "Hatikvah," 1912. 165
6.2 Choir, Kibbutz Gan Shmuel, 1945. 180

Acknowledgments

This book began as a lecture at the University of Nanjing, where I was invited in 2019 by my colleague, Professor Lihong Song, to speak to his students. A year later, Prof Song Invited me again to Nanjing, this time to give a graduate seminar based on that lecture. By the end of it, he suggested that I turn the seminar into a book. Both the lecture and the seminar were based on a course I developed and had been teaching at the University of Cambridge, mostly to students of Arabic. I mention these audiences, Chinese students, and Arabists because none is typical of people who usually engage in this subject. It's a difference that shaped a book which tries to do two things at once: to introduce a familiar subject to people who are not too familiar with it; and to speak about a fraught subject with caution. I hope I have managed it. Since some of the cultural aspects the book deals with are outside my usual remit, such as civic culture, architecture, art, and music, I want to thank generous colleagues and friends who read versions of this book and advised me, including Hizky Shoham, Haim Yacobi, Derek Penslar, Vincenzo Vergiani, Yirmi Pinkus, Yair Qedar, Raz Kohn, Ruth Cats, and Assaf Shelleg, who has been especially generous with his time and attention. I also want to thank my long-time friend and colleague Eran Kaplan, whose wisdom continues to inspire me. My harshest critic by far was my partner, Thiago, who argued passionately about the thorny issues this book raises. The fact that many of these issues were new to him challenged me and made me look at them afresh. I hope the book is better for it.

I also want to thank the dedicated staff of the Beit Ariela Public Library in Tel Aviv, especially Olga Filatova, the archivist of the Felicja Blumental Music Center and Library in Tel Aviv, who has been extremely kind and generous with her knowledge and time and helped me navigate the rich sea of materials in her care. Orna Granot from the Illustration Library, Youth Section at the Israel Museum was also very helpful, as was Rotem Kaplan from the Shenkar College archive.

Introduction

The Zionist claim to Palestine was based on a very old story: so old that it became a myth. And since the distance between the Jewish present and the Jewish past was vast, the wish to make Palestine a home for a modern Jewish nation called for creating that nation anew. It was an immense claim that required an equally immense innovation. Zionist ideology took it upon itself to do that, to recreate Jews as a modern nation by canceling the culture of the Jewish Diaspora and at the same time preserving parts of it in the spirit of New Hebraism. This book explains why and how this daring experiment came about.[1]

Zionist culture was not only premeditated, during its formative years it was continuously debated and closely monitored for ideological fitness. Two events bracket this formative period and define it historically: the meeting of the First Zionist Congress in Basel, Switzerland, in 1897; and the establishment of the state of Israel fifty-one years later, in 1948. The Zionist Congress marks the initial push for the creation of a Jewish national community in Palestine–Eretz Israel. Its recognition by the international community as the state of Israel in 1948 marks the end of that period.

Cultural engineering is not unique to Zionism. Modern nationalism is based on the ideological molding of human groups into distinct communities. Zionism was simply an intensive example of a change that began in the modern era in Europe, whence it spread to the rest of the world, often by force. The violence that usually accompanies nationalism gave rise to Zionism first and foremost because of the difficult

---

[1] On the singularity of this experiment see the political philosopher Eyal Chowers, who credits it to a unique moment in Jewish history, a moment of temporal crisis, as he calls it, that can serve "as a springboard for reflection on the temporal imaginations of modernity" more generally. See the introduction to his book, *The Political Philosophy of Zionism: Trading Jewish Words for a Hebraic Land*, Cambridge University Press, 2012.

2   *Introduction*

conditions the national idea created for European Jews: a condition commonly referred to as the Jewish Problem.

The Jewish Problem

Europe's so-called Jewish Problem intensified during the nineteenth century following changes to the legal and civil status of Jews at the time. With the spread of liberalism after the French Revolution and Napoleon's campaigns, European society opened up to its minoritized Jews, who until then had been excluded from full participation in it. One by one, European societies began to admit Jews as equal members into the various nation-states that took shape on the continent. However, while there was increasing willingness to include Jews as part of various national communities, the growing familiarity with them in Western, Central, and finally in Eastern Europe also bred a new kind of contempt. Unlike the former resentment toward Jews, which was mostly religious in nature, the Age of Reason saw the development of a resentment that was couched in pseudo-scientific terminology, an antipathy based on alleged racial differences between Jewish and Christian Europeans.

The new antagonism toward Jews was shaped by four major revolutions, which came to define European modernity during the nineteenth century: the secular revolution, the national revolution, the scientific revolution, and the gender revolution. All four gave rise to what came to be known as antisemitism. The secular revolution made the old religious antagonism toward Jews obsolete. The creation of the nation-state rebranded Jews as pariahs, an ultimate Other. The scientific revolution provided a rational framework for identifying Jewish difference. The gendering of the European bourgeoisie and the creation of the nuclear family as a way to ensure the stability of the new national community was another defining argument for singling out Jews. Toward the end of the nineteenth century, then, many Jews found themselves increasingly isolated within the new ethnic nation-states of Europe – isolated as a minority whose difference became progressively more problematic in various ways and to various degrees, depending on time and location.

Labeling Jews, especially Jewish men, as effeminate came to represent many of the prejudices against them. The label had a lasting influence on the formation and development of Zionism later. The pejorative

The Jewish Problem 3

meaning of the epithet was based on the longstanding bias against women, a prejudice that shaped the modern European middle class as well with its division into men, who work outside the home, and women, who stay inside. The contrasting ideal of a traditional Jewish society, which encouraged men to study while women worked to support them, even if it wasn't widely practiced, painted Jewish men as passive and effeminate. If we add to this the fact that few Jewish men engaged in traditionally masculine professions before the modern era – in the military, in politics, and in farming – and the legally subordinate status of Jews since late antiquity, we get a general image of Jews as passive, weak, and powerless.

The revolutionary idea of Zionism was to accept this power dynamic but to make it work for Jews, not against them. Since getting over these negative associations in Europe seemed impossible, Zionists suggested doing it by establishing a Jewish state outside the continent, in what they and fellow Europeans regarded as the Jewish ancestral land, the Land of Israel. By mimicking European non-Jewish culture, especially the assertive or manly sides of nationalism, Zionists hoped to shake off associations of passivity and effeminacy and prove the fitness of Jews, as individuals and as a community. They believed that the establishment of a sovereign state would prove the agency of Jews and their right to join other nations as equals on the world stage.

It is worth noting that Zionism was such an unusual solution for the problems Jews faced in modern times that it was never supported by a majority of them, either in the past or in the present. When European Jews found themselves increasingly displaced in a continent crowded by a growing number of new nations, many of them left. Between the 1880s and 1920s close to 3 million Jews left Europe. The majority headed to North America. As for millions of other European migrants at the time, financial and political security were the major reasons for moving. Ideology was a minor consideration for most migrants, Jews and non-Jews alike. The number of Jews who went to Palestine increased only after the United States imposed immigration quotas in 1924. Even today, the majority of the world's Jews reside outside the state of Israel.

At the same time, from shortly after its establishment in 1948 Israel came to represent world Jewry, for Jews and non-Jews alike. International politics and military skill certainly played important roles in this transformation. But what this book suggests is that the cultural revolution of Zionism was at least as important for turning the ancient Jewish nation into a modern national community. By creating a distinctive new Jewish culture in Palestine, Zionists solved one of the most persistent challenges Jews faced in modernity, except that instead of an individual solution, such as assimilation or migration, Zionism came up with a communal program that turned it into a leading force in twentieth-century Jewish civilization. Politics was crucial in making sure Zionism survived, but it was culture that gave it a distinct shape and a specific meaning.

This book goes back to the first fifty years of Zionism and looks at the ideological crucible in which Israeli culture was forged. It traces the sources of Zionist culture, the premises that helped to create it, and the great passion that secured its success. But in doing so, the book also reflects on the unraveling of the Zionist vision today, the vision of a secular Jewish nation and of a unitary Jewish people, and the legacy of the violence that shaped it.

Most of the cultural innovations Zionists developed were reactions to various difficulties Jews met in their attempts to assimilate into a secular and increasingly nationalist Europe, where they eventually became pariahs. Again, the genius of Theodor Herzl as the founder of political Zionism was to turn this weakness into strength by suggesting that Jews establish a country of their own. Only in Palestine, claimed Herzl, would Jews become real Germans – that is, equal members in the (inter)national order.

In creating a modern Jewish nation in Palestine, early Zionists were inspired by many of the cultural sensibilities that were at play in the new nations of Europe during their formative years, values that were adapted to the realities of Palestine but included reworked elements from traditional Jewish culture at the same time. This book looks at six of those innovations, which became the core of the new Jewish culture in Palestine and later Israel.

- The first is language and literature, the attempt to turn book Hebrew, a language of devotion and law, into the language of a modern Hebrew literature and a modern Jewish life.
- The second is the creation of new space, farms, and towns that would embody Jewish sovereignty and the socialist values of early Zionism.
- The third is the creation of muscular Jews, the reshaping of diasporic Jews into strong and independent Jewish farmers and soldiers.

The Jewish Problem   5

- The fourth is the creation of a festival calendar that enshrined many of these innovations by emphasizing the ancient agricultural elements of Jewish festivals and the glory of the Jewish military past.
- The fifth is the creation of new Jewish aesthetic sensibilities and the development of a distinctly Jewish art.
- The sixth is the creation of nationally distinct music that infused Western music with Arab tunes and traditional Jewish ritual music.

The book looks closely at these innovations; it traces their origins and examines the transformations they went through under a passionate national ideology. In doing so, it highlights the central role of culture in modern nation formation and suggests how the kind of culture Zionists created early on – fiercely patriotic, defiant, and proud – has had a decisive influence on the development of the state of Israel and the directions it took after its establishment.

* * *

A few words on some of the unresolved issues that continue to complicate discussions about Zionism. The first is the complex relationship between Zionism and colonialism and the discourse of power it has engendered. Both have made it increasingly difficult to speak about Zionism without provoking extreme reactions. For the Jews of Europe, colonization began after the Enlightenment with the changes they accepted in order to integrate more easily into a European society that always thought of them as different. To shed their perception as Others, many Jews adopted new languages, clothing, customs, and tastes. It was not an easy transformation, but the Jews who chose it did so because of the reward it promised: the reward of becoming Europeans, or, as we would put it today, becoming white. This act of self-colonization predated the arrival of Zionists in Palestine, where tensions between West and East, origin and mimicry continue to occupy Israeli society to this very day.

This is partly why Zionism paid little attention to the inhabitants of the land they settled, the Arabs of Palestine, despite early and urgent calls to do so. Yitzhak Epstein warned his fellow Zionists about it as early as 1907. Epstein came to Palestine in 1886 and witnessed the high-handed way in which Jews who bought land in Palestine drove away Arab tenant farmers who had lived on that land for generations. "We seem to have forgotten one small thing," Epstein told his fellow Zionists in an essay he titled "An Unresolved Question" (שאלה נעלמה), "that

6   *Introduction*

there is another people in the land we desire, a people that had been living on it for hundreds of years and have no plans of leaving."[2] Most Zionists were too absorbed in their own revolution and too focused on Europe to heed such calls, and all but ignored the Arabs of Palestine.

Another issue is the role of women in a socialist movement that claimed to be egalitarian but in actuality replicated traditional gender roles and continued to marginalize women. In many ways this was exacerbated by the masculine anxiety Zionism inherited from a European nationalism that usually cast women in supporting roles.

Yet another issue is the role of non-Ashkenazi or non-European Jews in the formation of Zionism. As a national movement, Zionism originated in Europe in response to a set of challenges that were unique to Jews there and as a solution for these challenges. Non-Ashkenazi Jews related to Zionism differently and began subscribing to it later because they lived otherwise. As a result, relatively few of them were involved in the formation of the movement in ways that were compounded by the differences between West and East.

A last point worth remembering is the vast difference in the condition of Jews at both ends of the twentieth century. At the beginning of the 1900s Jews were at the bottom of the power hierarchy in Europe as a community, especially in the eastern parts of the continent, where most of them lived. The Holocaust was a devastating example of this power dynamic. By the end of the century Jews had gained significant power in the state of Israel and in the United States, where most of them now live. Although early Zionists could not have imagined this enormous change, Zionism was devised in the hope of bringing it about. Any consideration of the movement needs to take this difference into account.

Finally, many of the issues this book raises have been studied in depth elsewhere. It is not meant to replace any of those valuable studies. Instead, it brings them together in a singular combination that highlights the intensity of the cultural revolution Zionists staged, a revolution so fervent that it altered the course of Jewish history and set in motion one of the most enduring transformations in a century crowded with radical changes.

---

[2] For the essay see https://benyehuda.org/read/38385.

1 | *Modern Hebrew Language and Literature*

Jewish immigrants who approached the coast of Palestine by sea were deeply moved by their first glimpse of the legendary land.

The land of Israel! Can you see it ... ?

Behind the dark mist above the mountains a bright red light began to rise and paint the sky a delicate purple that filled the air with soft pale light, as in a dream. There was an awesome stillness, no wind, no waves. A moment later the mountain tops caught fire, great big glowing embers that sent sparks into the heavens. And then the sun burst out of the depth with a mighty force and great speed, young, vigorous, burning with deep, pure, blinding brilliance. Dark reddish clouds floated above and then vanished one by one like melting snow. The sky cleared, and the air radiated silently, steeped in the soft, sweet warmth of dawn. The small group of people on the ship's deck stood as if spellbound. Mr Cederbaum was the only one who broke the silence.

- But this is our sun! he called out with excitement and awe at the bright sun ... - Our sun, the sun of our fathers, the sun of the land of Israel, our land, the sun that had shone here in the days of Abraham! Our sun has risen!

This is an excerpt from a 1938 novel, *The Days of the Messiah*, which Y. D. Berkowitz wrote in a vibrant Hebrew that could hardly have been imagined a few decades earlier. Hebrew never died, but for almost two millennia it was a religious language confined to books of prayer and legal texts. Few people used it outside of that context – the poetic tradition of Spanish Jews in the Middle Ages was a brilliant exception – and fewer still spoke it. And so the Zionist decision to return to Hebrew was neither obvious nor predetermined. Theodor Herzl, for instance, believed that the Hebrew language was antiquated and unfit for modern national life. "Who among us knows Hebrew well enough

8   *Modern Hebrew Language and Literature*

to ask for a train ticket in that language?" he famously quipped.[1] He later changed his mind and even tried to learn Hebrew, though he remained uncommitted to the future of Hebrew and thought people should decide for themselves which would be the "precious homeland of their thoughts," as he put it.[2]

At the same time, the role of Hebrew in the Zionist revolution was probably a historical imperative. First, because nationalism was preoccupied with origin and heritage. Second, because the cultural genealogy of Jews was tied to the Hebrew language as a proof and as a symbol of their antiquity. But the process wasn't simple and took more than a century.

Most historians locate the beginning of modern Israeli Hebrew in the Jewish Enlightenment, the Haskala, of the nineteenth century and the new uses it found for Hebrew. A neat idea, but not necessarily accurate. The Modern Hebrew of the Haskala is different from Israeli Hebrew and developed in response to a specific set of circumstances. Jewish nationalism was not one of them. In fact, the opposite was true. Paradoxically, the modern chapter in the history of Hebrew began as a way to ease the integration of Jews into non-Jewish society in order to enable them to eventually forget about Hebrew and other identifying markers that set them apart from non-Jews. At the same time, the linguistic creativity of Haskala writers and the modern Hebrew literature they composed was an important evolutionary stage in the history of contemporary Hebrew, even if it was unintended, and even if we can only say so in retrospect.

The Haskala was a belated Jewish Age of Reason that advocated liberty, tolerance, religious and political freedom, and a belief in scientific progress, ideas which allowed Jews to integrate into European society for the first time since the Roman era. And since most Jews had until then lived in separate communities of faith, the work of the first *maskilim*, the proponents of Haskala, focused on eliminating the barriers that separated Jews from non-Jews.

---

[1] The quip appears in Herzl's political pamphlet: Theodor Herzl, *Der Judenstaat*, 1896, available at Project Gutenberg, www.gutenberg.org/files/25282/25282-h/25282-h.htm.

[2] Shimon A. Shur. "The Complete Return to Hebrew and the Israeli-Zionist Nation-Building: A Bibliographical Essay," *Jewish Studies* (מדעי היהדות) 36 (1996): 73–107, available at www.jstor.org/stable/23381998, p. 75.

Modern Hebrew Language and Literature 9

Language was the biggest of those barriers, for while Jews had lived outside the Land of Israel since antiquity – they had settled in Babylon(ia) in the sixth century BCE and in Athens in the third – they tended to develop separate Jewish languages. In Europe it was Ladino and Yiddish. Both languages were based on local idioms – Ladino on Spanish, Yiddish on German – but they were written in the Hebrew alphabet. It was a peculiar practice, perhaps, that promoted communal cohesion amongst Jews, who tended to be geographically dispersed. But it also set Jews apart. Despite living side by side in many towns throughout the Pale of Settlement, a swath that stretched across Europe from the Baltic to the Black Sea, Jews and non-Jews barely communicated. "Ivan!" shouts the rabbi in Bialik's story "The Short Friday," moments before his drunk sled driver hurls the two of them into a snowbank. The learned rabbi has lived among Russian speakers his entire life, but knows only one word in that language, the name of his Gentile driver.

Language, then, almost immediately became one of the most urgent matters for *maskilim*. Until the end of the nineteenth century literacy levels among Jews were relatively high, particularly among Jewish men, who had some form of religious education. But like the rabbi in Bialik's short story, Jewish literacy was limited almost exclusively to Jewish languages: Hebrew for rituals and religious study, and several vernaculars such as Yiddish, Ladino, and Judeo-Arabic for everyday use.

Maskilim who wanted to spread their ideas among their coreligionists were limited to the Jewish languages they knew. In Germany, where the Haskala began, it was either Yiddish or Hebrew. Yiddish was the most obvious choice because Hebrew was considered an elevated language of religion and law. Yiddish, on the other hand, was the language of everyday life and understood by all, including women, who were less proficient than men in Hebrew because they were barred from religious education. The *maskilim* chose to write in Hebrew – Biblical Hebrew, to be exact – the old and stylized language of the Bible. It was an odd choice.

Consider one of the first major projects of the Haskala, Moses Mendelssohn's *Bi'ur*, his translation of the Five Books of Moses from Hebrew into German, using Hebrew letters. Mendelssohn (1729–1786) was a pioneering *maskil*, who wanted to teach German to his fellow Jews so he could share the ideas of Enlightenment with them. Still, his choice of alphabet seems counterintuitive. If his goal was to teach Jews a new language that would give them access to the world around them, why use letters that represented their isolation? There were two

10   *Modern Hebrew Language and Literature*

good reasons for it. The first was the intimacy of Hebrew, which lent a familiar context to Mendelssohn's novel ideas and constructed a friendly Hebrew bridge on the way to enlightenment. The second was to appease a rabbinic establishment that was suspicious of the Enlightenment.[3]

Using the traditional layout of Rabbinic commentaries, Mendelssohn placed the original Hebrew text in the middle of the page and inserted the translation into Hebrew-German on the side:

Translation into German using Hebrew letters   Leviticus 27:34:
with Yiddish orthography (ע for 'e' and א for
'o' or 'a'):

(לד) דיזע זינד דיא גבאטי, וועלכי דר עוויגי אם בערג   (לד) אֵלֶּה הַמִּצְוֹת אֲשֶׁר צִוָּה
סיני דעם משה פיר דיא קינדר ישראלש   יְהֹוָה אֶת־מֹשֶׁה אֶל־בְּנֵי
אויפֿגעטראגן: יִשְׂרָאֵל בְּהַר סִינָי:

Transliterated into standard German, the text reads, "Diese sind die gebote, welche der Ewige am berg Sinai dem Moshe für die kinder Israels aufgetragen," or in English, "These are the commands that the Eternal commanded Moses for the Children of Israel on Mount Sinai."

The choice of Hebrew over Yiddish was also emotional. Hebrew was the language of Jewish origins, Jewish history, and a Jewish identity that spanned time and space. For many *maskilim*, however, Yiddish was the language of a minority, of subjugation, a language that stood for an antiquated way of life. Even Mendelssohn, a sophisticated linguist, thought Yiddish too plain to express the high ideas of the Enlightenment. *Maskilim* spoke of Yiddish as a jargon, an impure idiom that was unfit for refined cultural expression. It was a resentment that transferred to Zionism later.

The Hebrew of the Jewish Enlightenment

But if the choice was between Hebrew and Yiddish, why choose the antiquated language of the Hebrew Bible? Why not choose a more accessible idiom, such as Rabbinic Hebrew? Jews who knew some Hebrew were more familiar with its medieval varieties used in the Talmud, the most important legal codex in Judaism. Both versions of the Talmud, the Palestinian and the Babylonian, were composed in late

---

[3] Joshua A. Fishman, ed., *Readings in the Sociology of Jewish Languages*, Brill, 1985.

The Hebrew of the Jewish Enlightenment 11

antiquity and the early Middle Ages, and their Hebrew was influenced by Aramaic and other languages. But that was precisely the problem. *Maskilim* thought of Rabbinic Hebrew as a contaminated language that, like Yiddish, reflected an obsolete way of life.

As the *maskilim* saw it, Biblical Hebrew was both pure and ancient, and as such it accomplished two goals. It cleansed Jewish life of religious obscurantism, and it reminded Jews of past glories that even non-Jews acknowledged and respected. And it was timely too. The Haskala unfolded one hundred years after the Age of Reason, during the rise of nationalism. Ancient Hebrew emphasized the antiquity of the Jews just when other nations in Europe were scrambling to establish their own pedigrees.

The reference to the biblical kingdoms of Judea and Israel was not part of a political program to restore Jewish independence. Not yet. That would come later, with Zionism. Biblical Hebrew was a sentimental device. It gave Jews a greater sense of self-worth, and elevated them in the eyes of others. The idea was to look beyond the reduced Jewish present to a future that was inspired by a distinguished past, a vision that would allow Jews to enter non-Jewish society as equals.

In 1853 Abraham Mapu (1808–1867) captured these sentiments in his runaway bestselling novel *The Love of Zion* (אהבת ציון), a love story set in biblical times and written in Biblical Hebrew throughout. Historical novels are always about the present, not the past, and so the love story and its political context in the novel provide important clues to its agenda. The pastoral romance teaches about personal fulfillment through love; the religious reforms of King Josiah resonate with the reformative program of the Haskala. Mapu worked on the novel for nearly twenty years and used a literary technique called *shibutz* in Hebrew, roughly translated as "mosaics." He collected words, phrases, and names from the Hebrew Bible and rearranged them to create an entirely new text, a secular work of art that used a sacred language. The technique itself was not uncommon, in Hebrew as in other languages, though usually for shorter works such as letters or poetry. Mapu used it to write an entire novel. It was remarkable and unprecedented, a modern story that recalled the illustrious Jewish past and gave Jewish readers a sense of personal and communal agency.

Because Mapu restricted himself to the language of the Hebrew Bible and cherry-picked dramatic elements from well-known stories, readers of the novel get an uncanny impression that they are reading

12   *Modern Hebrew Language and Literature*

the holy book. Here is the opening to the novel, which draws on the book of Job, the book of Kings, stories of the patriarchs, and the story of the prophet Samuel:

איש היה בירושלים בימי אָחָז מלך יהודה ושמו יוֹרָם בן אֲבִיעֶזֶר, אלוף ביהודה ושר אלף, ויהי לו שדות וכרמים בכרמל ובשרון ועדרי צאן ובקר בבית לחם יהודה; ויהי לו כסף וזהב, היכלי שן וכל שכיות החמדה, ושתי נשים היו לו, שם האחת חַגִּית בת עִירָא, ושם השנית נַעֲמָה. ויאהב יורם את נעמה מאד, כי יפת תואר היא. ותקנא בה חגית צרתה ותכעיסנה, כי לחגית היו שני בנים ולנעמה לא היה ולד.

In the days of Ahaz, king of Judea, there was a man in Jerusalem named Yoram ben Aviezer, a chieftain in Judea and captain of a thousand, he had fields and vineyards in Carmel and Sharon as well as sheep and cattle in Bethlehem of Judea, he also had silver and gold, ivory palaces, and lovely crafts, and he had two wives, one named Hagit daughter of Ira, the other named Na'ama. Yoram loved Na'ama very much for she was beautiful. Hagit, her rival, was jealous of her and tormented her, for she had two sons and Na'ama had no child.

The Love of Zion	Biblical Source[4]	English Translation
איש היה בירושלים	Job 1:1	There was a man [in the land of Uz]
בימי אָחָז מלך יהודה	Isa. 7:1	In the days of Ahaz … king of Judea
ושמו יוֹרָם	2 Sam. 10:8	His name was Yoram
בן אֲבִיעֶזֶר	Josh. 17:2	Aviezer
אלוף ביהודה	Gen. 36:15	Chieftain
ושר אלף	1 Sam. 18:13	A captain of a thousand
ויהי לו	Gen. 12:17	And he had
שדות וכרמים	1 Sam. 22:7	Fields and vineyards
בכרמל	Josh. 18:26	In Carmel
ובשרון	1 Chron. 27:29	In Sharon
ועדרי צאן ובקר	Gen. 12:16	Sheep and cattle
בבית לחם יהודה	Judg. 17:7	In Bethlehem of Judea

---

[4] Only the first occurrence of a word in the biblical text is noted in this table. The translation is based on a variety of sources.

The Hebrew of the Jewish Enlightenment

The Love of Zion	Biblical Source[4]	English Translation
ויהי לו כסף וזהב	Gen. 24:35	Silver and gold
היכלי שן	Ps. 45:9	Ivory palaces
שכיות החמדה	Isa. 2:16	Lovely crafts
ושתי נשים היו לו	1 Sam. 1:2	And he had two wives
שם האחת	Gen. 4:19	The name of the one
חַגִּית	1 Sam. 3:4	Hagit
בת עִירָא	2 Sam. 20:26	Ira
ושם השנית	Gen. 4:19	And the name of the other
נַעֲמָה	Gen. 4:22	Na'ama
ויאהב יורם את נעמה מאד	Gen. 29:18	And Yoram loved
כי יפת תואר היא	Gen. 29:17	Beautiful
ותקנא בה חגית	Gen. 30:1	Was jealous of
צרתה	1 Sam. 1:6	Her trouble
ותכעיסנה	1 Sam. 1:7	And would torment her
כי לחגית היו שני בנים ולנעמה לא היה ולד.	Gen. 11:30	Had no child

The book brought tears to the eyes of many a young man who read it in secret at night – the Hebrew of the book limited it almost exclusively to yeshiva students, who were not allowed to read such secular "trash." "I would wait until my parents turned the light off in their bedroom," remembered author Shlomo Tzemach, "shut the door to my room, turn the light on, and read Hebrew books my conservative parents disapproved of," among them, Mapu's *The Love of Zion*.[5] "My desire to speak Hebrew began after I secretly read *The Love of Zion*," wrote Eliezer Ben-Yehuda, who longed to speak Hebrew "like Amnon and Tamar and the other young people I met on the pages of that book."[6]

The *maskilim* believed that modernity could provide Jews with a more comfortable place in the world. And if they wrote in Hebrew,

---

[5] Shlomo Tzemach, My Life Story (סיפור חיי), available at https://benyehuda.org/read/25934#fn:4.

[6] Eliezer Ben-Yehuda, "Changes, the Beginning of Hebrew Speech" (תולדות ותמורות, תחילת הדיבור העברי), Hebrew Academy website, Archival Collection, available at https://hebrew-academy.org.il/2020/08/26/לקט-תעודות/.

14   *Modern Hebrew Language and Literature*

the language would only be a temporary measure, a bridge to ease the crossing from the Jewish to the other side. "I was a young married man then, boarding with my wealthy in-laws in a small Russian town," wrote Micha Yosef Berdichevsky (1865–1921) in his short story "Across the River." "The town had two sides, an upper part of wealthy Gentiles and a lower and poorer part, where the Jews huddled." The protagonist is frustrated by these differences, which go beyond socioeconomics. "I am not sure what I feel or think, I only know I am confined here, I lack the space to think." And so, "one summer night, after evening prayers, I snuck out of the study house and headed for the bridge. I walked across it slowly ... struck by the knowledge that I am going from a place of darkness to a place of light."[7]

In some ways the Haskala in Europe was a success; in others it was a failure. Enlightenment fulfilled its promise by helping Jews integrate into the modern world as individuals. But it failed to create an alternative communal framework for them. Modernization often led to complete assimilation. Consider this: four of Mendelssohn's six children converted to Christianity, and their offspring, including the composer Felix Mendelssohn, left the Jewish community completely. And although this failure continued to needle many *maskilim*, it set the scene for the next stage in the modern history of Hebrew, which focused on the language as an end in itself. The idea was first suggested by Peretz Smolenskin in 1868. "Other nations put up stone monuments, they build towers, and fight bloody wars to be remembered," he wrote in the inaugural issue of his journal, *The Dawn* (השחר):

They look forward to that great day when they shall be restored to their land, and they never let up. Whereas we, who have neither monuments nor land, neither name nor remnant except our one and only record, the last testament that survived our destruction, the Hebrew language, we are ashamed of it and turn away from it. ... Those who turn away from Hebrew despise the Jewish people ... and betray their nation and its faith.

Smolenskin (1842–1885) and likeminded *maskilim* never specified exactly how Hebrew might bring more meaning into modern Jewish life, how the language could create a new communal framework. But they didn't have to. The idea was powerful because it relied on the

---

[7] Micha Yosef Berdichevsky, "Across the River" (מעבר לנהר), available at https://benyehuda.org/read/7645 (my translation).

A Hebrew Revival? 15

centrality of Hebrew in Jewish culture. "We write Hebrew," wrote Y. H. Brenner a bit later, "because we cannot help it, because only this flame sparks the divine in us."[8] Their stubborn work – in isolation, often unrewarded – created a new Jewish library – an alternative to the vast traditional library Jews had created over the millennia – that had the potential to inspire a new Jewish community if and when it came to life. When historians speak about the genealogy of modern Israeli Hebrew, they speak of this library as its foundation.

A Hebrew Revival?

Mordechai Zeev Feierberg (1874–1899) was one of the first Hebrew authors who gave the cultural agenda of Hebrew a distinctly political turn. Whither? he asked in his 1899 novella of that name; where should Jews go now that many avenues of acculturation have been closed off to them, primarily in Eastern Europe? Nahman, the tortured protagonist of the novel, thinks of his fellow Jews as "a miserable people, used to a life of slavery and scorn, confinement and dirt." But he has also noticed that they are beginning to wake up: "The accursed prisoner is breaking out of his cell." Where should this freed prisoner go? wonders Nahman, who comes up with a solution by the story's end. "I do believe," he urges, "that if the Jewish people truly has a purpose, [it should live up to it] by going to the East," to the Land of Israel, "not as an enemy of the East but as its loving brother." It will not be easy, he warns his listeners, but there is no doubt it shall come about. "I see it, though not now, I behold it, yet it is not near," he quotes the prophet Balaam, and ends his own prophecy with the call, "To the East! To the East!" (מזרחה).

Feierberg wrote those words at about the time Zionism appeared on the world stage. It was not a coincidence, except that Feierberg and other Hebrew writers focused on culture, not on diplomacy, and, naively perhaps, hoped that language would bring those changes about. Few writers summed this up as well as Shalom Jacob Abramovitch (1836–1917), better known by his penname, Mendele Moikher Sforim, Mendele the Book Seller. Abramovitch began his career as an unremarkable Hebrew writer in the 1850s. In the 1860s he switched to Yiddish, and became a celebrated writer. In the 1880s he took up Hebrew again, and became a founding father of modern Hebrew literature. His story is the story of Jewish modernity in Europe and the fortunes of Hebrew as part of it.

[8] Shur, "The Complete Return to Hebrew," pp. 77, 88.

Early in his career Abramovitch wrote in a grand Biblical Hebrew that matched the lofty vision of the Haskala but limited his appeal. When he switched to Yiddish he extended his reach and spread the ideas of the Enlightenment further afield. But when anti-Jewish sentiments in Eastern Europe escalated toward the end of the nineteenth century, they challenged many of those ideas and drove Abramovitch back to Hebrew again. The return signaled a new stage in the Jewish struggle toward modernity, one that reconsidered some of the unfulfilled promises of the Haskala and looked for other ways to work them out.

In 1878 Abramovitch published a short novel in Yiddish, *The Travels of Benjamin the Third*, a story about a lovable ignoramus named Benjamin, who plans an expedition in search of Jewish dragons and other fanciful creatures. If the story parodied traditional Jewish backwardness, it saluted curiosity, the desire to leave the narrow confines of the shtetl (a Jewish townlet in Eastern Europe) and learn about the world outside. When Abramovitch reissued the work in Hebrew in 1897, the emphasis of his critique shifted, and the joke was no longer on the Jews alone. Benjamin and his travel companion are kidnapped and forced to serve in the Czarist army. But because they make such terrible soldiers they are eventually discharged and sent back home. On one hand, the ending presents traditional Jews as unfit for "service" in European national culture. On the other hand, militarism is revealed as the kind of patriotic rubbish that people, including Jews, can do without. "Tell me, Sendril," Benjamin asks his mate, as the two bungle their marching drills, "who cares if I use my left foot or my right foot to turn around, isn't it all the same?"

The 1870s Yiddish version was a hopeful gesture that helped Abramovitch reach many of his fellow Jews and encourage them to embrace the world around them and become part of it. The 1890s Hebrew version celebrated the nation's heritage as a defiant response to the disappointments of the Enlightenment. And something had happened to Abramovitch's Hebrew in the intervening years. It had become less biblical and lofty, more relaxed, "contaminated" by Yiddish and other European languages. If it made Hebrew less pure, it also made it more pliant, a more modern idiom that was soon picked up by other writers.

The New Life of Hebrew in Palestine

But if Abramovitch and his colleagues were busy compiling a modern Jewish library, their readership continued to decline. Most Jews were occupied with the ordinary stuff of an increasingly secular life and had little time or use for Hebrew. Many emigrated overseas in search of a better life, and those who remained in Europe continued to hope for integration. Hebrew became increasingly useless for both groups. "The Hebrew language," wrote David Frishman in 1901, "is bereft of speakers and readers, we have no people, no literature, no movement, no revival. We have nothing."[9]

Zionism was a game-changer, and it turned the fate of Hebrew around. It was yet another paradox, in which Hebrew flourished by breaking away from Jewish life in the Diaspora and by cutting ties with the very culture that had preserved it for centuries. If the *maskilim* were the first to imagine Hebrew in a secular context, Zionists gave that context a political turn. It was only when Zionists finally formulated a concrete political agenda that Smolenskin's call to take up Hebrew as a solution for the Jewish Problem became clear. With the establishment of a Jewish community in Palestine, Hebrew became a transcendent expression of it almost immediately. It was a singular historical moment, as Benjamin Harshav showed, a convergence of traditional Hebrew, modern literary Hebrew, and Zionism, a meeting that jolted the Hebrew language back to life; not a revival, perhaps, as Hebrew had never died, but a full return to the language.[10]

The fortunes of Hebrew under Zionism were very different from the previous history of the language. Since the late 1700s Modern Hebrew had led a rarified existence as a cultural conceit. In Palestine it became a cultural imperative. Joseph Klausner described it as a drama in three acts: the romantic act of the Haskala, the cultural act of the Revival, and the political act of Zionism.[11] It was a remarkable journey. When the First Zionist Congress met in 1897, subscriptions to Hebrew periodicals had fallen sharply and only about half of all schoolchildren in the Yishuv, the modern Jewish community in Palestine, were studying Hebrew.[12] By

---

[9] Quoted in Nurit Gertz, *Not from Here* (אל מה שנמוג), Am Oved, 1997.

[10] Shur, "The Complete Return to Hebrew," p. 84.

[11] Rachel Elboim-Dror, *Hebrew Education in the Land of Israel, Volume 1: 1854–1914* (החינוך העברי בארץ ישראל), Yad Yitzhak Ben-Tzvi, 1986, p. 310.

[12] Ibid., p. 203.

18   *Modern Hebrew Language and Literature*

1926 Hebrew was one of the official languages of the British Mandate in Palestine, together with English and Arabic. A decade later it was the principal language of about 400,000 residents of the Yishuv, a critical mass that sustained a vibrant culture in Hebrew.

It was neither an easy nor a simple change. In the early 1900s fewer than ten families in the Yishuv spoke Hebrew at home. The rest spoke a variety of languages that served them so well they were in no hurry to replace them. But the new immigrants who began arriving then were determined to change that. On his first day in Palestine in the winter of 1904, Shlomo Tzemach was shocked to hear the farmers in Rishon Letzion, a Jewish agricultural village that was set up in 1882, "speaking Yiddish, and Russian and French." Hebrew was nowhere to be heard. Disappointed and angry, he got up at the next town meeting and "in my bad Polish Hebrew [I told the townsfolk] never mind my young age, I will still fight you! Everyone laughed at me [and made fun of my Hebrew]." [13] But Tzemach and his fellow immigrants, who were consciously Zionist, turned Hebrew into a communal project. They forced themselves and others to speak Hebrew at home, at work, to the grocer, to the butcher, and even on their sickbeds. Nehama Puhachevska recalled how, when one of her friends fell ill with a high fever and started groaning in Russian, a Hebrew teacher who was present "demanded that the patient groan in Hebrew." Everyone got very upset.[14] It was an obsession, and almost all Yishuv members eventually subscribed to it, including writers, linguists, educators, and then Zionist organizations, who were able to spread the language on a bigger scale.[15]

Take the enthusiasm of one man, the legendary linguist Eliezer Perlman (1858–1922), better known as Eliezer Ben-Yehuda, an early champion of Hebrew nationalism. In Zionist historiography Ben-Yehuda is what the British historian Thomas Carlyle called "a Great Man," an extraordinary person who singlehandedly changes history by the power of their actions. Reality was not as neat, of course. In the early 1880s, almost two decades before the rise of Zionism, the twenty-three-year-old

---

[13] Tzemach, *My Life Story*. At this town meeting Tzemach spoke up against the Uganda plan, but he made a point of doing so in Hebrew as a critique of the linguistic mishmash of the townsfolk.

[14] Nehama Puhachivska, "People Spoke Hebrew in Public" (דיברו עברית בחוצות), 1890, Hebrew Academy website, Archival Collection, available at https://hebrew-academy.org.il/2020/08/26/לקט-תעודות/.

[15] Elboim-Dror, *Hebrew Education*, ch. 4, pp. 204–403.

The New Life of Hebrew in Palestine 19

Perlman published a series of fiery articles in the Hebrew press in support of Hebrew. In an 1881 article he wrote:

Our Hebrew language is our national language ... our forefathers shed blood like water ... over every word of it, every letter, every dot. Why, the number of words in the Hebrew language is equal to the number of the victims sacrificed on its altar. It is the only precious thing left to us of our former glories. How can we abandon it? How can we add insult to the injury of our forefathers and let the angel of death take it? Our predecessors sinned by preferring foreign languages to Hebrew. Let the blood they shed and that of their children be their penance. For what is our excuse? How long will our language and our literature survive if we don't teach it to our children, if we don't revive it, if we don't turn it into a spoken language? And how can we do so if not by making it the language of instruction in schools?[16]

It was a striking idea that excited intense debates. Many thought it ridiculous, irrelevant, and especially impractical. But it didn't deter Ben-Yehuda, who went on to promote it as a writer, journalist, publisher, cultural entrepreneur, and visionary linguist. The trail he blazed began with his own children. Ben-Yehuda spoke only Hebrew to his first-born son, shocking many in the Yishuv. "Don't you feel sorry for the child?" Eliezer and his wife Dvora were asked when word about their Hebrew homeschooling got out. "Reviving Hebrew is all well and good for grownups ... but why torture your child? ... It's a crazy idea, nothing like it has ever been tried ... Latin died as a spoken language, ancient Greek too, may it rest in peace, and here you are with plans to take a language that has not been spoken for two thousand years" and make it talk again. "Leave the child alone."[17] When their son Ben-Tzion (later Itamar) Ben-Yehuda, started speaking Hebrew, people journeyed from afar to witness the wonder: a native speaker of Hebrew. "What happened after God has opened [the child's] mouth to speak in Hebrew is hard to describe," remembered a local Jerusalem sage; "the news quickly spread around the city and became the main topic of conversation. People came in droves to marvel at it."[18]

---

[16] Eliezer Ben-Yehuda, "The Banner of Nationalism" (דגל הלאומיות), *Hamagid* 37 (Winter 1881), available at https://benyehuda.org/read/2635.

[17] Itamar Ben Avi, *The Dawn of Our Independence: The Memoirs of the First Hebrew Child* (עם שחר עצמאותנו: זכרונות-חייו של הילד העברי הראשון), https://benyehuda.org/read/15014.

[18] Ibid.

The sensation was the age of the young speaker, not just the Hebrew he spoke. There were people who could speak Hebrew – men mostly – but it was a foreign language to them, and their speech was formal and stilted. Most Jews were familiar with a few set phrases from prayers and blessings, and the revival of spoken Hebrew owed a lot to that knowledge. But it was a passive and limited proficiency that was acquired with age and learning. Few if any people used Hebrew on a daily basis, and no one spoke the language fluently as a native. Ben-Yehuda changed that, and the change was thrilling. It was an important moment in the evolution of a language, which sprang out of the mouths of babes in the most literal sense. Ita Yelin, the wife of the well-known Hebraist David Yelin, confessed that her family "spoke Yiddish at home, and I only started learning and speaking Hebrew after my children enrolled in the first Hebrew kindergarten in Jerusalem" in 1903. As a "Hebrew mother [I] had no choice but to learn Hebrew from [my] children."[19]

Ben-Yehuda also helped to set up a Language Committee, a voluntary organization dedicated "to facilitate Hebrew as a spoken language in every aspect of life, at home, in schools, in public life, in commerce, construction, industry, art, the humanities and sciences," and to ensure the preservation of the Eastern character of the language.[20] Later named the Academy of the Hebrew Language, the committee thought of itself as the vanguard in an ongoing language war and acted accordingly. In its October 1911 meeting, Ahad Ha'am told those present, "I don't know if Hebrew is a living language yet, but since it is the language of instruction in all schools," and since every school makes up its own vocabulary, "we need to come up with one lexicon for all of them."[21] "The committee for color terms met this week," reported the secretary, S. Eisenstadt, in a letter to Bialik. "Tomorrow I'll start to organize new committees ... we still haven't completed the list for construction terms and [the terms for] tailoring need attention too."[22] Ben-Yehuda

---

[19] Aharon Bar-Adon, "'Mother Tongue' in the Beginning, or, rather, 'Father Tongue' First? The Incipient Deprivation of the Woman's Role in the Revival of Hebrew," in *Proceedings of the World Congress of Jewish Studies*, World Union of Jewish Studies, 1989, division D, vol. 1, p. 106.

[20] Shur, "The Complete Return to Hebrew," p. 99.

[21] Minutes of the Language Committee meeting, October 1911 (ט"ז חשון תרע"ב), Hebrew Academy website, Archival Collection, available at https://hebrew-academy.org.il/2020/08/26/לקט-תעודות/.

[22] Letter from S. Eisenstadt to Bialik, May 26, 1932 (כ אייר תרצ"ב), National Library of Israel, Bialik House Archive.

The New Life of Hebrew in Palestine   21

himself coined hundreds of new Hebrew words, neologisms such as newspaper (עִיתוֹן), airplane (אֲוִוירוֹן), police (מִשְׁטָרָה), towel (מַגֶּבֶת), and ice-cream (גְּלִידָה). He also coined the word for dictionary (מִילוֹן) and went on to compose one, the monumental Ben-Yehuda dictionary of Modern Hebrew, which was completed after his death.

Others, such as Yehuda Leib Metmann (1869–1939) and his wife Fania (1874–1980), translated Ben-Yehuda's romantic ideas into more concrete educational programs, and established the first Hebrew high school in Jaffa in 1906. The idea for the school first came to the couple during a lecture Ahad Ha'am gave in Odessa in 1899. He had just returned from Palestine, and was depressed with the level of Hebrew he heard there. How can one develop respect for Hebrew if even teachers speak it in an "artificial, deficient, poor and wooden," way and lack the most basic vocabulary, he lamented. Teachers admitted to it themselves. "We had no words for towel, socks, interesting, seriousness. ... "[We spoke] a broken language and used our hands and eyes" a lot.[23]

Moved by the address, the Metmanns organized what they called a Revival Army, a group of fellow Hebraists who vowed to change things by becoming Hebrew educators in Palestine. The first item on their visionary agenda was a Hebrew gymnasium (high school) in Palestine dedicated to encouraging young Jews to love their land; fostering the spirit of the Hebrew national revival in parents and students; and developing Hebrew into the spoken language of the Land of Israel.[24]

In 1906, seven years on and wielding Swiss PhDs in education, the couple moved to Palestine, took on a Hebrew name, Matmon-Cohen, and opened a Hebrew school for ten students in their two-room apartment in Jaffa. Four years and 195 students later, the school moved to a beautiful new building in Tel Aviv under a new name, the Herzlia Gymnasium, and became a leading educational institution in the Yishuv. This extraordinary story was less an exception than the rule during those heady times, in which Hebrew educators advanced the cause of Hebrew, probably more than anyone else in the Yishuv.

And while early education in the Yishuv eventually became the domain of women, at first their limited access to Hebrew hampered their professional development. Some of the first women teachers were wives of Hebrew educators, such as Fania Matmon-Cohen, who

---

[23] Elboim-Dror, *Hebrew Education*, p. 367.
[24] Ibid., pp. 242–243.

taught math at the Herzlia Gymnasium or high school in Tel Aviv and wrote one of the first math textbooks in Hebrew; during the first years she also helped by washing the floors of the school. Later, the number of professional teachers grew, especially kindergarten teachers, who taught the first generation of native Hebrew speakers. When Yehudit Eisenberg (later Harari) (1885–1979) started her stint at the college for kindergarten teachers in Jerusalem – after running a kindergarten in Rehovot at the age of sixteen! – she was excited about the chance to "Jewfy [*sic*] seven hundred girls ... and inspire a proper sense of nationalism in them." She was encouraged by a former teacher, who wrote her, "How wonderful it would be if you taught six hundred, even a thousand girls, who would then go on to teach another thousand. Is there anything more gratifying than this?"[25]

But it was a formidable task, especially in the beginning. "I was in charge of 16 children aged 2 to 7," wrote a young woman in the late 1890s. "I couldn't do much with them because we didn't have proper materials ... the only option was to go outside ... tell stories and sing songs out in nature."[26] Another teacher, who trained in Germany in the early 1900s and was preparing to go to Palestine, remembered how she "collected songs I learned in Germany and asked [a poet friend] to translate them into Hebrew. Later on my trip I met author David Frishman, who let me have translations he made of some of Hans Christian Andersen's fairytales."[27] It was a dedication well rewarded. In 1888 an enthusiastic visitor to a school in Rishon Letzion reported how "during class time, only Hebrew is heard in the school. Occasionally, the teachers take the children out for hikes. ... It's a pleasure to see the children play, joke and squabble in Hebrew. During the outing, the teachers tell the kids the Hebrew names of everything they see – mountain, valley, hill, stream, field, etc., as well as the names of plants and animals."[28]

Eventually, eclectic materials were replaced with more programmatic texts, written especially for children by local songsters and musicians;

---

[25] Margalit Shiloh, *The Challenge of Gender: Women in the Early Yishuv* (אתגר המגדר, נשים בעליית הראשונות), Hakibbutz Hame'uhad, 2007, p. 128.

[26] Miriam Snapir, Shosh Siton, and Gila Ruso-Zimet, eds., *One Hundred Years of Kindergarten in the Land of Israel* (מאה שנות גן ילדים בארץ ישראל), Ben-Gurion University Press, 2012, p. 45.

[27] Ibid., p. 50.

[28] *Hatzvi*, May–June 1888.

The New Life of Hebrew in Palestine

texts that not only taught Hebrew but "Jewfied" students as well, as Harari put it, by instilling a sense of Hebrew nationalism in them: textbooks that celebrated the flowers and animals of Palestine, introduced changes to the Jewish festival calendar, and served the Hebrew Bible as a national tale of action and adventure. "We now have 150 Hebrew schools in Palestine with more than 20,000 students and 1,000 teachers," noted one of them with pleasure in 1929. "I feel proud and heartened when I think how much of our nation's revival is owed to [our work]."[29]

In the 1920s some of those dutiful students must have made their Hebrew teachers proud by composing poems that demonstrated the lessons they learned:

In the Homeland, Esther Hananit, 8th grade

I love you, O homeland, on long hot days,
when the sand burns the feet and the air is as hot as a furnace,
lips cleave together,
and the world is thirsty.

I love you on calm, bright, moonlit nights,
when the world is covered with a dappled sheet of lights and shadows.
I love you on joyous days,
when I feel like dancing and singing forever.
And on sad days, when eyes tear up,
And the heart shrinks with sorrow – I love you always.[30]

But the most dramatic moment in the transformation of Hebrew from an affectation to an everyday reality was the language war of 1913–1914, which secured the status of Hebrew as the lingua franca of the Yishuv. The conflict broke out because the first university in Palestine, the technical college in Haifa, later named the Technion, announced its intention to use German as the language of instruction. The decision made sense because there were no textbooks in Hebrew at the time and because the college was planned and funded by German Jews. But the initiative was passionately opposed, at first by the students themselves, who wrote to the college to say they were "shocked and dismayed to

---

[29] H. A. Zuta, "We Have Made it" (אשרינו שזכינו לכך), 1929, Hebrew Academy website, Archival Collection, available at https://hebrew-academy.org.il/2020/08/26/לקט-תעודות/.

[30] David Shahar, *Myth and Education* (מיתוס וחינוך), Resling, 2021, p. 199.

24 *Modern Hebrew Language and Literature*

hear that Hebrew will not be the language of instruction in the technical college in Haifa. As graduates of Hebrew schools in the Land of Israel, we won't accept it."[31] Led by those students, who pulled their parents into it and eventually also their teachers, and then the entire Yishuv, protesters staged strikes, organized marches, and held rallies in support of Hebrew.

In one of the biggest rallies, 2,500 enthusiasts gathered in the Herzlia Gymnasium with banners displaying slogans such as "Long live the Hebrew Language!" "War against defilers of our language!" and "Hebrew means independence!" One of the teachers who was at the rally later wrote about "speeches and battle cries" that were so rousing that some people in the crowd fainted. "My own heart was pounding … I know many others who, like me, are willing to fight [for Hebrew] until their last drop of blood. Is there anything holier than [our national language]?" he concluded the letter with dramatic flair.[32]

Fundraising dinners were held to collect money in support of the cause, and local businesses in Jerusalem announced discounts for protesters, who marched through the city, singing, "Rejoice, make merry / the public we carry / a day full of joy / let us Hebrew employ (גילו גילו/ המעגל הגדילו/ יום זה לשמחה לנו נכון/ העברית השיגה ניצחון)."[33] The campaign ended with a decisive victory for Hebrew and marked the rising power of the Yishuv in world Zionist politics. The war also stressed the difference between Zionism and the diasporic Jewish culture that gave birth to it. Yiddish was one of the first casualties in a culture war that later turned against Jewish life in the Diaspora more generally and eventually developed into what came to be known as the Zionist Negation of Exile, which, so to speak, canceled Jewish life outside of Palestine/Israel.

A more eccentric example of the passion for Hebrew was an organization called the Language Defense Brigade (גדוד מגיני השפה), a free association of high-school students, teachers, and intellectuals who devoted themselves to the cause. They volunteered to teach Hebrew, organized public events to promote it, and were not squeamish about shaming people who failed to use Hebrew. Their most notorious encounter was with the venerated poet Haim Nahman Bialik, who was reprimanded one day by a brigade member for speaking Yiddish in public. When

---

[31] Elboim-Dror, *Hebrew Education*, p. 326.
[32] Ibid., pp. 335–336.
[33] Ibid., p. 336.

A Hebrew Accent 25

the offended poet scolded the lad for his chutzpah, the young man filed a suit against him. In his statement to the court, Bialik described how

> my friend Mr. Rawnitzki and I were walking along Allenby Street, speaking quietly with one another in Yiddish, as we have done for the past twenty-eight years, when I noticed a man walking next to us listening to our conversation. A moment later the man turned to us and had the audacity to demand, 'Why aren't you speaking Hebrew? You should speak Hebrew!' I replied to him, in Hebrew: 'It is none of your business. No one asked you. Go away, damn you.' The gall!"

The poet was acquitted.[34]

A Hebrew Accent

Accent became an ideological issue too, complicated by the various reading traditions of Hebrew as the language of Jewish scripture and, sometimes, as a language of communication between Jews from different parts of the world. The best-known example of such connections comes from Benjamin ben Yona, who in the twelfth century traveled from Tudela in Spain to Jewish communities as far away as Babel and Yemen. Benjamin of Tudela used book Hebrew to speak with the Jews he met on his journey, and when he returned home after ten years on the road he published a Hebrew account of his travels entitled *The Travels of Benjamin*; *The Travels of Benjamin the Third* by Abramovich is a reference to this original travelogue. As a native of Tudela in the north of Spain, Benjamin probably spoke Sephardi Hebrew,[35] one of three distinct varieties, together with the Ashkenazi Hebrew of Central and Eastern Europe, and the more isolated form of Hebrew spoken in Yemen.

Zionists opted for the Sephardi pronunciation of Hebrew. First, it was common in Palestine. "Most of the [Jewish men] speak [some form of] Hebrew," reported a visitor to Jerusalem in 1857, "and foreigners who wish to deal with them but cannot speak Hebrew in the manner of

---

[34] For a short description of the incident and the protocol of the trial see Avner Holtzman, "Then Bialik Told Him, Go to Hell," *Davka: Eretz Yiddish Vetarbuta* 3 (2007): 18–19, available at https://bethshalomaleichem.co.il/wp-content/uploads/2021/08/Davka_3_New_2021.pdf.

[35] *Sepharad* is the Hebrew word for Spain. Sephardi is an adjective that describes anything connected with the Jews who were expelled from Spain in 1492 and dispersed primarily across the Mediterranean rim.

26   *Modern Hebrew Language and Literature*

Spanish [Jews] will not make much headway."[36] Second, they believed
it was closer to the sound of ancient Hebrew than any other extant
Hebrew accent. There was no way of knowing this, of course, but
Sephardi Hebrew fit the Romantic Nationalism of Zionists and served
their rejection of Ashkenazi culture.

Sephardi Accent vs. Ashkenazi Accent

Modern Israeli Hebrew retained very few of the so-called Sephardi
features:

1. An ultimate stress: Sha<u>bbat</u> instead of <u>Sha</u>bbos;
2. An open A sound instead of O: Shabb<u>a</u>t instead of Shabb<u>o</u>s;
3. No difference between stressed T (t) and unstressed T (s): Shabba<u>t</u>
    instead of Shabbo<u>s</u>.

The vocal tradition of Biblical Hebrew was fixed early in the Middle
Ages by Jewish grammarians in the Galilean town of Tiberias. Hebrew
had fallen out of everyday use by then, and efforts to record and preserve
the pronunciation of the consonantal language led scholars to develop
annotations that helped readers vocalize it. The system consisted of small
strokes and dots, called diacritic signs, that were marked above, below,
and through the script and indicated proper pronunciation, similar
to the function of vowels in the Latin alphabet. Dubbed the Tiberian
tradition or Masora, the signs were adopted as a standard throughout
the Jewish world, although actual pronunciation of these marked texts
differed from region to region depending on a number of variables.

א בְּרֵאשִׁית, בָּרָא אֱלֹהִים, אֵת הַשָּׁמַיִם, וְאֵת הָאָרֶץ. ב וְהָאָרֶץ, הָיְתָה תֹהוּ וָבֹהוּ, וְחֹשֶׁךְ,
עַל-פְּנֵי תְהוֹם; וְרוּחַ אֱלֹהִים, מְרַחֶפֶת עַל-פְּנֵי הַמָּיִם. ג וַיֹּאמֶר אֱלֹהִים, יְהִי אוֹר;
וַיְהִי-אוֹר. ד וַיַּרְא אֱלֹהִים אֶת-הָאוֹר, כִּי-טוֹב; וַיַּבְדֵּל אֱלֹהִים, בֵּין הָאוֹר וּבֵין
הַחֹשֶׁךְ. ה וַיִּקְרָא אֱלֹהִים לָאוֹר יוֹם, וְלַחֹשֶׁךְ קָרָא לָיְלָה; וַיְהִי-עֶרֶב וַיְהִי-בֹקֶר, יוֹם אֶחָד.

Genesis 1:1–5 with the Tiberian annotation system, developed to help readers pronnce th consnntl lngge (or: pronounce the consonantal language).
Modern Hebrew dispensed with the signs, which means that reading the

---

[36] Yosef Ofer, "The Beginning of Israeli Accent" (ראשיתו של המבטא הישראלי),
in A. Maman, F. E. Fassberg, and Y. Breuer, eds., *Sha'arei Lashon: Studies in
Hebrew, Aramaic and Jewish Languages Presented to Moshe Bar-Asher*, vol. 3,
Mossad Bialik, 2007, p. 166.

A Hebrew Accent

27

language today is a kind of guessing game, which slows the learning process but speeds up reading later.

Another benefit of the Sephardi accent was its connections with Arabic, a sister language that, for Zionists, affirmed the Jewish link to Palestine. The decision to use it was never taken officially, but rather was spontaneous. It is only natural, said the Hebraist David Yelin, that "an Eastern language, should be spoken as such."[37] Schools were instrumental in instilling it, and teachers became its important cultural agents. "Politically speaking," said the Zionist leader Menachem Ussishkin, echoing Ben-Yehuda's earlier words, "the prattle of small children, the study of botany in school ... even a street sign in pidgin Hebrew, are more important for our national revival than the greatest literary or poetic work."[38] And because schools educated the young, what happened between their walls shaped the cultural reality of the Yishuv. "It is now impossible to speak Ashkenazi Hebrew in the Land of Israel," reported Joseph Klausner in 1912, "because children think it wrong" and make fun of you.[39]

But was the new Hebrew of the Yishuv a Semitic language? It was a surprising question that came up early in the revival of Hebrew. Some scholars claimed that spoken Hebrew owed its rapid growth to the existing infrastructure of Yiddish, a Germanic language, which the revivers of Hebrew speech had allegedly dressed up with a square Aramaic script and given a Semitic lexicon that made it look old. In other words, they felt that Modern Hebrew only looks Semitic, but is in fact Indo-European at its core.[40] It's an academic question that has never shaken the belief of most Modern Hebrew speakers that they are indeed speaking the language of the Hebrew Bible. The fact that Israelis can generally understand their Bible with little difficulty may have something to do with that belief, as well as with the mandatory schooling they receive in it.

What did not change, of course, was the wealth of associations Hebrew carried with it into modernity. That was the price paid for

[37] Ibid., p. 170.
[38] Abraham Ussishkin, *Ussishkin Book* (ספר אוסישקין), Hamol, 1933, p. 188.
[39] Elboim-Dror, *Hebrew Education*, pp. 373–374.
[40] Shur, "The Complete Return to Hebrew," p. 90. The latest iteration of this debate took place in 2008, when Ghil'ad Zuckermann argued that Israeli Hebrew is not a Semitic language: *Israeli – A Beautiful Language* (ישראלית שפה יפה), Am Oved, 2008.

28 *Modern Hebrew Language and Literature*

reanimating an ancient language that for most of its long life had been used primarily in faith-based contexts. Even if those associations were secularized by modern users of the language, Israeli Hebrew retained many of the old theological connotations, as Gershom Scholem famously pointed out in 1926. "If we teach our children this secret language and revive it, the religious force it packs may one day blow up in their faces," he wrote to a friend, the philosopher Franz Rosenzweig. "This modern Hebrew is very dangerous. It cannot and will not remain [a secular tongue]. ... We speak a ghostly language" that may one day come to haunt us, Scholem continued, warning that the revival of Hebrew would likely also revive the rich sacred traditions that were imbedded in it. Anyone who thinks otherwise, he prophesied, is deluding themselves.[41]

From Hebrew to Israeli Literature

The growth of a Hebrew-speaking community in Palestine did not change the nature of Hebrew literature to the same degree that it changed the language. The expansion of the Yishuv shifted most of the creative work in Hebrew from Europe to Palestine, but with more than a hundred years of history by then, modern Hebrew literature did not require the monumental revival efforts that the spoken language needed. Literature became an integral part of Yishuv culture, which it predated by a century and, in some ways, laid the ground for. It was not many years before it was bound up with Yishuv life in the natural way of all living literatures.

And yet the rapid adoption of Hebrew as a vernacular had visible effects on poetry and prose. One predictable change was an expanding vocabulary and more natural ways of expressing it. The Hebrew authors who predated the Yishuv were consummate Hebraists, but their literary Hebrew was ultimately artificial, no matter how talented they were. It was a made-up language that had no relationship to a lived linguistic experience because none existed. It was only inevitable that, once the language began circulating more widely, older works of literature would become progressively outdated. Even the works of writers who predated the Yishuv by a few decades, gifted writers such as Abramovitch and

---

[41] Franz Rosenzweig, "An Oath to our Language" (הצהרת אמונים לשפה שלנו), in a collection of Scholem's writing, *Another Thing* (עוד דבר), ed. Avraham Shapira, Am Oved, 1989, pp. 59–60.

From Hebrew to Israeli Literature   29

Berdichevsky, began to be overshadowed by more contemporary works. It was not only a question of language but of life too.

Subject matter was another change, a shift in focus from Jewish life in the Diaspora to life in the Yishuv. The early work of Moshe Smilansky is a dramatic example of it. In the 1910s Smilansky published a collection of tales under the exotic title *The Sons of Arabia* (בני ערב), short stories that were inspired by his contacts with the Arabs of Palestine. The work fascinated readers in the Yishuv and abroad, who were drawn by its blend of Hebraism and orientalism. As Europeans, they felt superior to the Arab "noble savages." As Jews, they felt a special connection to them as fellow "orientals."[42]

As the Jewish settlement in Palestine grew, poets and writers turned their attention to the new reality that was taking shape all around them. At first the shift was more deliberate, guided by programmatic editors. But as the Yishuv took root, editors became less heavy-handed. In the 1920s and 1930s poetry and prose grew progressively more enthusiastic about life in the new country. The restoration of Jewish self-rule was felt to be so momentous that writers often spoke of it in spiritual terms. For a society that tried to recreate itself as both Jewish and secular, it was a paradox that yielded a rich poetic harvest.

כפרקי נבואה בוערים ימותי בכל הגילויים, "My days burn like prophecies in all their revelations," wrote Uri Zvi Greenberg in his 1920s poem "With my God, the Blacksmith":

> My days burn like prophecies in all their revelations,
> my body pressed between them like a metal block about to be melted.
> Over me stands my blacksmithing God and bangs down heroically:
> Every wound, that time has cut in me, opens a gash
> that lets out the pent-up fire in time sparks.

The Romantic motif of the suffering poet receives a distinctly Zionist expression in this poem through the sanctification of hard, physical labor, a central tenet of Zionist ideology, which is stressed in the next stanza:

> This is the fateful lot I serve daily till dusk.
> And when I lay down my banged-up block of a body,
> my mouth is an open wound,

---

[42] Yaron Peleg, *Orientalism and the Hebrew Imagination*, Cornell University Press, 2005.

30 *Modern Hebrew Language and Literature*

and naked I speak to my God: you have toiled.
Night has come; let us both rest.[43]

The poem paints two complementary images, one in which the aching poet is validated as a laborer, the other in which physical labor turns into prophecy. The biblical allusions, especially in the first stanza, endow both poet and laborer with spirituality and transcendence. Language and labor are consecrated in this poem by Greenberg, who was not unusual in this regard. Many of his contemporaries wrote works that expressed the solemnity with which they regarded their own lives and times.

In this poem by Esther Raab, one of the first native Hebrew poets of the Yishuv, the Land of Israel is quietly hallowed:

> A white day celebrates your bareness,
> you, who are so impoverished and rich,
> a mountain freezes like a wall,
> as clear as mirage,
> cleaving to the offing.
> Noon. Your sweeping fields burst into flame
> and your depths rise up playfully
> against the white sky,
> like a never-ending curtain,
> drawing, quivering.
> In the plain
> a hill jots like a round breast,
> a white tomb on top;
> and in the empty fields after the harvest,
> a thorny, lonely bush.
> And should the eye tire
> of the blinding light,
> let it dip in the green of the thorny bush,
> as in a pool of fresh water.
>
> Impoverished, you with your red slits
> in the golden distance
> with your dry, white riverbeds –
> How beautiful you are![44]

[43] Uri Zvi Greenberg, "With my God, the Blacksmith," in Uri Zvi Greenberg, *Midworld in Midtime: A Selection of Poems from the 1920s and 1930s*, selected by Binyamin Harushovsky (באמצע העולם ובאמצע הזמנים שירים), Hakibbutz Hame'uhad, 1979, p. 74 (my translation).

[44] Esther Raab, *Collected Poems* (כל השירים), ed. Ehud Ben-Ezer, Zmora-Bitan,

From Hebrew to Israeli Literature 31

Although the tone of Raab's poem is not as grand as that of Greenberg's, the land is still an ethereal vision, not a rich or lush land but rather dry and empty. The intense heat and the blinding light summon up an arid landscape, a desert, to which the tomb and the thorny bush add an unforgiving aspect. And yet this stark landscape is pronounced beautiful, and its feminine attributes – the breast, the vaginal allusions – give it intimacy and intensity.

Similar feelings toward Jewish history, the Hebrew Bible, land, and labor were shared by many writers at the time, who focused again and again on the astonishing transformation Jewish life in Palestine was undergoing in the first decades of the twentieth century with quasi-religious and high-flying lines such as "Massada, open your gates and give me refuge! / I shall place my crumbling soul at your feet – / lay it on the anvil of your rocks and hammer it into/something new!" (Yitzhak Lamdan, "Masada"); "My Land, my [en]lighted land – a chariot of fire among the world's mountains" (Yocheved bat Miriam, "Eretz Israel"); "Oh, blessed are the fingers / which hold the sickle on harvest day" (Abraham Shlonsky, "Labor" [עמל]); "The sea of wheat swells / The flock bells ring / This is my land and its fields / This is the valley of Jezre'el" (Nathan Alterman, "Song of the Valley" (שיר העמק).

Later, as some of these transformations became more commonplace, lofty expressions of this kind subsided as well. Writing in the 1980s, the literary critic Gershon Shaked summarized the role of Hebrew literature in modern Jewish life by drawing an arc that began in the late eighteenth century and ended with the eventual establishment of a Hebrew-speaking Jewish state almost two hundred years later. While a great variety of historical and other causes led to the establishment of Israel, wrote Shaked, it was the textual world of modern Hebrew poetry and literature a century earlier, he claimed, that first suggested its possibility.[45]

Some decades earlier, in 1924, the critic Yaacov Rabinowitz had a less programmatic view of Hebrew literature in the Yishuv, which would naturally be different from literature in Hebrew that was written elsewhere. And as if anticipating Scholem's words two years later,

---

1988, pp. 9–10 (my translation). For a selection of Raab's poems in English see Esther Raab, *Thistles: Selected Poems of Esther Raab*, trans. Harold Schimmel, Ibis Editions, 2002.

[45] Yaron Peleg, "The Critic as a Dialectical Zionist: Gershon Shaked's Hebrew Fiction 1880–1980," *Prooftexts* 23: 3 (Fall 2003): 382–396.

32   *Modern Hebrew Language and Literature*

he imagined that it probably "won't be Jewish in the same way, but human, multifaceted. Its Jewishness will be different, adapted to life in Palestine as a natural part of it. ... It would be pointless to rejoice or grumble about it, we simply need to look ahead with understanding."[46]

---

[46] Yaacov Rabinowitz, *Our Literature and Life* (ספרותינו וחיינו), in *The Paths of Literature* (מסלולי ספרות), 1971, quoted by Avner Holtzman in https://onegshabbat.blogspot.com/2022/05/blog-post_20.html.

2 | *Hebrew Space and Architecture*

We came to the Land[1]

To build and be built by it

אָנוּ בָּאנוּ אַרְצָה

לִבְנוֹת וּלְהִבָּנוֹת בָּהּ

This pioneering song became very popular from the 1920s. Of unknown origin, its lines were repeated over and over again in Hasidic fashion, another example of the spontaneous cultural generation that was common during early Zionism.

Zionists saw themselves as colonizers and spoke of themselves as such because, among other things, it boosted their credentials as Europeans. But they also considered the land they came to settle as their historical legacy. And if they wanted to reshape space in Palestine according to modern European standards, they also thought of their colonization project as an act of restoration, a contemporary expression of an ancient patrimony. It was a unique aspect of the Zionist colonial project and the Zionist immigration model, defined by Itamar Even-Zohar as rejecting the old culture they left behind but not adopting the new culture they encountered, the Arab culture of Palestine.[2] Instead, Zionists wished for something altogether new and different.

For Zionists, the desolation of Palestine was a historical accident they were intent on fixing by removing what they thought of as the layers of grime that had accumulated on it for generations and restoring it to

---

[1] The Land of Israel is often referred to in Jewish culture as simply the Land, without further identification, indicating its singularity and cultural significance. For historical recordings of the song see www.zemereshet.co.il/m/song.asp?id=717.

[2] Itamar Even-Zohar, "The Emergence of a Native Hebrew Culture in Palestine," in Yehuda Reinharz and Anita Shapira, eds., *Essential Papers on Zionism*, New York University Press, 1996, pp. 727–744. The connections between Zionism and colonialism have been debated at length. For a summary of the discourse see Avi Bareli, "Forgetting Europe: Perspectives on the Debate about Zionism and Colonialism," *Journal of Israeli History* 20: 2–3 (2001): 99–120. Derek Penslar has also written an excellent commentary on it in *Zionism: An Emotional State*, Rutgers University Press, 2023.

34   *Hebrew Space and Architecture*

its original Jewish condition. "Is this my land? The land of Abraham, Moses, Salomon, Judah Maccabee, Bar Kokhba and mine as well?" asks David, a young immigrant in a 1920s short story by Yosef Luidor.[3] Writing about his own childhood, S. Yizhar recalls a similar notion when he describes how his father

continued to press as hard as he could on the handles of that iron plow; it was hard for the plow and hard for the mule and hard for the man, and he was not sure if it was so hard because the stubborn soil with its packed crust was undisturbed for thousands of years, or ever, no one has touched it, no one has violated its purity ... but now we thrust a peg in, as the saying goes, and redeem another strip of land with our hands, unnoticed yet in the great expanse that lies wasting in the sluggish heat.[4]

Zionists considered the history of the Land an exclusively Jewish affair. But while Herzl's vision for a Jewish state was audacious, grand, and biblical in its proportions, in practice it was very difficult to carry out. Initially, Zionists had relatively few means at their disposal and few opportunities to use them. With limited funds, a small, irregular, and untrained work force, arbitrary access to land, political obstacles, and increasing resistance from Arabs in Palestine, they could not implement their ambitious national vision with predictability and regularity until the establishment of their state in 1948. The spatial consequences of these challenges meant that settlements were somewhat randomly spread over the country, that they were built intermittently, and that they were modest in scale and design.[5]

At the same time, the Zionist colonization project was an organized affair, paid for, planned, and managed centrally, and this also had an impact on the construction of the Yishuv. In other words, and unlike most colonial settlement projects, the Jewish colonization of Palestine was a group effort. "Settling the Land of Israel is not a personal matter but a communal one," wrote Ahad Ha'am in 1891; "anyone can just pick up and go to America, but the settlement of Jews in the Land of Israel should be arranged by the people as a whole ... and managed

---

[3] Josef Luidor, "Yoash," in *Recklessness* (נער פחז כמים), Pardes, 2022, p. 64.

[4] S. Yizhar, *Preliminaries* (מקדמות), Zmora-Bitan, 1992, pp. 13–14 (my translation).

[5] Zvi Efrat, *The Israeli Project: Construction and Architecture, 1948–1974* (הפרויקט הישראלי: בניה ואדריכלות 1948-1974), Tel Aviv Museum of Art, 2004.

A Hebrew Countryside

thoughtfully and with purpose by our leaders."[6] The communal nature of the Zionist colonial project shaped every inch of the land Jews acquired in Palestine, rural as well as urban.

A Hebrew Countryside

The modern idea of farming or work on the land as purifying or redemptive goes back to the ancient Greek concept of the pastoral, a harmonious life in the bosom of a welcoming nature. It was always more of a literary notion, in ancient Greece as well as in early modern Europe, where Romantic poets used the figure of the shepherd to symbolize it. But as life in Europe began to change, as factories replaced farms and cities replaced villages, the poetic notion of the pastoral transformed as well. From the late eighteenth century onward, farming and the allegedly cozy community it fostered began to be seen as an antidote to the ills of industrialism and the alienation brought on by urbanization. In the European Romantic imagination, farmers came to symbolize the new nation and its attachment to its ancestral soil.

The pastoral idea in its Greco-Christian version entered Jewish culture late, at the beginning of the nineteenth century. It also took on a different form because the modern Jewish experience was different, shaped by the ancient legacy of the Jews and their minority status in the societies they inhabited. In the Hebrew Bible, shepherds often represent freedom and a critique of settled society; both King Saul and his successor, King David, began their careers as shepherds.[7] If we go back to Abraham Mapu's 1856 novel *The Love of Zion*, we find one of the first modern formulations of the pastoral idea in Jewish culture. The love story at the center of the novel takes place in a rustic biblical setting, populated by young men and women who frolic and make love in the fields and vineyards of Judea. "The sons and daughters of the noblemen had come up to Bethlehem to enjoy the spring weather. Tamar, radiant with beauty ... went with her maid ... to the shepherd's pastures, where Amnon was feeding his flocks."[8] At the same time, the novel is also

---

[6] Ahad Ha'am, "Truth from the Land of Israel" (אמת מארץ ישראל) *Hamelitz* 13, June 30, 1891 (כ"ד בסיון תרנ"א).

[7] Herbert Schneidau, *Sacred Discontent: The Bible and Western Tradition*, Louisiana State University Press, 1976.

[8] Abraham Mapu, *The Shepherd Prince or The Love of Zion* (אהבת ציון), Brookside Publishing, 1922, p. 44.

set in a densely built and culturally refined city, in a Jerusalem of fine palaces, teeming markets, and learned societies. The novel gives two separate and somewhat contradictory aspects of European modernity a distinctly Jewish context, the desire for a highly developed national culture alongside a romantic belief in a return to the land as an escape and expression of that culture.

The Jewish design of colonial space in Palestine mixed rustic and urban in ways that had begun in the construction of *moshavot*, the farming villages that were built in the 1880s by proto-Zionist immigrants to Palestine, who used their own capital to buy land and establish agricultural settlements as private farms. Unlike the Zionist immigrants, who would arrive twenty years later, these early Jewish immigrants did not have a coherent national agenda yet. They came to Palestine hoping to build a better and healthier Jewish life close to a land they considered theirs.

Moshava

Land ownership in Palestine was regulated and documented, and anyone who wanted to settle on it had to buy it from its legal owners. Until the establishment of the state of Israel, land could not be seized by force. This was another peculiarity of the Zionist project, which allocated considerable amounts of money for land acquisition.[9] Some of the land was occupied by Arab tenant farmers who had lived on it for generations, and removing them was not easy or pleasant. "When we come to our [*sic*] land," wrote Yitzhak Epstein in 1907, "we must not think of it as conquest, we must not wrong anyone" already living there. But his prophetic warning was largely ignored by the new Jewish owners, who were eager to reshape the land they had just acquired and considered virgin soil.

The question was, how? What shape should the new owners give the land they had bought? Like other colonialists, Jewish settlers could choose between two models, villages they knew back home, mainly in Eastern Europe, and local Arab villages. They chose neither.

---

[9] In some early European colonies, Manhattan, for example, or New Zealand, European settlers made land contracts with the indigenous peoples who lived on the land but whose concept of ownership differed from that of Europeans. Acquisition by force was a more common colonial practice.

A Hebrew Countryside   37

Instead, they developed a unique model that borrowed elements from both, but was based on a third model, the Templer village.

The Templers were members of a German Protestant sect, who believed that the second coming of Christ was imminent and that it would take place in or around Jerusalem. In preparation for it, they arrived in Palestine during the second half of the nineteenth century and built a number of agricultural villages in anticipation of their Messiah. The Templers were part of a larger Christian messianic trend, which took advantage of the decline of Ottoman rule to strengthen a Christian foothold in the Holy Land. Like many of the Christian projects that were developed around Palestine at the time – convents, hospitals, hostels – Templer villages were designed by European architects and engineers, many of whom were later engaged in the *moshavot*.[10] "The settlement I have seen," said Kaiser Wilhelm II to Theodor Herzl when the two met in Jerusalem on November 2, 1898, "the German ones as well as those of your people, may serve as indication of what can be done with the land."[11]

While a number of considerations determined the clustered shape of Templer villages – security, isolation in a new land, scant infrastructure – they had a curious "suburban" look to them: angular street plans, spacious houses, red-tiled roofs, and gardens with decorative trees and shrubs. They looked more like garden cities, a contemporary planning concept that combined city and country living. The notion developed in Europe in response to urban congestion, and it influenced design in the Yishuv in important ways. Templer villages were praised by contemporaries for "their well-cultivated fields, trim gardens, and substantial white stone mansions." In a sparsely populated Palestine they looked very distinct, "a most agreeable and unexpected picture of civilization upon this semi-barbarous coast," wrote Laurence Oliphant

---

[10] Yossi Ben-Artzi, "The Moshavot and the Beginning of Farming Architecture in Palestine – a Reassessment" (המושבות וראשיתו של תכנון פיסי כפרי בא"י – הערכה מחדש), in Yehoshua Ben-Arye, Yossi Ben-Artzi, and Haim Goren, eds., *Studies in Historical Geographic Settlement of the Land of Israel*, Yad Ben Tzvi, 1988, p. 105.

[11] Theodor Herzl, *The Complete Diaries of Theodor Herzl*, Herzl Press and Thomas Yoseloff, 1960, pp. 755–756, available at https://archive.org/details/TheCompleteDiariesOfTheodorHerzl_201606/TheCompleteDiariesOfTheodorHerzlEngVolume2_OCR/page/n165/mode/2up?view=theater.

Fig. 2.1 The first Templer colony in Haifa, before 1874, when the square houses were retrofitted with red-tiled roofs following a freak winter and heavy snows. Süddeutsche Zeitung Photo/Alamy Stock Photo.

(see Figure 2.1).[12] Visiting the colony in 1883, Oliphant was delighted to observe how,

> leaving [Haifa] by the western gateway, we ride for about a mile parallel to the seashore between high cactus hedges, and suddenly find ourselves apparently transported into the heart of Europe. Running straight back from the beach for about half a mile and sloping upward for about a hundred feet in that distance, to the base of the rocky sides of Carmel, runs the village street. On each side of it is a pathway, with a double row of shade-trees, and behind them a series of white stone houses, of one and two stories, generally with tiled roofs, each surrounded with its garden, and each with a text in German engraved over the doorway.[13]

---

[12] Laurence Oliphant, *Haifa: Or, Life in Modern Palestine*, William Blackwood & Sons, 1886, p. 20; Yossi Ben-Artzi, *The Hebrew Moshava in the Landscape of the Land of Israel, 1882–1914*.) 1914–1882 המושבה העברית בנוף ארץ ישראל), Yad Ben Tzvi/Hebrew University, 1988, p. 282.

[13] Ibid.

A Hebrew Countryside

Most of the early *moshavot* adopted the clustered shape of Templer colonies, with two facing rows of rectangular white houses and slanted red roofs, separated by a main road that ran through them. It was a common village configuration, in the old countries as well as in colonies overseas, that changed over time for different ideological and security considerations.[14]

Isolation and poor infrastructure forced both German and Jewish farming villages to establish communal institutions that added a municipal flair to their settlements, an urban aspect that was not alien to the traditional founders of the *moshavot*. As modern farming communities, the *moshavot* were unprecedented in Jewish history. But since most of their founders had grown up in shtetls, small Jewish towns in Eastern Europe, their idea of community was informed by their upbringing and was reflected in the institutions they added to their farming communities, "rabbi and butcher, cantor and choir, a doctor and a pharmacist and a medic, an infirmary ... a school, and a store," as Agnon wrote: institutions that were more typical of a town than a farming community, in Europe or in Palestine.[15] The writer Y. D. Berkowitz left this exuberant note about a trip he took around the country a few years after he settled in Palestine in 1928 (see Figure 2.2):

The Jewish settlements stand out almost immediately. After you see the charred Arab villages with their houses jumbled on top of bald, rocky hills, with no windows and not a spot of greenery, looking like old, abandoned nests, it's lovely to see the Jewish settlements with their fresh green grass, young red roofs, and tall water towers that jot into the blue sky and look to the future.[16]

This unique combination of town and country was passed on to future communal settlements in the Yishuv.[17]

---

[14] Ya'acov Shavit, "Regulations of the First Moshavot Concerning the Practicality of Utopia" (תקנות המושבות הראשונות: מתקנות הקהל לניסיון באוטופיה מעשית), *Katedra* 72 (1994): 50–62, at p. 52.

[15] S. Y. Agnon, *Only Yesterday* (תמול שלשום), Shocken Books, 1971, p. 193.

[16] Y. D. Berkowitz, "Tel Aviv," in *Collected Writings* (כתבי י"ד ברקוביץ), Dvir, 1963, p. 354.

[17] See Shavit, "Regulations of the First Moshavot," pp. 50–62; Yisrael Bartal, "Old Yishuv, New Yishuv" (ישוב ישן וישוב חדש), *Katedra* 2 (1976): 1–17 (esp. nn. 1, 3). On the urban character of the shtetl see Allan Sokolova, "The Podolian Shtetl as Architectural Phenomenon," in G. Estraich and M. Krutikov, eds., *The Shtetl: Image and Reality*, Routledge, 2000. Templer

Fig. 2.2 New Jewish settlements, such as Rosh Pina, pictured here around 1896, impressed visitors, including the writer Y. D. Berkowitz. Photo by Leon Katz, Pritzker Family National Photography Collection, National Library of Israel.

House design on *moshavot* was also influenced by the innovations of the Templers, who rejected both the crammed and irregular farmhouses of traditional German villages and the closed and almost windowless houses of local Arab farmers, the *fellahin*. Instead, they enlarged the square shape of Arab houses into roomier stone structures, added tall windows, and, following a freak winter in 1874, when heavy snows caused their flat roofs to collapse, they replaced them with slanted terracotta roofs.[18] The founders of the *moshavot* simplified these designs, duplicated them on a smaller scale, and standardized them to ensure their communities "are built attractively and in good order ... with well-regulated houses."[19] Later, the design became a template

villages had many of the same services as well, including schools, medical facilities, churches, and sometimes a hotel. See Oliphant, *Haifa*, p. 24.

[18] Gil Gordon, "Roofs in the Wind: The Introduction of Roof Tiles and a Terracotta Industry to Palestine" (גגות מתעופפים ברוח: כניסתם של רעפים ותעשיית החרסית לארץ ישראל), *Zmanim* 96 (2006): 58–67.

[19] Shavit, "Regulations of the First Moshavot," p. 59: 1879 ordinances of Petah Tikva.

A Hebrew Countryside

Fig. 2.3 The simplified design of houses on *moshavot* became the model for country housing, usually on kibbutzim. Kibbutz Bet Alfa, 1948–1951. Pikiwiki.

for the iconic Israeli house: a rectangular white house – or cottage, as it was popularly called – topped by a triangular roof of red tiles (see Figure 2.3).

The selective choices of the early Jewish settlers and their new designs were the first example of Even-Zohar's Zionist immigration model. But because these early settlers were not guided by a well-defined national vision, their construction of space was considered pragmatic rather than ideological.[20] It was not until the next wave of immigrants, who started arriving in the early 1900s, that space in Palestine began to change on a bigger scale and followed an ideological program in ways that had unexpected consequences.

[20] A few people did speak about a grander national vision at the time. In 1882 Z. Dubnov wrote that "I and several other people have a lofty and far-reaching goal in mind. Our end goal is to take eventual possession of the Land of Israel and reestablish the national independence that was lost to the Jews for two thousand years." See https://benyehuda.org/read/43514.

The Creation of the Kibbutz

The kibbutz (pl. kibbutzim) was the next stage in the evolution of modern farming space in Palestine and one of the earliest attempts to give the natural environment an ideological shape as part of the Zionist restoration project. Communalism played a major role in it, as it had in other settlements Jews set up in Palestine during the nineteenth century – in 1868 a man named Wolf Kalisher drew up plans for a communal farming village near Jerusalem and proposed that members give up their private property and share everything.[21] There were two reasons for this. The first was the absence of a modern infrastructure in Ottoman Palestine, which made cooperation necessary. The second was the communal traditions of the Jews who established these settlements.

The first reason is fairly obvious. Establishing settlements in a new and unfamiliar land that was not rich in resources required capital, expertise, organization, and cooperation. The second is more unusual, and came from the cooperative nature of traditional Jewish communities. Centuries of existence as minoritized communities led to an advanced collective culture amongst Jews. These traditions came in handy during the Jewish settlement of Palestine. They also contributed to the urban character of the *moshavot*. The establishment of the first kibbutzim in the early 1910s took these communal traditions to a new level, not only in Jewish history but in world history as well, and redefined Jewish space in the process.

Unlike the first group of middle-class Jewish immigrants, whose settlements soon turned into small towns, some of the settlers who arrived in Palestine in the early 1900s were very different: young, single, fiercely ideological, and with a clear national vision they were eager to realize. "He felt like a stranger" in Palestine, says a young immigrant in Luidor's short story "Harvest." "Nothing bound him to it yet, no land of his own, no footing, no family, a brother, a sister, no one, only his love for the land of his fathers."[22] But within a few years of landing on the shores of Palestine this group of young men and women came up with a completely new settlement configuration. Eventually called

---

[21] Haim Gvati, *One Hundred Years of Settlement: The History of Jewish Settlement in the Land of Israel* (שנות התיישבות 100), Hakkibutz Hame'uhad, 1981.

[22] Josef Luidor, "Harvest" (ימי הקציר), in *Recklessness*, p. 34.

A Hebrew Countryside 43

the kibbutz, it was a unique communal setup that became one of the earliest and most well-known innovations of Zionism.

Ironically, the creation of the kibbutz was a historical accident, a meeting of ideology, demography, physical conditions, and coincidence. Between 1909 and 1912 Zionists experimented with three kinds of cooperative settlements that were influenced by contemporary trends of social and economic justice in Europe. We often think of socialism and communism in this context, but in many ways Zionism belonged to those trends as well. Some of the Jewish immigrants who arrived in Palestine in the early 1900s were deeply moved by those ideas, especially the redemptive power of labor and Jewish self-sufficiency. But since most of them had no agricultural experience, they were sent to vocational farms that were set up by Zionist organizations specifically for that purpose. The idea was to train them as farmers and then help them set up private farms; no one envisioned cooperative farming yet. In practice, the plan did not work very well. First, because farming in Palestine was not very profitable. Second, because work on the training farms created tension between capital and labor, between the Zionist central organization and the agricultural students. That tension generated the first kibbutz.

Specific problems started when a group of agricultural students at a training farm near the Sea of Galilee, known as Kvutzat Kinneret, became upset with the manager of the farm, who had hired local Arab laborers as additional farm workers. As the students saw it, it was a question of profit over ideals – nationalist ideals about Jewish labor and self-sufficiency. They walked off the job in protest, and were persuaded to come back only after management agreed to let them run part of the farm on their own and set up "an independent farm ... with no managers or overseers."[23] The harvest was good that year, and when the rookie farmers turned a profit, the managing Zionist organization agreed to continue the experiment on a more permanent basis, making history in the process; a socialist experiment in the service of national-capitalism, if you will.

A year later, in 1910, the second farming cooperative, Degania, was established and laid the foundations for what soon became a phenomenally successful settlement scheme, based on a bottom-up approach that

---

[23] Gvati, *One Hundred Years of Settlement*, p. 126.

contributed to its strength and endurance.[24] Cooperatives helped the young settlers to cope with the harsh conditions and compensated for their inexperience. Later, when Arab resistance to Jewish colonization grew, farming cooperatives were instrumental as training grounds and as shelter for the Jewish militia, the Hagana.

The failure of a third experiment in collective farming, Merchavia, clearly demonstrated the benefits of the first two. Merchavia was established in 1911 as the brainchild of the German economist and sociologist Franz Oppenheimer (1864–1943), who envisioned an agricultural settlement that would combine capitalist and communist principles in accordance with the socialist maxim "From each according to their ability, to each according to their needs" – the same idea that inspired Herzl's New Society in his utopian novel *Altneuland*. Although Merchavia was temporarily abandoned in 1918 following a series of difficulties, its plan for communal space had a lasting effect on the layout of kibbutzim later.

Plans for the cooperative were made by another German architect, Alexander Baerwald (1877–1930), who happened to be in nearby Haifa at the time to plan the Technion, the first institution of higher learning in Palestine. Baerwald's task was to create a space that would express the common ownership of the land and the cooperative nature of labor and the means of production while accommodating differences in individual needs and abilities. Inspired by housing projects for German farm workers, the initial design included a large central yard, flanked by living and farming facilities. "On the north side," wrote the secretary of the cooperative, "cowsheds, a stable and warehouses. … On the east side, residence buildings, and on the south more residences, a dining hall and other communal facilities. On the west, by the outside wall, farm sheds, a carpentry and a smithing shed."[25] The geometric shape emphasized cohesion and cooperation and outlined the community clearly in the open setting of the land (see Figure 2.4).

In essence, Baerwald shrank an entire village and arranged it in a neat square that included all the different parts of the community in one place – shopping malls are designed on a similar principle. It is difficult to guess what spatial form the unique composite of communism and capitalism would have taken had Merchavia prospered. Baerwald only

---

[24] Galia Bar-Or and Yuval Yaski, curators, *The Kibbutz: Architecture without Precedent. The Israeli Pavilion at the 12th International Venice Biennale* (הקיבוץ: אדריכלות בלא תקדים), Keter, 2010.

[25] Merchavia Visitor Portal, available at https://merchavyard.org.il/.

A Hebrew Countryside

Fig. 2.4 Aerial photo of the restored yard in Merchavia, 1937, originally designed by Alexander Baerwald in 1912 as a cooperative village. Baerwald was an eclectic architect who incorporated local elements into his designs. His plan for the cowshed, stable, and storehouse reflects local Arab aesthetics in the arched windows, flat roof, and limestone bricks. The shape of the residential section of the farm, with its big square windows, quoins, and red-tiled roof, reflects Templer aesthetics. Israel Government Press Office.

managed to articulate its first and more communal phase, and in doing so gave a clear physical expression to abstract ideas that circulated almost simultaneously in Kvutzat Kinneret (see Figure 2.5), in Degania (see Figure 2.6), and in Merchavia.

The closed geometry of early kibbutzim was a sensible plan for a small and isolated collective. But as cooperative farms grew in size and number during the 1920s and 1930s, the division of space evolved as well. Two architects in particular helped to redefine it: Richard Kauffmann (1887–1958) and Lotte Cohn (1893–1983). Their major challenge was the novelty of the task. There were no precedents for planning a kibbutz. Existing farm models were not useful because most of them were private properties planned for profit. It was a completely new concept.

Fig. 2.5 Hatzar Kinneret, the first Zionist farming cooperative, in 1912. Some of the principles that informed Baerwald's design for Merchavia in 1912 are visible in this earlier layout as well, such as cohesion, cooperation, and the clear outline of the farm in the surrounding open space. Photo by Ya'acov Ben-Dov, Bitmuma, Aharon Israeli collection, Pritzker Family National Photography Collection, National Library of Israel.

Kauffmann and Cohn came up with an odd solution for this challenge: they took the principles of the garden city and applied them to rural space. "We are actually the first in the world," said Kauffmann, "to take modern principles of urban planning and apply them to country life."[26] The solution was odd because Palestine was sparsely populated and mostly rural at that time.

When we first came to Palestine we were impressed by the beauty and splendor of [a] country … unchanged yet by the intensive agriculture that altered it later. … The unusual modest yet heroic beauty of the land struck us like no

---

[26] Similar solutions were suggested for Templer villages and in housing design in Tel Aviv. See Marina Epstein-Pliouchtch and Michael Levin, eds., *Richard Kauffmann and the Zionist Project* (ריכארד קאופמן והפרויקט הציוני), Hakibbutz Hame'uhad, 2016, p. 111.

A Hebrew Countryside

Fig. 2.6 Aerial photo of Degania in 1918. On the left is the yard, comprising barns, workshops, and granary. The two-storied house outside the yard to the right is the members' living quarters. Pritzker Family National Photography Collection, National Library of Israel.

other land before. It seemed to us that the landscape – perhaps including its "charred Arab villages with their houses jumbled on top of bald, rocky hills, with no windows and not a spot of greenery, looking like old, abandoned nests," as Berkowitz put it[27] – challenged architects to dare and build on it.[28]

After a few years of trial and error, and with input from members of kibbutzim, architects such as Kauffmann, Cohn, and others broke the original farm square and shaped it into an expansive "socialist" space.[29] The major aspects of communal life, which were placed on different sides of the original kibbutz square, were now separated into different areas or

---

[27] Berkowitz, "Tel Aviv," p. 354.
[28] Epstein-Pliouchtch and Levin, eds., *Richard Kauffmann*, pp. 108–109.
[29] Early plans for kibbutzim were neater and more symmetrical, and set aside small private spaces for members. See Ruth Enis and Yosef Ben-Arav, *Kibbutz Gardens and Landscape* (גנים ונוף בקיבוץ), Defense Ministry, 1994, pp. 34–38.

48

zones that were easily negotiated on foot. There was a communal zone for dining, cultural facilities, and children's dorms; a zone consisting of small apartment blocks for members; and a third zone with barns and workshops. They were placed in a park-like setting that was free of cars and broke the traditional division between private and public. The main landscaping challenge here was how to shape the kibbutz "park," how to release the landscape from the boundaries of the (ornamental) garden, as Christopher Tunnard put it, free it from the capitalist constraints of the parcel and the plot and fit it to the classless kibbutz society.[30] Since green space surrounded the entire community on a kibbutz, turning it into an ornamental garden was impractical and irrelevant, as members of Degania soon realized. When they first arrived at the shores of the Sea of Galilee and saw the "bare valley, without tree or shade," they quickly "arranged a little garden with neat flower beds ... they planted alfalfa that carpeted everything with green, built a little round pool with a fountain," and arranged garden paths around it.[31]

But the refined design felt wrong and out of place. Another configuration was needed, one that would fit a cooperative community that was "neither a city nor a village ... nor ... a [recreational] park."[32] And it had to be practical too, a landscape or a garden that would redefine the relationship between private and public space. "As farmers of a commune," recalled a member of Kibbutz Bet Zera, "we ignored Kauffmann's plans for small vegetable gardens next to members' apartments" and his fondness for symmetry.[33] A more fitting solution was offered by Architect Shmuel Bickels, who suggested thinking of the kibbutz as "a garden for the whole day," a green space where people live, work, and rest.[34]

---

[30] Elissa Rosenberg, "Landscape Modernism and the Kibbutz: The Work of Shmuel Bickels," in Inbal Ben-Asher Gitler and Anat Geva, eds., *Israel as a Modern Architectural Experimental Lab, 1948–1978*, Intellect Books, 2019.

[31] Enis and Ben-Arav, *Kibbutz Gardens*, p. 21. The Deganians were not alone in that. Ornamental pools cropped up in other kibbutzim even after gardening was made to match the communal ideology better. See ibid., pp. 38–39. For a picture of Degania's first ornate garden see https://commons.wikimedia.org/ wiki/File:Jewish_colonies_and_settlements._Various_Jewish_colonies,_etc._ Degania_(A)_near_Semakh._approximately_1920_to_1930._matpc.02346.jpg.

[32] Kibbutz architect Shmuel Bickels in Rosenberg, "Landscape Modernism."

[33] Enis and Ben-Arav, *Kibbutz Gardens*, p. 31.

[34] Rosenberg, "Landscape Modernism," p. 101.

A Hebrew Countryside 49

Lawns became an important element in the whole-day kibbutz garden, even if they were unusual in the context of the Middle East. They required a lot of water and stood out as green oases in the semi-arid environment, as did the kibbutz landscape in general, a literal representation of the Zionist colonial project with its aspirations of making the desert bloom. The social value of lawns was first suggested by the gardener of Kibbutz Ashdot Ya'acov, who took generic plans for his kibbutz and modified them to better fit the nature of his cooperative community. "We wanted to imbed our community in green and create large lawn areas that would blend with the natural environment more harmoniously," he wrote later, no doubt as someone who had grown up in Europe, a stranger to the dry land around him. "We planted ornamental plants around the lawns and arranged trees for shade by the houses."[35]

Toward the end of the 1930s lawns became an iconic element of kibbutz life, an open living-room for members to hang out in, to socialize, to play, to celebrate, and, before the introduction of air-conditioning, to stay cool as well. Lawns also contributed to the final evolution of the original kibbutz square into a deconstructed home, whose various rooms – kitchen, dining room, living rooms, bedrooms, etc. – were extended outside and blended with the external environment, mixing inside and outside as well as private and public. A garden for the whole day indeed (see Figure 2.7).

Houses were integral to the garden and designed to suit its communal logic. On the first communal farms, houses looked very similar to those on *moshavot* and Templer villages. Standing two stories tall and built of stone, with decorative elements and red roofs, the first houses in Degania looked oddly bourgeois amidst the barns, warehouses, and open land around them. But as the original square yard of the first kibbutz was abstracted and diffused, architecture was changed as well.

Curiously, building conventions on many kibbutzim developed two distinct orientations, public and private. Public buildings, like dining halls and performance spaces, children's houses, and schools were modernistic in shape, while the private apartments of kibbutz members – measuring about 25 square meters (apartments were called

[35] Enis and Ben-Arav, *Kibbutz Gardens*, p. 45. For a picture of one these first kibbutz lawns see www.bitmuna.com/?s= יעקב+אשדות&jig_custom_ search=nextgen.

Fig. 2.7 The introduction of large lawn areas on kibbutzim integrated the different zones of the community and extended the communal living space to the outside. The biggest lawn area was usually set up next to the dining hall, the center of kibbutz life. In this picture it occupies the center of the diagonal rectangle around the dining hall with rows of trees planted at the edges of the rectangle. Smaller lawns can be seen throughout the community, around the children's houses (bottom right) and next to members' apartments (bottom left). Kibbutz Nir David, 1946. Wikipedia.

"rooms" on kibbutzim) – had more rustic features, such as red roofs. The difference was another expression of the unusual combination of town and country that marked the kibbutz experiment and the Jewish colonization project in general.[36]

The most distinctly urban aspects of kibbutz life were education and culture, and the modernistic structures that housed them conveyed it in their simple, angular shapes. Dining halls were the focus of communal life on kibbutzim, and not just because all meals were taken there. They

[36] A picture of Kibbutz Nir David shows 1930s rustic apartment houses of kibbutz members, with red terracotta roofs, on the right. The modernistic, two-story building at the center-top is the children's house. See https://commons.wikimedia.org/wiki/File:A_VIEW_OF_KIBBUTZ_TEL_AMAL_(NIR_DAVID)._(ניר_דוד)_מראה_כללי_של_קיבוץ_תל_עמל).D14-018.jpg.

A Hebrew Countryside

51

also had an important cultural function as meeting places for leisure and entertainment. Kibbutzim had a rich cultural calendar – the culture committee had a big role in kibbutz life – of lectures, music concerts, and festivals, especially Jewish festivals. These were adapted by kibbutz members to life on the land and were marked on a grand communal scale that was unprecedented in Jewish history. In traditional Jewish communities, holidays were usually marked in the synagogue and followed by a family meal at home. Kibbutzim took those rituals out of the synagogue and incorporated them into the communal festival meal as part of an integrated cultural program, blending traditional religious elements with elements from the agricultural cycle that were meant to recall biblical times. The celebrations were held in the kibbutz dining hall, which was transformed into a festive space that attracted guests from all over the country.

The cultural aspects of kibbutz life were not confined to the dining hall. Many kibbutzim built dedicated cultural institutions, such as reading rooms, museums, performance spaces and memorial halls, that housed various cultural activities. Some of these events took place outside in the open spaces of the whole-day garden, where festivals, dance performances, concerts, and a variety of shows could be easily hosted; this set the kibbutz apart as a unique community, a farming community designed by townsfolk for other townsfolk who had become farmers, a vivid example of the kind of cultural engineering that went into the making of Zionism.

Farmland

The Bible had tremendous influence on the human imagination, especially in the Christian world, and shaped the perception of the Land of Israel for millennia. Most of the visitors to Palestine who left a record of their journeys – some 3,500 journals in total, 2,000 of them in the nineteenth century alone – made the journey because of the Bible and experienced the land through it.[37] Many of them, though not all, were disappointed with a land that seemed to them empty and desolate.[38]

[37] Rachel Gottesman, Tamar Novick, Iddo Ginat, Dan Hasson, and Yonatan Cohen, eds., *Land. Honey. Milk: Animal Stories in Imagined Landscapes*, Israeli Pavilion, Biennale di Venezia and Park Books, 2017, p. 46.

[38] Ruth Kark, *The Land that Became Israel: Studies in Historical Geography*, Magness Press, 1989. Laurence Oliphant, for one, praised the Jezreel Valley for

Their disillusionment was likely shaped by the temperate climes of Europe and North America, whence most of them came. But it was also formed by the radiant picture they had of ancient Israel, whose spiritual value was expected to manifest in real life and take on familiar images. "We were only one little hour's travel within the borders of the Holy Land," wrote Mark Twain excitedly about his well-publicized visit to Palestine in 1867, "we had hardly begun to appreciate yet that we were standing upon any different sort of earth than that we had always been used to and see how the historic names began already to cluster! ... They were all in sight." But the meeting with the earthly Palestine was sorely disappointing. Twain saw a land "where prosperity has reigned, and fallen; where glory has flamed, and gone out; where beauty has dwelt, and passed away; where gladness was, and sorrow is."[39] The expectation was as unrealistic as the abstract nouns Twain used.

The Hebrew Bible colored the view of Zionists as well, but with one crucial difference. The comparison of contemporary Palestine with the milk and honey of biblical times didn't depress Zionists, it inspired them. In fact, the vision of the modern Jewish settlement project was predicated on it. Zionist ideology promised to turn the present desolation of Palestine into a fertile future that was based on an idyllic past.[40] Jewish patriotism, said Berl Katznelson, is a literary patriotism "born out of the Book, out of verses and historical names." And while it may be an abstract patriotism, it has become "a mighty force."[41]

Nineteenth-century photographs and early twentieth-century films of the Palestinian countryside show a land with little tree coverage, stony hills, and small valleys, dotted with villages of stone houses, usually bunched on hilltops, surrounded by small, uneven fields and hillside terraces. Vegetation looks sparse and consists of subsistence crops such as cereals and vegetables, small plantations of fruit trees, like olives and citrus, and a distinct central American import, the cactus plant. Also known as prickly pear, or *sabar* in Arabic, the cactus spread throughout the Mediterranean via Spain and was commonly used for marking out

---

looking "like a huge green lake of waving wheat ... one of the most striking pictures of luxuriant fertility which it is possible to conceive": Oliphant, *Haifa*, p. 60.

[39] Mark Twain, *The Innocents Abroad*, available at www.gutenberg.org/files/3176/3176-h/3176-h.htm, chapters 56 and 57 respectively.

[40] Yohai Oppenheimer, *Barriers: The Representation of the Arab in Hebrew and Israeli Fiction, 1906–2005* (מעבר לגדר), Am Oved, 2008, pp. 46–47.

[41] Ibid., p. 47.

A Hebrew Countryside   53

property boundaries in the way hedges, tall trees, walls, or fences are used in other countries. These were the sights that greeted visitors to Palestine in the nineteenth century, pilgrims and Jewish settlers alike.

The attempts of Jewish farmers to transform this landscape and "restore" it to its biblical glory went through several stages that grew progressively distant from the initial romantic vision of an agricultural Jurassic park based on old literary descriptions – it was a romantic vision that was shared by the British Mandate authorities, which governed Palestine from 1918 to 1948. Moreover, ancient Israel stretched over the hilly land west of the Jordan River and the Dead Sea, in the areas known as Judea and Samaria. But since that land was crowded with Arab villages and farms, it was not for sale. Zionists had to get what they could, less populated and less arable land on the coastal plain of Palestine and the Jezreel Valley in the north. If the open land they bought looked less biblical, it lent itself better to industrial farming and geometric field shapes that produced an orderly and modern look.

Excited by the first attempts at Jewish farming since antiquity, the settlers of the *moshavot* tried to revive a biblical agriculture of cereal crops and fruit trees, "a land of wheat and barley, and vines and fig-trees and pomegranates," as it says in Deuteronomy 8:8. But excitement was not a substitute for experience, and the early idyllic stage didn't last long. "Our Jewish colonists came full of ideals, and some of them with money too, but none of them have the necessary skills or habits fit for farming," wrote Ahad Ha'am in 1891.[42]

In the 1880s Baron Edmond de Rothschild was persuaded to help the struggling Jewish farmers start a wine industry in Palestine. Rothschild, who owned renowned vineyards in France, sponsored the planting of thousands of acres of vines in the *moshavot*. But the attempt proved problematic, and the project was eventually abandoned. "All of our colonies are following the baron's gardeners blindly," wrote Ahad Ha'am, even though "we have no idea if the vines will do well here." Many of them did not, but for a while vineyards replaced seasonal crops and marked the landscape of Jewish Palestine.

By the early 1900s vineyards began to be replaced by orange trees. Citrus traveled to the Middle East from Asia and was cultivated in the region long before the arrival of Jewish settlers, who adopted it enthusiastically. Perhaps it was the relative ease of growing the sturdy fruit, storing it, and moving it to market that made it such a favorite.

---

[42] Ahad Ha'am, "Truth from the Land of Israel."

54   *Hebrew Space and Architecture*

From the 1920s on, Jewish farmers began to expand what was already a considerable Palestinian citrus sector. They surrounded their settlements with dark-green groves of the short, round trees and soon turned oranges into part of Zionist folklore, art, and literature. Writing about a memorable visit to one of those orchards, Y. D. Berkowitz described how

> they were greeted by the coolness of shaded orange groves that stretched before them right and left and across the gentle hill country to the distance, a fresh carpet of green leaves, dappled with golden red spots that twinkled in the morning light. The sun ... was warm and pleasant here, redolent of a soft and gentle spring, shining brightly on the whitewashed trunks of the small trees, on their rich green leaves, and on the golden ripe fruit that hung peacefully in their fullness.[43]

The final form of the Yishuv's landscape came with the purchase of larger tracts of land and the establishment of cooperative farming. Unlike the smaller private plots on *moshavot*, the open land of kibbutzim and their intensive farming practices created bigger and more geometric field shapes that were often marked by rows of tall trees. Jewish farmers were not fond of the ubiquitous prickly pear and chose another import for that purpose, the Australian eucalyptus, as well as the local cypress tree. Both trees stood taller and were more orderly and manageable than the cactus, "a strange, wild plant covered in sharp needles that burn like fire if you touch them," as Yishuv children were admonished in an early story, before the cactus, or *sabra*, as it was called in Hebrew, came to describe Jewish natives of the Yishuv and later Israel in an ironic twist.[44] By the 1940s the landscape of Jewish Palestine had been considerably transformed by Zionists, who turned it into an orderly agricultural space of large, even fields dotted with small communities of rectangular white houses topped by red roofs. Many of the stony hills that could not be cultivated were planted with trees, mostly pines and cypresses.[45]

---

[43] Y. D. Berkowitz, *The Days of the Messiah*, in *Collected Writings*, p. 486. See the 1935 picture of an orange grove on Kibbutz Na'an, available at https://commons.wikimedia.org/wiki/File:A_KIBBUTZ_MEMBER_IRRIGATING_ORANGE_TREES_IN_THE_PLANTATION_OF_KIBBUTZ_NA'AN. חבר_קיבוץ_נען_משקה_עצי_תפוזים_במטע_הקיבוץ.D18-034.jpg.

[44] Alexander Siskind Rabinovich, "The Hike" (הטיול), *Eshkolot*, issue 3, 1907; mentioned in *Onegshabbat* blog, https://onegshabbat.blogspot.com/search?q=אשכולות .

[45] Aerial picture of kibbutz Degania, 1931, available at https://en.m.wikipedia.org/wiki/File:Degania._Jewish_agricultural_colony._South_end_of_Lake_Galilee._1931_Oct._matpc.15823.jpg.g.

Woodland

The Eastern Mediterranean has been inhabited continually since prehistoric times, and the human impact on it was extensive early on, as the Bible tells us. In preparation for their entry into Canaan, God instructs the Israelites to "plant all manner of trees for food" (Leviticus 19:23). But he also tells them to clear the land for farming: "the high country shall be yours, for it is forest, and you shall clear it" (Joshua 17:18). By the nineteenth century, grazing, farming, and frequent wars in the region had used up most of the natural tree growth in Palestine and left large parts of it bare.

Still, Bible-reading visitors to Palestine were surprised to find the land so naked. It wasn't an unreasonable surprise, given the great variety of trees the Bible mentions. The word יער, meaning forest in Modern Hebrew, is mentioned forty-two times in the Bible, and its frequent poetic use, from Exodus to Ezekiel, indicates that ancient Israel must have been covered with all manner of trees. The clash between the poetic then and the very different now was disappointing. Palestine is "stripped and starved ... a carcass of a land," wrote the Scottish theologian George Adam Smith after his visit, expressing the disappointment of many visitors.[46]

Jewish settlers were also dismayed to find a dry and stony land when they first arrived. In 1927 the founders of Kibbutz Bet Zera looked at the Jordan Valley and saw "a flat plain, bare, burnt and scorching."[47] Even Jews who came from the dry Arabian Peninsula noticed it. "Our elders praised the Land of Israel," wrote Sa'adya Maswari, who came from Yemen in 1912, "but what I saw was very different, a dry and desolate land, hilly, full of thorny bushes and very few trees."[48] But such sights also strengthened the resolve of Jewish settlers to change it, to return the land to the glory of biblical times and soothe their own longing for some of the greenery they left behind in Europe. "Our first reaction was – shade. To plant a tree, to screen the burning light with green ... [to fulfill the biblical commandment] 'when you come to the land ... plant all manner of trees'" (Leviticus 19:23).[49]

---

[46] Roza I. M. El-Eini, "British Forestry Policy in Mandate Palestine 1929–1948: Aims and Realities," *Middle Eastern Studies* 35: 3 (July 1999): 75–155.

[47] Enis and Ben-Arav, *Kibbutz Gardens*, p. 23.

[48] Nitza Droyan, *The First Yemeni Immigrants, 1882–1914* (חלוצי העליה מתימן, פרקים בהתישבותם תרמ"ב-תרע"ד), Zalman Shazar, 1982, p. 101.

[49] Enis and Ben-Arav, *Kibbutz Gardens*, p. 23.

56 Hebrew Space and Architecture

The pitiful impression made by Palestine sent both Jewish settlers and the British Mandate authorities who followed them on a quest to restore the land to its imagined past. And if the exact nature of that wooded past was unknown, it didn't stop the Jews or the British from trying.

The Templers from Germany were among the first to bring modern horticulture to Palestine. They planted trees and flower gardens in their colonies and tended to the woods around them. The practice was picked up by the settlers of the *moshavot*, who mandated setting aside "four yards for a rose garden in front of every house" and planting trees that would sweeten the air.[50] The efforts must have been successful because a few years later visitors to those new Jewish villages were impressed with the "flower beds in front of almost every house, and [the] shaded boulevards of mulberry trees along the streets."[51] But most of these attempts were local and limited, even when they included larger projects, such as the grandly named Hadera Forest of Eucalyptuses that was planted in 1896 to help drain marshland around the *moshava*.[52]

Most of the trees that were planted by the German and early Jewish colonizers of Palestine were fruit trees. This was not necessarily because of the biblical injunction to do so; it simply made good farming sense, certainly for private farmers not thinking of themselves as founders of a future Jewish state. Zionists thought it was a good idea too. We need "to establish a national arbor association for planting trees in Palestine," Herzl noted in his diary two years before he visited the country. "Every Jew should pay for one or more tree," he added, so we can have "ten million trees."[53] It was a brilliant idea. When it was combined with a commemorative gesture after Herzl's death, the innovation became a highly effective foresting scheme that paid for the first Zionist plantation in Palestine: thousands of olives, almonds, apricots, and grapevines that were planted at Ben Shemen in 1908 in honor of Herzl. More orchard

---

[50] Shavit, "Regulations of the First Moshavot," p. 61. For an image of these early gardens see https://commons.wikimedia.org/wiki/File:PikiWiki_Israel_13752_Petah_Tikva_streets.jpg.

[51] Tal Alon-Mozes and Shaul Amir, "Landscape and Ideology: The Emergence of Vernacular Gardening Culture in Pre-State Israel," *Landscape Journal* 21: 2 (2002): 37–50, at p. 46.

[52] For an image of Hadera Forest see https://commons.wikimedia.org/wiki/File:PikiWiki_Israel_1120_hadera_ שמירה_ביער_בחדרה.jpg.

[53] Orly Rechtman, "The Development of Forestry in Israel" (של התבססותו 1960 מדיניות מעשים ותוצאות מתחילת הייעור ועד משאב היער בישראל,), *Ya'ar* 18 (December 2017), at p. 6.

A Hebrew Countryside 57

than forest, it was a romantic reenactment of Leviticus 19:23 and, in good Zionist fashion, a pragmatic attempt at a cash crop as well.

But orchards and forests are two different things, and the project flopped, prompting Zionists to take another look at the challenge. "We cannot speak of forests in Palestine in a European sense," wrote Max Bodenheimer in 1911. "Let's plant woodland trees like eucalyptus, pine and cypress," he suggested more sensibly; in other words, not an emotional act of restoration but a project of environmental engineering that was supported by scientists, botanists, and agronomists who set up experimental nurseries for that purpose. Bodenheimer worked for the Jewish National Fund (JNF), an organization that was set up in 1901 to collect money for land acquisition in Palestine. Most of that land was used for settlements and farms. Land that was unfit for either was planted with trees, mostly pines and cypresses because they grew fast.

As the Yishuv developed and expanded, forestry became a strategic settlement device. Forests extended Zionists' dominion over land they owned but could not cultivate, either for logistical reasons, such as manpower and money, or for more objective reasons like topography or arability. Planting forests also provided work for a growing force of unskilled workers. Moreover, Zionists thought of tree planting as an act of *tikkun* or holistic repair, an environmental improvement and an aesthetic gesture, a civilizing expression of high culture. "Woe to the land whose woods were cut off and chopped and is left uncovered," a 1921 JNF report waxed poetically. "The absence of forests disturbs the creative harmony of nature and invites evil spirits which befoul the air and spoil it for human habitation," the report continued.[54] Planted forests became symbolic of the rejuvenating spirit of Zionism, which rededicated to it the ancient tree day of Tu Bishvat, 15 Shevat, and used it to organize tree planting events that involved the entire Yishuv.[55]

---

[54] Nili Liphschitz and Gideon Biger, "Forestry Policy of the Zionist Movement in Palestine 1895–1948" (1948–1895 מדיניות הייעור של התנועה הציונית בא"י), *Katedra* 80 (1996): 88–108, at p. 96.

[55] For studies on this see Shaul Amir and Orly Rechtman, "The Development of Forest Policy in Israel in the 20th Century: Implications for the Future," *Forest Policy & Economics* 8 (2006): 35–51; Lifschitz and Biger, "Forestry Policy of the Zionist Movement in Palestine, 1895–1948"; Nurit Kliut, "Ideology and Forestation in Israel" (אידאולוגיה וייעור בישראל – יער מעשה אדם באמצעות הקרן הקיימת לישראל), *Mehkarim bege'ografia* 13 (1993): 87–106; Nili Liphschitz and Gideon Biger, "British Mandate Forestry Policy in Palestine" (מדיניות

58 *Hebrew Space and Architecture*

The British colonial administration in Palestine advanced the cause of trees even more than the Zionists. In their first year the Mandate authorities planted 370,000 trees. A year later, in 1920, the number of planted trees rose to 2 million. The British were surely inspired by the Bible and showed a metaphysical reverence for restoring the Promised Land to its ancient botanical beauty; a beauty which the "virile [Hebrew] race" bestowed on it, as Claude Jarvis put it; he was the British colonial governor of the Sinai Peninsula between 1923 and 1936.[56] But they tempered that reverence with experience gained in other parts of their empire.[57] Joining science to romance, the British approached forestry in Palestine more scientifically, considering the practical aspects of trees for preventing soil erosion, stopping the advance of sand dunes, and supporting a timber industry.

If the local Arabs and Jews who helped them in their work had "never [seen] a forest since there are no forests in Palestine," the British were determined to change that. In 1929 the high commissioner to Palestine, John Chancellor, assured the League of Nations that he intended "to allocate ten million dunams for forest reservations." Unlike the Zionists, who were confined to land they had bought, the British could plant trees anywhere they wanted in Palestine, and that was precisely what they did. They set up woodland reservations and planted a variety of local trees that proved much sturdier and longer lasting than the more homogeneous and faster-growing Zionist woodland.

But if the British and the Zionists shared a biblical dream, it meant little to local Arabs, who often disregarded new tree plantations and continued to use the land for grazing. "The Jews have started planting increasing numbers of pines and other trees," wrote T. J. Tear of the Palestine forestry division in 1931. "Arabs, on the other hand, have no interest in forests, they only want olive and other fruit trees"; and they "wantonly destroy everything for which they could find no immediate

---

(הייעור של הממשל הבריטי בארץ ישראל), *Ofakim bege'ografia* 40–41 (1994): 5–16.

[56] Robert S. G. Fletcher, *British Imperialism and the Tribal Question*, Oxford University Press, 2015, p. 196. 22

[57] Alon Tal, "British Planting, an Unfulfilled Mandate" (הנטיעות הבריטיות -מנדט שלא התגשם, מרחבים בשינוי: תמורות גיאוגרפיות בא״י וסביבתה), *Merhavim* 7 (2016), ed. Yaron Balslav, Yossi Katz, and Yitzhak Schnel: 159–188, at p. 162.

A Hebrew Countryside

use," Jarvis wrote elsewhere.[58] It was an economic issue. Many Arabs were subsistence farmers who depended on grazing for survival, and none of them was consulted anyway about the landscaping initiatives of the Jews and the British. And although Tear did add in his report that "Arabs began to understand the importance of forest preservation as well and several of their learned men have begun to plant forests," the economic differences between Arabs and Jews were eventually channeled into a growing national rivalry that led to deliberate sabotage of tree plantations.

A charming initiative that was not directly connected with Jewish nationalism or British colonialism was an ecological project called the Men of the Trees in Palestine.[59] It was the brainchild of Dr. Richard St. Barbe Baker, an Englishman who worked for the British colonial forestry division in Kenya and Nigeria, where he set up similar tree clubs in 1922. In 1929 he founded a Palestinian chapter that did speak of the need "to beautify the Holy Land" but was much more focused on "developing an affinity for trees in every person and encourag[ing] everyone to plant and love trees ... [since] forest work is one of humanity's oldest and most respected activities, unselfish and constructive." As an English peer, St. Barbe Baker was able to enlist key British figures in support of his project, which called on everyone in Palestine, "irrespective of religion, race, or wealth," to take part in it and plant trees on their private land and anywhere else they could. The club planted trees with money collected from both Jews and non-Jews. Some of its initiatives included planting competitions for high schools, with points given for soil preparation, planting methods, choice of trees, and cultivation practices.

In 1953 St. Barbe Baker was invited to Jerusalem for an exhibition called Defeating the Wilderness. In an open letter to the organizers he wrote how happy he was "to be part of the exhibition and thankful for all those who help beat wilderness and hold back the desert. The fertility of the soil in Israel depends on trees, and the dry bones – the exposed lime rocks – are coming back to life. It won't be long before

---

[58] Liphschitz and Biger, "British Mandate Forestry Policy," p. 7; Fletcher, *British Imperialism*, p. 196.

[59] Uri Rosenberg, "Developing a Tree Sense: The First Land Preservation Project in the Land of Israel," available at www.kalanit.org.il/firsttreesassoc2020/.

60   *Hebrew Space and Architecture*

the mountains will be covered with green, and the land will be a fruitful garden again" – a romantic, perhaps, after all.[60]

By the end of the Mandate period in 1948, about 35 million trees had been planted on 85,000 dunams. It was less than 3 percent of Palestine and far below the 10 percent Zionists aimed for – the current forest coverage of Israel is about 6 percent. More than two-thirds of the trees were planted by the British, a mixture of pines, cypresses, pistacias, and other varieties. Most of it was planted on rocky hills and mountain slopes that could not be farmed and gave the Israeli countryside much of its current look.

Hebrew Cities

Cities occupied a peculiar place in Zionist thinking, which was more concerned with farming. This was understandable, given some of the old connections between city and decay – the pastoral idea in ancient Greek culture was an early critique of the corrupting influences of urban life – and between the city and Jews; for various historical reasons Jews had settled in towns and cities outside the Land of Israel. Herzl made several references to it in his diaries. Max Nordau, his right-hand man, premised his popular 1895 *Degeneration* on "the evils which follow the uprooting of the people from fostering Mother Earth, and the incubation of [the] urban industrial proletariat," and based his famous call for a muscular Judaism on it.[61]

One of the express aims of Zionism was to sever these damaging connections, to take Jews out of their unhealthy ghettos and turn them into wholesome farmers again. But since city life was ingrained in Jewish diasporic civilization, it was integral to Zionist ideology as well. It influenced the formation of farming communities in Palestine, and had an impact on the Zionist imagination. Highly developed cities were part of most future visions of a sovereign Jewish state in the various utopias written by the likes of Theodor Herzl, Elhanan Leib Lewinsky, Edmund Menachem Eisler, and Boris Schatz, who named his 1918 utopia *The*

---

[60] Richard St. Barbe Baker, "Shall These Bones Live?" (התחייינה העצמות האלה), *Laya'aran, Agudat Haya'ar Beyisra'el* (Israel Forestry Newsletter) 4: 1–2 (1954), p. 23, available at www.kkl.org.il/files/Accessible-1/afforestation_and_environment/afforestation_and_environment_publications/layaaran_magazine/layaaran-1-2-1954.pdf.

[61] Max Nordau, *Degeneration*, tr. William Heinemann, 1898, p. 163.

Hebrew Cities 61

Built Jerusalem (ירושלים הבנויה). And it was clear to all that the viability of the Jewish settlement project in Palestine required an urban base, cities that would "encourage building, commerce and industry," like the city "Herzl envisioned in [his novel] *Altneuland*" and named Tel Aviv.[62] Talking about it, however, was not as exciting as talking about the bosom of nature.

In the early 1900s Palestine had two principal towns or cities, Jaffa and Jerusalem. The descriptions we have of them by contemporaries are not glowing. "Here we are in Jaffa: again, poverty and misery and heat in gay colors," Herzl wrote in his diary on October 27, 1898.[63] A month later he described his last day in Jaffa as "exceptionally unpleasant, full of beggars and spies." Meir Dizengoff, the first mayor of Tel Aviv, described Jaffa as "filthy" and "ugly," lacking "comfort and aesthetic beauty."[64] Jerusalem did not fare better. Herzl though it looked charmingly picturesque in the moonlight or from afar: "so much can be done with this [spectacular] view," he noted complacently as he stood on the Mount of Olives looking over the city. But the filth and beggary he saw there on closer inspection upset him so much that he jotted down how to improve it "by a loving hand that will make it a gem of a city."

While these were the views of people who were at home in cities such as London, Vienna, and Paris, the small and ancient cities of Jaffa and Jerusalem could not logistically absorb substantial numbers of immigrants. And yet many of the Jews who arrived in Palestine during the first decade of the twentieth century settled in Jaffa, in particular, for lack of other options. The need to accommodate them prompted several initiatives for building new and more spacious neighborhoods outside the walls of both cities on land bought for that purpose. Although the first such initiative began in Jerusalem in 1860, urban development on the coastal plain around Jaffa grew more quickly than in the hills around Jerusalem. Jaffa was closer to the country's main port, where most immigrants disembarked, the sand dunes to its north were fairly flat, they were sparsely populated and little farmed, and had no religious

---

[62] Akiva Arye Weiss, one of the Tel Aviv's founders, in Edna Yekutieli Cohen, "Akiva Arye Weiss and the First Hebrew City" (עקיבא אריה ויס והעיר העברית הראשונה), *Katedra* 135 (2009), at p. 134.

[63] Herzl, *The Complete Diaries*, p.739.

[64] Mark Levine, "A Nation from the Sands," *National Identities* 1: 1 (1999): 15–38, at p. 17.

62   *Hebrew Space and Architecture*

significance. Most importantly, large chunks of it were for sale. It made for a good canvas.[65]

Ahuzat Bayit, later named Tel Aviv, was not the first community that was built for Jews on the sands north of Jaffa; the first one, Neve Tzedek, was built in 1887. But it was the first properly planned community, and its founders had big hopes for it. Although it was described in its bylaws as "a modern Jewish quarter of Jaffa," plans for the gated community were strongly influenced by contemporary ideas about the garden city, ideas that set the neighborhood apart from its surroundings and shaped its growth.[66] Almost everything about it was different, from the land area that was bought and exceeded its needs, the professional plans that were drawn for it, "with roads, sidewalks, electricity ... and running water, like a modern European city,"[67] to the vision of its founders, who long before the first house was built spoke of it as "a new kind of Hebrew settlement ... a city of Jews in the land of the Jews ... the New York of [Israel]."[68] In many ways the building blocks of Ahuzat Bayit were like stem cells that later grew into the urban organs of a much larger city that became the hub of the Yishuv. This was the revolutionary aspect that set Tel Aviv apart from earlier Jewish settlements.[69]

[65] For an aerial view of Jerusalem around 1920, looking west, see https://commons.wikimedia.org/wiki/File:Jerusalem,_Temple_area_from_S.E._corner_showing_a_great_part_of_the_Old_City._ppmsca.18914.jpg. The new construction outside the walls is primarily to the left (west) of the old city, where the first Jewish neighborhood outside the city walls, Mishkenot Sha'ananim, was built in 1860. For an aerial photo of Jaffa, looking from the north east toward the southwest in 1917, see commons.wikimedia.org/wiki/File:אויר_צילום_.29%_1915_28%_._ב-אביב_-תל_פו.-PHKH-1278800 .png. The city of Jaffa juts out into the sea at center top. The white triangle of sand extending north of Jaffa to the right is crowded with new Jewish neighborhoods. Ahuzat Bayit is at bottom left of a triangle whose urban base is Jaffa. Arab-owned citrus groves comprise the dark part of the picture on the left of the photo.

[66] Levine, "A Nation from the Sands," p. 20.

[67] Yekutieli Cohen, "Akiva Arye Weiss," p. 135.

[68] Ibid., pp. 133, 136–137.

[69] This garden-city plan for Ahuzat Bayit by the Jewish-Austrian architect Wilhelm Stiassny was not officially adopted by the community, which nevertheless implemented many of its principles, including the grid, the space between houses, gardening ordinances, and the construction of a main road and public buildings at the center of the community. For an image of Stiassny's plan see www.researchgate.net/figure/Stasianis-scheme-for-Ahuzat-Bayit-Source-Avigdor-Droyanov-The-Tel Aviv-Book-Tel_fig1_263520167.

Hebrew Cities 63

Organic growth aside, the expansion of Tel Aviv, which was quickly dubbed the "first Hebrew city," posed several challenges. In addition to the logistical difficulties imposed by rapid expansion, there were more ideological and aesthetic challenges: the parts, quarters, zones, or areas the city should contain and the form these parts should take; the layout of streets; the shape of houses etc. that would fit its original plan. This was not a *moshava* or a kibbutz anymore but something bigger, a city. The fact that it was to be a Jewish city begged another question. Given the charged nexus between cities and Jews, and given that Yishuv society wished to change it and was focused on farming, how would urban culture fit into it? This tension dogged the image of Tel Aviv for decades and became the stuff of literature too. Here is how Y. D. Berkowitz put it:

The pioneering farmers look askance at Tel Aviv, especially the fanatics among them, those sworn slaves to toil who never crack a smile, who vowed to till the nation's soil with solemn dedication for the glory of Hebrew labor. Tel Aviv is the devil to them, a symbol of urban decay, land wasted for petty commerce and a specter of the Jewish Diaspora. But the city is also home to Jewish culture, and it pulls at the heartstrings of those farmers, especially on festival days. On Hanukkah or Passover, some of them come to celebrate in Tel Aviv, and the city makes them smile.[70]

Part of this tension was eased by the novelty of the concept of the "Hebrew city." A majority of Jews may have lived in cities throughout history, but always as a minority, and frequently as a discriminated-against minority. One of the commonplaces of early Yishuv culture was to give various everyday phenomena the pair of adjectives "first" and "Hebrew": the first Hebrew child, the first Hebrew cow, the first Hebrew streetlight. These sobriquets were theatrical perhaps, but they reveal the civic exuberance of the Zionist settlers and their appreciation for the Jewish historical moment they were living in. "When the small wheel began to scrape against the wire, its voice carried to the entire length of Herzl Street," reminisced Nahum Gutman about the lighting of the first streetlight in Tel Aviv:

---

[70] Berkowitz, "Tel Aviv," p. 356.

64   *Hebrew Space and Architecture*

People in the street grew silent and approached the lamp post that was put up a few days earlier on the corner of Herzl Street and Rothschild Boulevard. ... A green light flickered in the small mesh inside the lamp ... and with a hum that sounded like a tired bee it grew and spread, sending long fingers across the street and over to the sand dunes ... let's call it the hum of culture, which has just set foot on this quiet place and stood among us.[71]

Calling an entire city "first" and "Hebrew" expressed a much higher aspiration, one that already implied the next stage, a sovereign Jewish state.

In principle, the challenges of constructing a so-called Hebrew urban space were not different from those of shaping a Hebrew countryside. Similar questions could be asked here as well: What does the term Hebrew city mean, and how does one give concrete shape to such an abstract idea? If none of these questions was asked directly, answers to them were formulated in quick succession during the three evolutionary stages Tel Aviv underwent, following the shifting fortunes of Zionism.

During the first stage, between 1909 and 1914, Ahuzat Bayit was a small, landscaped neighborhood for middle-class Jews whose first priority was to leave the congestion of old Jaffa and the provisional Jewish neighborhoods around it.[72] This is how Agnon described it:

Camels and donkeys carry sand over, wheelbarrows come and go, hammers come down, and a steamroller presses down on the stones [that] level the plain. ... 'Tis the sound of building and the smell of a dwelling place ... the beginning of a road, a firm footrest. And men, women and children come from Jaffa and try the road for firmness and behold, the road is unyielding, their feet do not sink into the sand anymore.[73]

In its first years Ahuzat Bayit looked like a *moshava*. With its cream-colored, one-family homes, topped by red roofs and spruced up with gardens, the neighborhood looked like a peaceful suburb of a metropolis rather than the beginning of one (see Figure 2.8). "Tourists who later

---

[71] Nahum Gutman, "The First Streetlight" (פנס רחוב ראשון), Ben-Yehuda Project, available at https://benyehuda.org/read/30638. Gutman dedicated a drawing to that auspicious moment in his memoir about early Tel Aviv, *A Small City with Very Few People* (עיר קטנה ואנשים בה מעט), Am Oved, Dvir, 1959.

[72] Levine, "A Nation from the Sands," p. 21.

[73] Agnon, *Only Yesterday*, p. 439.

שדרות רוטשילד (לצד מערב) — 1911.

Fig. 2.8 Stage 1: Rothschild Boulevard in 1911 during Tel Aviv's initial "suburban" stage. Most houses have one story and red terracotta roofs, characteristic of the architectural style of the *moshavot*. The front gardens facing the street were mandated by community ordinances to add to the beauty, peace, and health of the neighborhood. At the back of the photo, toward the shore, is the older and more crowded neighborhood of Neve Tzedek. Photo by Abraham Soskin, Pikiwiki.

came to Palestine saw a neat new neighborhood of sixty houses called Tel Aviv," wrote Agnon, "houses with gardens around them, and clean streets, and boys and girls playing in the streets, and old people leaning against their canes basking in the sun."[74] And although the modest scale of Ahuzat Bayit reflected the limitations of the Zionist movement at the time, the neighborhood did have one imposing building, the Herzlia Gymnasium or high school, visible proof of its greater urban aspirations.[75]

---

[74] Ibid., p. 141.
[75] The Herzlia Gymnasium was completed in 1910. The building was designed by Joseph Barsky and Boris Schatz in the eclectic style, a mixture of Western and Eastern elements. Barsky was an early practitioner of the style. Schatz was the founder of the Yishuv's first art academy, the Bezalel School of Arts and

The second and more organic stage, 1919–1925, began with the British Mandate in Palestine and the surge in Jewish immigration that changed the garden suburb into a more chaotic town that grew in all directions. By the 1930s, twenty years later, the fortunes of Zionism had changed dramatically. Even though a majority of Jews did not answer the call of Zionism, Palestine had by then become the third most vibrant Jewish community in the world, after New York and Warsaw. Tel Aviv benefited from this increase (see Figure 2.9). The city grew exponentially after the end of World War I and the arrival of the British, far beyond its initial remit. Much of the planned suburban character of the city's original neighborhood was lost as it filled sideways and upward with houses, as living cities do, jostled on all sides by new neighborhoods. It was time for another master plan, one that would be more suited to the swelling town and the growing capacities of Zionism.

The third stage in the evolution of Tel Aviv was shaped by the 1925 Geddes plan, named after its forward-thinking Scottish architect, Patrick Geddes, who was called in to address the growing needs of the first Hebrew city. In many ways Geddes modified the founding principles of Ahuzat Bayit to fit a bigger urban context. His plan brought together two modernistic trends that singled out the city and accounted for its putative Hebrew character. The first was the emerging discipline of urban planning. The second was the growing popularity of modernist architecture. It was their chance convergence in Tel Aviv that lent the city its distinct "Hebrew" urban character.

Tel Aviv at that moment in its history provided an exceptional opportunity for innovation: the need for a new urban plan, available land, new trends in urban planning that combined country and city life, architectural sensibilities that put together form and function with a revolutionary social awareness, as well as ready practitioners of these trends, Jewish refugees from an increasingly uncomfortable Europe who were looking for employment. In yet another historical coincidence, the

---

Crafts. Their initial design for the building was criticized as "too oriental" and had to be modified to look less like a mosque, to mollify the critics. The school building became iconic almost immediately and was an aesthetic monument to a brief cultural exchange between Jews and Arabs in Palestine – and not just in architecture – that ended after the civil unrest in 1929. For an image see https://commons.wikimedia.org/wiki/File:PikiWiki_Israel_49237_Gymnasia_Herzliya_Tel_Aviv_1910.jpg.

Fig. 2.9 Stage 2: Rothschild Boulevard in the 1930s during its more organic growth stage. Most houses have two stories by now, space between them is smaller, and some of the front gardens have been eliminated in favor of more urban landscaping of the street. Rothschild Photo Collection of Professor Shaul Ladani, Pikiwiki.

Fig. 2.10 Stage 3: Rothschild Boulevard in the late 1930s during Tel Aviv's third planned stage, the modern urban stage. The character of the street has become distinctly urban by now, with four-story apartment buildings lining the landscaped boulevard. Zoltan Kluger, Wikimedia.

68 *Hebrew Space and Architecture*

unplanned meeting of these elements created something new and singular. The more utopian parts of Geddes's plan for Tel Aviv, such as urban agriculture and temples of culture, did not materialize. His plans for a peaceful city of low-rise, unconnected apartment buildings, surrounded by gardens and unfriendly to cars, with easy access to street-level commerce, were, however, adopted in full. They characterize Tel Aviv to this day and set it apart from other major cities, in Israel and elsewhere.

With the swelling of Tel Aviv and the arrival of young, German-trained architects, the outline Patrick Geddes made for a garden city started taking modernist shape. The streets of Tel Aviv began to fill with angular buildings that reflected the simplicity in form and function of its designers as well as those of New Hebraism itself. None of the people who put these elements together was native to Palestine. The elements themselves were developed elsewhere and for reasons unconnected to the Yishuv. But it was their unusual blend under the ideological aegis of Zionism that mixed all of them together into something altogether new that eventually became "Hebrew" (see Figure 2.10).

In 1947 the JNF marked its fiftieth anniversary by publishing a map showing the development of the Zionist settlement project since 1917. Edited by Ernst Mechner, and designed by S. F. Loeb, the map was issued in three editions: Hebrew, English, and Yiddish. Theodor Herzl was quoted on the back of the map: "The ancient land grows young under their diligent hands. It again bears flowers, it again bears fruit, and perhaps one day, one beautiful day, it will again bear the happiness and the honor of the Jews. Herzl, 1896."[76]

Another change the map shows is that modern Jews settled in parts of Canaan/Palestine different than those of their claimed biblical predecessors. If the ancient Israelites occupied the hill country between the Jordan River and the sea, Zionists settled on the coastal plain and in valleys in the north, areas that were occupied by other biblical nations in the past. It was a historical irony that dictated the shape of space in the Yishuv. The flat lands Zionists developed had few natural constraints and little Jewish history. They constituted a relatively empty canvas on which drawings could be made from scratch of geometric shapes and airy houses that came to typify the space Zionists designed in Palestine as both a colonial gesture and a romantic restoration project.

[76] National Library of Israel map collection, https://blog.nli.org.il/en/hoi_zionist_map/.

3 | A New Hebrew Body

Judah was a young man of about thirty, a broad-shouldered and powerful giant. When he stood up with his legs apart, wearing high sandals, hands deep in his pockets and his huge chest projecting out, he looked like a firm rock or a solid marble statue. No one could take their eyes off him.[1]

Yosef Luidor, "Judah the Watchman," Palestine, late 1910s

The transformation of the Jewish body was perhaps the most radical change Zionists came up with, and it had far-reaching consequences for Jews and non-Jews alike. The yearning of German Jews in particular for a physical presence – to be seen, acknowledged, respected – was a major force behind the Zionist cultural revolution, which resolved to put Jews back into history in the most concrete sense of the word. After losing their political sovereignty in the second century CE, Jews turned their creative energies inward and built one of the world's first and most enduring imagined communities. For almost two millennia Jews thought of themselves as living in exile, cast out of their homeland. They retreated into isolated faith communities and rarely took any active part in the affairs of other nations. In the Christian world the animosity of the Church perpetuated their minority position. In the Muslim world their inferior status, along with that of Christians, was sanctioned by law. In both realms their political subordination exacerbated these conditions.

In Christian Europe Jewish minority status was especially fraught because of the combination of religious and political forces that shaped it. Religiously, Jews were considered the killers of Christ. The belief that they had not even possessed the courage to commit that crime directly, but did so by proxy, by betraying Jesus to the Romans, who executed him, proved their inherent cravenness to Christians. Politically, surrendering

---

[1] Luidor, "Judah the Watchman," in *Recklessness*, p. 47.

70   *A New Hebrew Body*

agency to others meant that Jews were almost always at the mercy of their host societies, sometimes resulting in physical attacks, along with other humiliations. And since resistance would have been severely punished, their reluctance to do so painted Jews as weak and cowardly. Moreover, since few Jews engaged in armed combat until the modern era, and since the concept of courage was often linked to combat, the image of Jews as physically unfit and mentally anxious prevailed in the popular European imagination. True valor is knowing how to suppress one's urges, says an old Hebrew saying: איזהו גיבור, הכובש את יצרו. The Jew as a clumsy coward was a recurring image in antisemitic visual culture during the eighteenth and nineteenth centuries.

The Enlightenment and its Jewish manifestation, the Haskala, saw the first conscious attempt since antiquity to fight these limitations and restore to Jews the status of political subjects. From a political perspective the agenda of the Haskala was limited: to make a place for Jews at the various national tables in Europe. The price: giving up part of the old Jewish identity and adopting modern ways that would make cultural and political inclusion easier. In addition to general education that introduced Jews to the culture around them – most Jews knew surprisingly little about it, especially in the eastern parts of Europe – physical education was an important part of acculturation as well. It would have a lasting impact on modern Jewish history, primarily in the Yishuv.

Jewish Athletes

During the nineteenth and early twentieth centuries sport figured prominently in the national education curriculum in Europe. It was considered an important component of forging a modern nation at the time, a way to develop healthy bodies and healthy minds and teach team spirit and cooperation. Exercising young people together prepared them in the most literal sense for membership in the coalescing national community. Training them to work as one and move together was a symbolic projection of the young nation, and coordinated calisthenic exercises were commonly practiced.

In the newer nation-states of Central and Eastern Europe, where most of the continent's Jews lived then, these dynamics were pronounced. In Germany, a major force in the constellation of emerging European nations after 1848, national *Bildung* or self-cultivation through physical exercise was pursued with particular vigor, and Jews were happy to share

Jewish Athletes 71

in it. The leveling quality of sports allowed them to take spontaneous part in building the new nation and at the same time to change their image as passive and weak. These aspirations were reflected in the names Jews gave their sports clubs: Maccabee, Bar Kokhba, Hasmonean, Hakoah. Judah Maccabee and Shimon Bar Kokhba were ancient Jewish generals, the Hasmoneans were an old Jewish dynasty, and Hakoah means power or force in Hebrew. The idea was not only to encourage Jews to take an active part in the contemporary national sporting culture, but to remind the world of the nation's glorious military past and cultivate Jewish athletes under its banner.

The physical modification of the Jewish body as part of a national regeneration was best expressed by Max Nordau when he spoke of a muscular Judaism. A doctor, Zionist ideologue, and political leader, Nordau was a harsh critic of the *fin de siècle* European bourgeoisie. He censured it for being disconnected from nature, for being inert, for wallowing in decadent pleasures, and he diagnosed it as degenerate. As a remedy, he suggested engaging in sports, getting closer to nature, and exercising a measure of asceticism. Nordau's ideas were not unusual at the time, but his categorical tone, and especially the Jewish context he gave it, were new, and they resonated loudly. Some of them had a lasting effect on Zionist culture and the shape it later took in Palestine.

The affinity between sports and Zionism came a bit later. The call for Jews to quit their old-fashioned ways and join the secular middle classes was a big part of the Haskala; as the poet Y. L. Gordon famously advised, "be a Jew at home and a person outside," היה אדם בצאתך ויהודי באהליך, be Jewish at home and act like regular folk (read: non-Jews) in public. It was a historic change that Zionism scaled up to the national level. Instead of limiting it to individuals, Zionists called for the creation of a national Jewish community that would fit more comfortably into the family of nations.

Initially, the physical regeneration of Jews involved sport mainly. It culminated in the first Jewish Olympic Games, the Maccabiah Games, held in Palestine in 1932. Named after Judah Maccabee, the games had three goals: to help Jewish athletes who were barred from various European competitions with the rise of Nazism; to showcase Jewish physical prowess in defiance of it; and to emphasize the emerging Hebrew nation in Palestine under Zionism. The games continue to this day, but the role of sport as an expression of Jewish strength evolved in the Yishuv to meet the more pressing needs of farming and then fighting.

Hebrew Farmers

If sport was an immediate way Jews could participate in the life of their nations and prove their mettle, life in Palestine posed other physical challenges. The biggest was the need to develop a land that would support a modern community, which left little time for recreation. Instead, farming and construction work replaced athletics as an expression of Jewish physical fitness and became central tenets of Zionist ideology. Sport continued to be practiced, but it never gained the importance it had for Jews prior to the establishment of the Yishuv.

Farming had become a priority for the proto-Zionists of the Hibbat Zion (Lovers of Zion) movement, which inspired some 30,000 Jews to move to Palestine in the last two decades of the nineteenth century and establish a new kind of Jewish life there that would be rooted in the soil. They built *moshavot* on land they had bought and began a Jewish agricultural renaissance, even if they were not always aware of it, as we learn from documentary evidence of a meeting between one of those new Jewish farmers and Theodor Herzl. In 1899, during his short visit to Palestine, Herzl stopped at the *moshava* of Rehovot. As his carriage approached the village, a mounted group of young men rode toward it with great fanfare, ready to escort the celebrated Zionist leader. An account of that meeting was left by both parties, by Herzl as well as by one of the riders, Moshe Smilansky. Both were deeply moved by it.

For the young Smilansky, who had immigrated to Palestine a few years earlier at the age of sixteen in order to become a farmer, Theodor Herzl was a detached politician, and his so-called Zionism was equally suspect, vague words that had little meaning for the struggling Jewish farmers in Palestine. And yet the sight of Herzl had a strange effect on Smilanskly, who recorded the incident in his journal, noting the leader's tall, dark, and brooding figure, which struck him with awe. "Never before did I experience the trembling that comes with solemn reverence," he wrote; "my knees shook."[2] The encounter with the messianic figure of Herzl contextualized for Smilansky the greater political meaning of his own work in Palestine. Herzl, for his part, was equally moved to see the manly Jewish farmers he had written about come to life before his eyes.

---

[2] Moshe Smilansky, "Herzl Day in Rehovot" (יום הרצל ברחובות), available at https://benyehuda.org/read/24093.

Hebrew Farmers 73

Describing the meeting in his diary, Herzl wrote how he "had tears in [my] eyes at the sight of those quick and brave horsemen, whom the Jewish peddler boys of Europe may one day resemble."[3] It was a meeting between the visionary and his vision, and a glimpse into history in the very process of its making.

Farming was even more important for the next group of about 35,000 Jewish immigrants, who came to Palestine between 1904 and 1914 with a clear political vision of establishing a Jewish state. They were a disparate group, but included a minority of enthusiasts who shaped the character of the larger group and laid the ideological foundations for the Jewish state-in-the-making in far-reaching ways. In fact, when historians speak about these early twentieth-century immigrants, also known as the Second Aliyah,[4] they often refer to a small coterie of single young men and women, who came to Palestine ready to launch a cultural revolution that would change the nature of the Jewish people and the course of Jewish history. Their passionate belief in working the land with their own hands was the single most important principle that brought that change about. "Only land that will be irrigated with the sweat of our brow will be ours," declared the Zionist apparatchik Menachem Ussishkin.[5]

The sacralization of physical labor by members of the Second Aliyah was fed by a number of trends, such as the desire to fight antisemitic stereotypes of Jews as weak, awkward, effete, and nervous, that were common in European culture, as well as the attraction to socialism as a contemporary political ideology. "He longed for backbreaking work," wrote Yosef Luidor in a short story that gives literary expression to these romantic dreams.[6] "It was delightful to spend the whole day among the fragrant heaps of corn," Luidor wrote in another story, so much so that "sometimes, he felt dizzy with joy and had the sudden urge to throw away the pitchfork, leave the wagon and the horses and jump into the corn and roll around it like a little child."[7] The fact that Palestine was

---

[3] Herzl, *The Complete Diaries*, vol. 2, p. 742, available at https://archive.org/details/TheCompleteDiariesOfTheodorHerzl_201606/.

[4] Aliyah means ascent in Hebrew, a term Zionists use to describe Jewish immigration to Palestine. Historians divide these early waves of immigration into periods, number the groups, and distinguish them by various attributes.

[5] Quoted in Ester Carmel-Hakim, *Hanna Meisel's Lifelong Mission* (שלהבת ירוקה), Yad Tabenkin, 2007, p. 31.

[6] Luidor, "Yoash," p. 63.

[7] Luidor, "Harvest," p. 33.

74 *A New Hebrew Body*

relatively undeveloped at the time allowed these European immigrants to think of it as empty, a clean slate on which to build a completely new society based on these principles.

Farming was practically fetishized by Zionists, even if most people in the Yishuv lived in towns. Consider the city of Tel Aviv, for instance, which was founded in 1909 and absorbed the bulk of Jewish immigrants who came to Palestine during those years. The rapid expansion of Tel Aviv – the city grew from 3,600 inhabitants in 1914 to 120,000 in 1936 – provided ample opportunities for construction work, and builders occupied an honorable place in the Zionist gallery of muscular Jews. And yet farmers far outranked them in the Zionist imagination as the highest expression of a cultural revolution that set out to renew the Jewish connection to the land and to create a new breed of Jews. "A nation who works its land will be strong and no storm shall move it," wrote the botanist Yitzhak Vilkansky, because "a farmer's plow is the best weapon."[8]

The New Jew or New Hebrew was first and foremost a cultural construction, the stuff of literature. Moshe Smilansky left one of the first sketches of it in a short story he wrote in 1911. Titled "Khawadja Nazer," it is a tale of a young Jewish immigrant, Lazar,[9] who comes to Palestine to work the land. Lazar is a twenty-year-old Russian lad of mixed heritage. Born to a Jewish father and a Russian Orthodox mother, he is drawn to the Land of Israel by the biblical stories he heard as a child. Lazar enters the story with dramatic flair: as he approaches the *moshava* on foot one night, he is ambushed and attacked by two Arab robbers. He overcomes them with ease and, when people from the village rush to his aid, they find that the robbers have been subdued by the strapping Lazar, who is standing over them, smiling calmly. "They didn't beat you?" the men from the *moshava* ask him anxiously. "Let them try," he replies confidently. "And they didn't try to get away?" they press. "All tied up?" he chuckles. In the village, Lazar quickly becomes an expert farmhand. "On his first day he worked the hoe as an expert and on his second day ... he left even the experienced Arab laborers behind." In his free time Lazar studies Hebrew and dreams of reaching the Jordan River, which looms larger in his biblical imagination than the Volga of his native Russia. When he finally reaches the Jordan he is

---

[8] Quoted in Carmel-Hakim, *Hanna Meisel*, p. 31.
[9] The hero's name, Lazar, is mispronounced by the Arabs in the story as Nazer. Khawadja is an Arab honorific meaning "sir" or "mister." https://benyehuda .org/read/37791.

Hebrew Farmers 75

disappointed to see how small it is. But the puny river belies its might; as the giant Lazar jumps in for a swim he is caught by an undercurrent and drowns. An attempt to give him a proper Jewish burial fails when the members of the Jewish burial society discover that he is not circumcised. His body is returned to the river, "and the current carried [it] downstream further and further away upon the waves. ... The Jordan has taken him!"

The image of Lazar is a literary manifestation of Nordau's muscular Jews, men who would "rise early and ... not weary before sunset ... have clear heads, solid stomachs and hard muscles" (see Figure 3.1).[10] The half-breed Lazar may not be Jewish according to *halakhah* (Jewish law), but that made no difference to an anti-clerical Zionism that looked for a new kind of Judaism or Jewishness based on history and heritage, not law. Lazar is a composite of Zionist fantasies. He is fit and strong: on his first day at work in the orchards of the *moshava* he handles back-breaking work with an ease that bewilders all and defies many accounts of the agonies suffered by Jewish immigrants unused to such work. He is brave and defiant: he is an easy match for the local Arabs and takes part in Bedouin war games as an equal. He is sexually attractive: the local Arab girls swoon at the sight of him. He is uncomplicated: Lazar is a man of few words, much better with his hands than with his head, the antithesis of the Jewish scholarly weakling. Finally, the biblical associations of the giant Lazar with both the Jewish Samson and the Gentile Goliath are sanctified by his symbolic death. By drowning in the Jordan River Lazar is baptized as a New Hebrew.

The literary prototype of Lazar and others like him was reinforced by Zionist ideologues such as A. D. Gordon, who touted the redemptive qualities of physical labor. Gordon believed that behavioral change would inspire an internal spiritual transformation; that working the land would figuratively ground Jews and make them into a new and more holistic community. Jewish pietism and mysticism, Hasidism and Kabbalah, provided Gordon with a more traditional context for his romance of individual agency, the idea that one person can make a difference and bring bigger changes. It resonated deeply with young Zionist settlers and provided them with a spiritual guide and a kind

---

[10] Quoted in George Mosse, *The Image of Man*, Oxford University Press, 1988, p. 152.

Fig. 3.1 A Zionist pioneer holding a pitchfork, 1937. Zoltan Kluger, Jewish National Fund archive.

of philosophy that sanctified their actions by creating a Zionist cult of labor.

"Cult" is not a misnomer. The conquest of labor, as Zionists called it, was the very essence of the Zionist cultural revolution, and it easily overshadowed every other aspect of Yishuv life. It was an anxious reaction to negative images of Jews as unproductive leeches feeding off the healthy body of the nation (see Figure 3.2). And it gave rise to a feisty socialist nationalism that cut into issues of labor and capital. Members of the Second Aliyah who were mistreated by Jewish farm owners

Hebrew Farmers

Fig. 3.2 Zionists wanted to get away from the image of of Jews as bookish and immured, men who looked like these members of Hamizrahi Educational Committee in Staszów, Poland, 1919. Yad Vashem Archive, Wikipedia.

Fig. 3.3 Zionist settlers rejected traditional Jewish images of masculinity, represented by Torah scholars. Influenced by Romantic Nationalist trends, they looked up to peasants as healthier models, people who lived a simple life close to the land. The first Zionist settlers at the beginning of the twentieth century mimicked the peasants they knew in Eastern Europe. But as they became acculturated to Palestine, fashion and body shape changed in response to local conditions, such as weather and an ideology that emphasized simplicity and reserve. Matson (G. Eric and Edith) Collection, Library of Congress.

Fig. 3.4 Workers in Kibbutz Gal-On, 1946. Zoltan Kluger, National Photo Collection of Israel, Government Press Office.

suffered their exploitation in the name of Hebrew labor and because they wanted to prove their ability to work as well as if not better than Arab farmhands. "You don't deserve [the sweat of] Hebrew workers!" wrote Alexander Zaïd, who felt used by his Jewish employers. Anyway, "we don't work for you ... the sweat of our brow is soaking a Hebrew soil in a Hebrew land" (see Figure 3.3).[11]

Zionist farmers wore their values on their sleeves, literally, and developed a fashion that fit their ascetic lifestyle. A survey of images from the Yishuv period shows that, while farmers in the *moshavot* and early kibbutzim were dressed like Eastern European peasants, including high leather boots and white shirts tucked into long trousers, by the 1920s Hebrew farmers began to reflect Zionist ideology more clearly. Some of these changes were objective, dictated by fashion, weather, or economic considerations, but others were more subjective, dictated by the ideological asceticism of the settlers, especially on the kibbutz (see Figure 3.4).

[11] Alexander Zaïd, *Diary* (לפנות בוקר פרקי יומן), Am Oved, 1975, p. 51.

Muscular Jewish Women?

If a sense of masculine deficiency was one of the deepest motivations behind the rise of Zionism, it was not an anxiety shared by Jewish women, who were objectified by non-Jews in other ways. Jewish men were often mocked for being effeminate. Jewish women were exoticized. "The figure of Rebecca might indeed have compared with the proudest beauties of England," wrote Sir Walter Scott in his 1819 popular historical novel *Ivanhoe.*

Her form was exquisitely symmetrical and was shown to advantage by a sort of Eastern dress, which she wore according to the fashion of the females of her nation. Her turban of yellow silk suited well with the darkness of her complexion. The brilliancy of her eyes, the superb arch of her eyebrows, her well-formed aquiline nose, her teeth as white as pearl, and the profusion of her sable tresses, which, each arranged in its own little spiral of twisted curls, fell down upon ... a lovely neck and bosom.[12]

Jewish religious education played a role in this mix. The Haskala often censured the immured Torah scholar as an obstacle to progress, by which it meant assimilation. Zionists considered him an irrelevant weakling. But since Jewish women did not study Torah, they were left out of this debate. What role, then, were they to play in the Zionist revolution? How could Jewish women relate to Nordau's ringing call for a muscular Judaism that involved more than athletics?[13] An early suggestion by Ahad Ha'am to cast women as wives and mothers in the service of the nation – a common call among nationalists at the time – had little attraction for Zionists, who were much more moved by the egalitarian promise of socialism. Or so they professed.

In reality, practice did not always follow preaching, and in the early days of the Yishuv few women worked in an agriculture that was devoted mostly to cereal production. This was partly because the work was backbreaking. "I spent the whole day out in the field," wrote a young woman who tried; "I grabbed the plow and the oxen ... but they

---

[12] Walter Scott, *Ivanhoe,* ch. 7, available at the Gutenberg Project, www.gutenberg.org/files/82/82-h/82-h.htm.
[13] Gerald M. Berg, "Zionism's Gender: Hannah Meisel and the Founding of the Agricultural Schools for Young Women," *Israel Studies* 6: 3 (Fall 2001): 135–165, at pp. 143–144.

80   *A New Hebrew Body*

ran away and took the plow with them. I ran after them and returned them to the field, but they kept running away from me again and again. When I returned to the barn in the evening, I was completely exhausted and irritated."[14] Women also tried to get into construction work, but progress was slow and frustrating there as well.[15] Most men "think that the role of the idealistic young women who come to Palestine is to serve them," wrote one of them, "and the inexperienced young women accept it and believe that by cooking and serving" they advance the cause of Zionism.[16]

There were a few exceptions to this. At the training farm in Sejera, women were encouraged to do all farm work, and newcomers to the farm were struck by it at first. "At some distance from us," wrote one of them, "[I saw] oxen pulling plows followed by people who didn't look like Arab farmers at all. When we came closer, we were surprised to see that they were women ... Esther, Sarah, Zipora, they were wearing *keffiyehs* like the men, long shirts, and wide trousers. So that's what the women here" are all about, the writer concluded with satisfaction.[17]

An attempt to expand the practice was made by Hanna Meisel, a pragmatic visionary, who came to Palestine in 1909 as part of the Second Aliyah and, unlike many of her fellow immigrants, wanted to give her mind to the revolution, not just her body. Labor, she thought, should be fortified with knowledge: agricultural knowledge. Meisel did not want to compete with men, she wanted to work alongside them. Rather than call for a muscular womanhood, she wanted Jewish women to become well-trained farmers and develop a "minor" agriculture of vegetables, dairy, and poultry. She called for the new Jewish woman to "leave the four walls of the house, not for the fields, but for the garden. And [to] bring science with her."[18] She was encouraged by the more egalitarian practices at Sejera, and in 1911 convinced the Zionist establishment to let her open an agricultural school for women.

---

[14] Quoted in Carmel-Hakim, *Hanna Meisel*, p. 25.
[15] See, for example, the story of Henya Pekelman, who worked as a construction worker in Palestine and left a diary with the story of her difficult experiences: *The Life of a Female Worker in Palestine* (חיי פועלת בארץ), Tel Aviv University Press, 2007.
[16] Quoted in Carmel-Hakim, *Hanna Meisel*, p. 21.
[17] Smadar Sinai, *Women and Gender in Hashomer* (השומרות שלא שמרו), Yad Tabenkin, 2013, p. 57.
[18] Berg, "Zionism's Gender," p. 142.

Muscular Jewish Women? 81

Surprisingly, Meisel encountered unexpected criticism from her own students, who were happy to study the principles of vegetable gardening and animal husbandry, such as dairy and poultry farming, but not too thrilled to learn household management, which they thought too traditionally feminine. "Kitchen work is a bitter necessity, but why make it into a cause"? wrote one of the students in the school.[19] And despite its early success, the Maidens' Farm (חוות העלמות), as it was called, was forced to close five years later because of World War I. But during its short life the school was a modest success that made a small dent in a cultural revolution that, otherwise, disappointed many women.[20]

Meisel did not feel inadequate as a woman, and she did not want to reform Jewish traditional education, which was not open to women anyway. She was interested in another kind of education, an agricultural education that would allow women to make meaningful contributions to Labor Zionism, and not just play supporting roles. Meisel's ideas inspired similar schemes, such as the Female Workers' Farm (משק הפועלות), a hands-on botanical school for women that was set up in Jerusalem in 1919, and the Bruria Group (משק ברוריה) in Petah Tikva, an agricultural school for observant Jewish women. These initiatives highlighted the great appeal that working the land as a revolutionary act enjoyed at the time and the wish of many women to join that revolution as equals. If Smilansky spoke of a Zionism that stressed the development of a new Jewish masculine body, Meisel spoke of a Zionism that stressed the development of a new Jewish feminine mind. In the context of traditional Jewish culture, both initiatives were revolutionary.

And while Jewish men demonstrated their revolutionary credentials by developing muscles, Jewish women showed theirs by taking off their clothes – by exchanging the layers that covered them in the traditional societies of the Jewish Diaspora for clothes that exposed their bodies and freed them to work in the heat of Palestine (see Figure 3.5). It was a bold statement. In the early part of the twentieth century most women in the West wore dresses. Skimpy fashion was limited to the wealthy, for evening wear or for summer leisure activities. By exposing their bodies, female farmers signaled their participation in the Zionist cultural revolution and found a way to be "womanly" as part of it. It wasn't

---

[19] Carmel-Hakim, *Hanna Meisel*, p. 45.
[20] For agricultural students at Meisel's Maidens' Farm, see https://commons .wikimedia.org/wiki/File:1912_3__העלמות_קבוצת)_מייזל_חנה_מקבוצת_עלמות ירק_גן_בעבודת_(כנרת_בחצר_btm11322.jpeg.

Fig. 3.5 At the beginning of the twentieth century, female laborers in Palestine still wore dresses. Merchavia 1917. Bitmuna Archive.

Fig. 3.6 Later, working women exchanged their dresses for shorter clothes that exposed their bodies and signaled their participation in the Zionist cultural revolution more visibly. The skimpy outfits of Zionist working women were, once again, the result of ideology and circumstance. Women's shorts were tailored from dresses brought over by settlers who had no use for them in Palestine. The first models were cut like skirts and fitted with elastic bands at the bottom to allow for freedom of movement without exposing the wearer too much. Later models were shortened for practical considerations of work, climate, and economy. Zoltan Kluger, National Photo Collection of Israel, Government Press Office.

Muscular Arab Jews? 83

a sexual gesture, even if men did not always understand it. As David Biale tells us in *Eros and the Jews*, the Zionist pioneers were ascetic and prudish.[21] If Jewish men announced their historical subjectivity by flexing their muscles, Jewish women did so by uncovering their bodies in a direct and forthright way (see Figure 3.6).

Muscular Arab Jews?

The historical forces that gave rise to Zionism were particular to Europe. First, because modern nationalism originated there. Second, because the economic and legal situation of Jews toward the end of the nineteenth century was particularly dire in the eastern parts of the continent. The liberating message of Zionism was received differently by Jewish communities in the Islamic world, though not by all of them. The Jews of Yemen were a notable exception, and in the 1880s a number of them began arriving in Palestine. But their integration into the Yishuv was not smooth. The main difficulty was the religious traditions of the Yemenis, which an anti-clerical Zionism found hard to stomach.

The fact that the Yemeni did not look – well – European did not help either. It did, however, raise hopes that as so-called locals, "who lived like the Arabs, and were also modest, undemanding, and hardworking people," they would be able to endure the climate and the hardships of farming better than Eastern European settlers. In 1912 a group of them was sent to settle a farming community in the north of the country by the Sea of Galilee (see Figure 3.7).[22] It was a miserable failure. None of the Yemenis had any farming experience. Moreover, their insistence on retaining their religious practices ultimately doomed their future as Zionist farmers. It cost them the sympathy and support of the Zionist–socialist establishment, which refused to finance religion.

The issue was widely debated at the time in the Zionist press, which was unanimous about the aim of Labor Zionism: to establish a productive Jewish community in Palestine based on socialist values. Levantine Jews, or Sephardim, as they were often called at the time, were welcome to join that project, but on condition that they adopt these values. "Are we against hiring Sephardi laborers?" asked some of the papers. Surely not. "But they must uphold our national socialist values. If not, what is

---

[21] David Biale, *Eros and the Jews*, University of California Press, 1997.
[22] Arthur Rupin, *My Life* (חיי), part 2, Am Oved, 1947, p. 103.

Fig. 3.7 A Yemeni Jewish family in their settlement by the Sea of Galilee, 1910s. Hundreds of Jews from Yemen emigrated to Palestine in the late 1800s and early 1900s. Most of them settled in Jerusalem. In the early 1900s some of them were encouraged to join Zionist farming communities. The experiment failed because of a fundamental clash between the religiosity of the Yemenis and the anti-clerical dogma of Zionism. Leo Kahn, Israel Archive Network project (IAN), Yad Ben Zvi Archive, the Ministry of Jerusalem and Heritage, the National Library of Israel.

the difference between a Levantine Jewish laborer and an Arab laborer? They dress the same, act the same, speak Arabic, and are indifferent to our national and socialistic ideals." [23]

After almost twenty difficult years the Kinneret (Sea of Galilee) Yemenis were finally moved elsewhere, and their settlement was dismantled. On a personal level many people sympathized with them. On an institutional level they were patronized, and their petitions to build synagogues and set up religious schools for their children were

---

[23] Yehoshua Kaniel, "Sephardi Jews as Part of the Second Aliyah" (אנשי העליה השנייה ובני העדה הספרדית), in Yisrael Bartal, ed., *Studies in the Second Aliya* (העלייה השנייה, מחקרים), Yad Yitzhak Ben-Tzvi, 1997, pp. 317–318.

flatly refused. "The lack of a quorum for prayers (minyan) depresses the Yemenis to no end," the authorities admitted, but they still insisted that "we most certainly cannot allow more people to join their community."[24] Like most revolutions, the Zionist cultural revolution was ruthless, and it imposed its values with rigor and severity. The Kinneret Yemenis were willing to work the land, but they didn't understand why they had to shave off their beards and stop praying. Unlike some of the Eastern European Zionists they did not believe there was anything wrong with their old Judaism, and the demand to become a new kind of Jew made little sense to them.

Jewish Fighters

If the Hebrew farmer in Palestine was created in reaction to antisemitic stereotypes in Europe, then its complement, the Hebrew fighter, was created in reaction to the realities of life in Palestine. Ironically, it was the success of the Yishuv that made it take up arms, as it were. As the Yishuv prospered and grew it displaced the Arab population, who resisted it with increasing determination.

At first, few Zionists imagined that the Arabs of Palestine would resent them. Zionist settlers saw themselves as returning sons and, anyway, believed that their progressive European culture would be welcomed by the natives of an underdeveloped land. "Were not the older inhabitants of Palestine ruined by the Jewish immigration?" asks a character in Herzl's utopian novel, *Altneuland*, "and didn't they have to leave the country" after the Jews arrived? "What a question!" replies the Arab host; "it was a great blessing for all of us."[25] But the realities of settlement changed that, and what began as an economic issue soon turned into a political rivalry that became progressively more violent.

Even before defense became an issue, Zionists thought of their settlement initiatives in surprisingly military ways. They drew heavily

---

[24] Gur Melamed, "The Kinneret Yemenis" (פרשת תימני כנרת), Master's thesis, Bar-Ilan University, 2005, p. 49, available at www.haskama.co.il/mediation/document/yaman.pdf.

[25] Theodor Herzl, *Altneuland*, book III, available at www.jewishvirtuallibrary.org/quot-altneuland-quot-theodor-herzl.

86   *A New Hebrew Body*

on a military lexicon, and used terms such as conquest, legion, and regiment to speak of farming, road building, and construction. The Labor Regiment, גדוד העבודה, was the name of an early construction cooperative. The word conquest, כיבוש, was frequently used to refer to settlement projects. Farming and construction became the Conquest of the Wilderness, fishing and shipping became the Conquest of the Sea, and the phrase Conquest of Labor instilled the cult of labor by inspiring Jewish workers and keeping Arab workers out.[26]

Military jargon reflected organizational realities and psychological needs. Most of the settlers who worked on those projects were young people with no property or capital, who came to a land that was unfamiliar and less developed than their homelands. Cooperatives not only fit their socialist leanings, they also made sense in the challenging environment of the Yishuv. They allowed for quick and flexible deployment, and they promoted a sense of urgency and mission that energized the self-anointed pioneers and eased the hardships they faced.

Before long, however, fighting became more than just a metaphor. As the Zionist political vision became clearer to Arabs, their objections to it grew. Initial resistance was economic and involved trespassing for the most part. Some of the land Jews bought in Palestine had tenant farmers on it, and they did not like being removed. Grazing habits, especially by nomadic Bedouin, were not always compatible with fixed property lines either. And so the need to protect their property was behind some of the first Zionist defense initiatives, such as Hashomer (The Guard), a security collective that was assembled in 1909 to protect Jewish farms. Hashomer was the biggest and most successful organization of its kind, but it was not the first or only one. The economic and political complexities that Jewish nationalism introduced to a region in turmoil after the dissolution of Ottoman rule led to the creation of other defense initiatives, most of them illicit. This was the background behind the emergence of the Hebrew fighter and an important moment in the evolution of Israeli militarism.

Since traditional Jewish culture idolized scholars rather than fighters, Zionists developed an original Jewish fighting type based on other

---

[26] Gershon Shafir, *Land, Labor and the Origins of the Israeli-Palestinian Conflict*, University of California Press, 1991 [1989].

Jewish Fighters 87

sources – none of them were modeled after the growing number of Jewish men who served in European armies or on the defense initiatives of Polish Jews in the early part of the twentieth century.[27] The first inspirational source were the Cossacks, the legendary horsemen of the Ukrainian steppes, who were romanticized in Russo-Ukrainian culture as freedom fighters (see Figure 3.8).[28] Strangely, their strong antipathy toward Jews did not prevent members of Hashomer from adopting them as models and from fantasizing about a "Cossack-like Jewish race" of farmer-soldiers who would lead simple lives close to the land and "develop bodies strong enough to take that land by force."[29]

The second were the Bedouin of Palestine, who were closer at hand and, at first, had more attraction for members of Hashomer, who adopted their dress and customs; they rode horses, covered their heads with the traditional Bedouin headdress, the *keffiyeh*, wore bullet chains across their chests, learned colloquial Arabic, and picked up other traits from the Arab natives of Palestine. The trend began earlier, in fact. In 1891 Zeev Yavetz joyfully reported how "as we were leaving one of the vineyards, we saw an Arab riding toward us, wrapped in a dark cloak and wearing a white cloth that was tied around his head with a rope … [suddenly] he called to us in [perfect] Hebrew… 'Are you an Arab?' I greeted the rider with a smile." Yavetz was delighted to learn that the rider was Jewish and went on to marvel at how authentic he looked, "Why, you are an Arab in every way, the way you speak, the way you ride."[30] The fighting culture and nomadic habits of the Cossacks and the Bedouin appealed to the first Hebrew guards, who lived on the fringes of Zionist settlements to provide protection. It was an unusual colonial paradigm that blended mimicry of the natives with a sense of settler superiority.

But the impact of the Bedouin on Jewish fighting culture was brief. As long as the native Arab population outnumbered the immigrant Jewish community significantly, it made sense to cultivate good relations with them and to borrow from their culture, even if not everyone approved

---

[27] Derek Penslar, *Jews and the Military: A History*, Princeton University Press, 2013.

[28] Yisrael Bartal, *Cossack and Bedouin: Land and People in Jewish Nationalism* (קוזק ובדווי), Am Oved, 2007.

[29] Ibid., p. 486.

[30] Zeev Yavetz, from a short report titled "Travels in Palestine" (משוט בארץ), quoted in Oppenheimer, *Barriers*, p. 43.

Fig. 3.8 Cossacks, 1855–1860. Wikimedia.

Fig. 3.9 Armed Bedouin, nineteenth century. Library of Congress.

Fig. 3.10 Members of Hashomer organization in Merchavia, 1913. Bitmuna Archive.

Jewish Fighters 89

of it (see Figure 3.9). Joseph Klausner mocked his contemporaries for their excitement at the sight of young men who "try to pass themselves off as Bedouins, Jews who ride a horse and handle a gun like pros ... and exhibit a spirit of savagery that strikes the Arabs with awe." He was certainly glad to see Jews "shedding their diasporic cowardice and scholastic idleness and returning to a vigorous life closer to nature." But not at the expense of adopting a "primitive" and "half-savage" culture, of exchanging one diaspora for another.[31] The issue was resolved after the Yishuv grew and the conflict with the Arabs escalated. Both killed the motivation for cultural identification.

Ultimately, the Cossack model had a greater influence on Zionist militarism because the Eastern European Jewish settlers were more familiar with it and, perversely, more comfortable with it too. "We shall raise our children to live together, work the land, and defend it," wrote the legendary guard, Alexander Zaïd, who went on to describe a Jewish Sparta, where "every boy and every girl, with no exceptions, will learn to use arms and ride noble mares."[32] It was a self-fulfilling prophecy that came to epitomize Yishuv life, an affinity born of necessity and strengthened by logistics. Since the Yishuv could not raise and sustain an army – it had little money, scant infrastructure, and was politically dependent – kibbutz communities became convenient training grounds that were used as barracks too. They kept servicemen hidden from the British and provided extra working hands during harvest times.

The image of the *shomer*-cum-soldier boosted the military credentials of Zionism as a national movement. At times it seemed that the combative spirit that developed in the Yishuv and the rhetoric that went with it were a delayed reaction to centuries of oppression as much as they were a reaction to Arab antagonism. In some cases it led to the abuse of power by members of Hashomer, whose founders adopted a disturbing motto: "Judea has fallen by blood and fire / by blood and fire Judea shall rise again" (see Figure 3.10) It did not bode well for future relations between Arabs and Jews.[33] "We felt the flutter of history's wings," waxed the young Zionist leader Berl Katznelson, after

---

[31] Joseph Klausner, "Fear" (חשש), *Hashiloach* 17 (1907), pp. 574–576.

[32] Zaïd, *Diary*, p. 62.

[33] Gur Alroey, "In the Service of the Colony, or Arrogant Tyrants?" משרתי המושבה או רודנים גסי רוח? מאה שנה לאגודת ‹השומר› פרספקטיבה היסטורית) *Katedra* 133 (2009): 77–104.

90 *A New Hebrew Body*

enlisting in the Jewish Brigade of the British Army during World War I. "We felt the intensity of the historical moment with unprecedented keenness ... and became privy to history's secret."[34] The secret was the opportunity Jews received to show their mettle and to finally avenge their long history of persecution. It became the ultimate expression of Nordau's call for a muscular Judaism. What began as an invitation for Jews to be more athletic turned into the cultivation of a Jewish working body and then a Jewish fighting body that represented the Zionist revolution in the most concrete and personal way.

Fighting Jewish Women

If women were among the founding members of the first Zionist defense societies, their role in those societies diminished with time. The first Zionist defense initiative was organized in 1907, a secret society called Bar-Giora, after a Jewish general who fought the Romans. In 1909 it evolved into a bigger outfit, Hashomer, a security collective that provided guards to Jewish farming settlements based on changing needs. In 1920, as Arab economic resentment became more political in nature, Hashomer was turned into a more permanent militia, the Hagana (Defense), which became the Israel Defense Forces (IDF) after independence. Women were integral to these societies from the very start. Three women, Manya Shochat, Rachel Yana'it Ben-Zvi, and Zipora Zaïd, earned their military credentials by helping to create these organizations and by serving in them with distinction. But as they grew and expanded, most of the women who later joined them did so in supporting roles.

The hatching ground for Bar-Giora was the Sejera training farm in the Galilee. Women worked side by side with men on the farm, but they were not given many opportunities to share guarding duties, except during emergencies. Rachel Yana'it Ben-Zvi recalled how, during one of those emergencies, she and "Esther stood by the window. Esther had a gun, and she gave me one too. It was my first time as a watchwoman, and in the Galilee too!" The Galilee was the Palestinian Wild West at the time, sparsely populated with Bedouin, who were not always happy about their new Jewish neighbors. "I felt excited and proud and didn't care anymore that I wasn't officially assigned to the post but volunteered for it."[35] During another emergency, Sejera guards were rushed to the

---

[34] Anita Shapira, *Berl* (ברל), Am Oved, 2000, pp. 135–136.
[35] Rachel Yana'it Ben-Zvi, *We Are Immigrating to Israel* (אנו עולים), Am Oved, 1962, p. 98.

Fig. 3.11 Zipora Zaïd, 1892–1968. One night, while on guard duty at the farm in Sejera, Zipora saw a figure she didn't recognize approaching her post. "Min haddah?" she asked, using the Arabic for "Who is it?," and drew out her gun. The alarmed figure quickly identified himself as one of her comrades, who had come to check up on her. "Don't ever do it again," she told him, "or else ..." From an oral interview with Zipora Zaïd, Central Zionist Archive. Tal Raveh Zeid, late 1920s–early 1930s. Wikimedia.

aid of a neighboring farm and did not allow women to join the expedition. After they left, Zipora and another woman followed the men and caught up with them midway. "The men were shocked to see us. Our doubters were ashamed to look us in the face, and our supporters rejoiced. When we arrived [at the farm] they divided everyone into shifts irrespective of gender"(see Figure 3.11).[36]

The women who joined Hashomer and those who hoped to do so worked hard to qualify for inclusion, but "it wasn't easy for [them] to gain the respect of the men," wrote Alexander Zaïd. "Ostensibly, we

[36] Sinai, *Women and Gender*, p. 69.

92   *A New Hebrew Body*

were equal members of the collective. In reality, the men were bona fide members while the women, who suffered with us, worked hard, and took care of us, were not officially recognized as members of the collective."[37] It had nothing to do with qualifications. Alexander Zaïd admitted that "Keila [Zipora's sister] was an especially good shot," and that Zipora, his wife, "was an expert horsewoman," better than he was.[38] Many of the women also cut their hair short, dressed like men, and walked around wearing *keffiyeh*s. "I wasn't used to seeing women dressed like men," wrote someone who saw the young Manya Shochat for the first time and thought, "My God, she's a man!"[39] But, beyond the few charismatic female founders, most of the women who later joined Hashomer did not do so as fighters. Even the two women who died defending Tel-Hai in 1920, a Zionist Alamo of sorts, did not change that. Most men still believed that women were not up to the rigors of the job, and farmers refused to hire them as guards. "Throughout my years of service at Hashomer I felt undervalued," wrote a frustrated member, who "could not accept the passive roles women were given. It made me very sad."[40]

The escalating conflict with the Arabs softened some of the resistance to the service of women in combat roles. "We don't want men guarding us anymore," said a delegate to a 1937 conference that finally changed things somewhat. She was probably referring to the feeling of being protected and monitored by men. Still, both farming and fighting in the Yishuv reflected many of the gender divisions of the traditional societies Jews left behind in the Old World. The Zionist revolution, it seems, only went so far.

Hebrew Dance: Sculpting a New Jewish Body

The Jewish body in Palestine was reshaped by labor, by war, and by the sun. The vibrant dance culture that developed in the Yishuv was meant to add grace to it as well. "Let the liberated, free [Jewish] body be created," Margalit Orenstein wrote in 1925, "straight, full of the rhythm, the power, and the essence of the old-new homeland."[41] Orenstein was a pioneering choreographer and dance teacher. Together with several

---

[37] Zaïd, *Diary*, p. 61.
[38] Sinai, *Women and Gender*, pp. 68–69; Zaïd, *Diary*, p.46.
[39] Sinai, *Women and Gender*, p. 33.
[40] Ibid., p. 78.
[41] Gabi Aldor, *And How Does a Camel Dance?* (איך רוקד גמל), Resling, 2011, pp. 50–51.

Hebrew Dance: Sculpting a New Jewish Body

other dance pioneers, most of them women, she laid the foundations for modern dance and folk dance schools in the Yishuv. Both came out of modern dance movements in Europe, like most, but not all, of the Zionist dance pioneers.

Early twentieth-century attempts to get away from classical dance traditions and create a new body language that would fit the post-World War I era better presented a great opportunity for Zionist dance teachers. They were especially keen on two contemporary dance trends. The first was expressionism; the second was mythology and ethnography. The first allowed Hebrew dancers the freedom to sculpt the new Jewish Palestinian space with their bodies, as Orenstein put it.[42] The second enabled them to give their creations a specifically Hebrew character by incorporating biblical and folk motifs.

Like many of the Zionist innovations, the creation of dance was deliberate and self-conscious. But unlike farming or fighting, dance as an art form allowed for a more symbolic expression of New Hebraism, one that could also be performed publicly and ritualized. It is not surprising that both art and folk dancing in the Yishuv began on stage, as choreographed performances for theater, for pageants, and especially for the renewed Zionist holiday calendar.

Artistic Dance

Zionist ideology permeated every aspect of life in Palestine, including the arts. Literature, visual art, music, and dance became symbolic channels for spreading and reflecting the revolutionary ideas of Zionism. But if ideology could be clearly expressed in words and through visual images, abstract arts such as music and dance presented a more difficult challenge.

One way to meet that challenge in dance was by creating works that incorporated ethnic elements and referred to the Bible. Rina Nikova (1898–1972), for instance, an orientalist dancer and choreographer, was adept at it. She traveled to remote corners of Palestine to study how Arab women walked, how they balanced heavy loads on their heads, and how heat and rain affected their movements. Back in her studio she transformed her observations into modern works she practiced with her Yemeni dance troupe.[43] Contemporary audiences were intrigued

---

[42] Ibid., p. 55.
[43] Nina Spiegel, *Embodying Hebrew Culture: Aesthetics, Athletics, and Dance in the Jewish Community of Mandate Palestine*, Wayne State University Press, 2013, p. 60.

94 *A New Hebrew Body*

by the results. "Rina Nikova is doing wonders in her achievements of teaching her Yemeni girls discipline without taking away their temper and natural graces," wrote one critic, who nevertheless thought Nikova's orientalism went a bit too far.[44]

Ethnography was a tempting option for choreographers who worked in a near vacuum, cultivating an art form that was relatively absent from Jewish traditional life. It was the first route for many Zionist dance pioneers, such as Rina Nikova, Baruch Agadati, Leah Bergstein, and Yardena Cohen, who tried to do two things at once: to refer to older Jewish traditions, and to give bodily expression to the new Jewish space in Palestine and to its spirit of New Hebraism.

In the early 1920s Baruch Agadati (1895–1976) made a splash in the Yishuv with a series of dance performances that mixed Hasidic, Yemeni, and Arab motifs in new and arresting ways. When he took it to Europe a few years later he was received enthusiastically as a representative of the new Palestinian Hebraism by both Jews and non-Jews. We are honored to have "the excellent and original Hebrew dancer," read a Lithuanian Hebrew newspaper in 1929. It went on to commend Agadati for "combining the devotion and yearning of Hasidic dances with the ecstasy of Yemeni dances and the vigor of the young pioneers in the Land of Israel ... [to produce] a most refined and original Hebrew dance."[45] Later, Agadati abstracted ethnographic details into more holistic works, such as a dance he based on anti-Jewish gestures or his popular version of the Hora, an Israeli folk dance based on Eastern European and Bedouin motifs (see Figures 3.12 and 3.13).[46]

The dancer and choreographer Leah Bergstein developed a different approach that mixed biblicism with ethnography, both Jewish and non-Jewish. Bergstein focused on the festival calendar, and her choreography for the Omer celebration on her kibbutz, Ramat Yohanan, became an iconic performance of a reconstructed Hebrew nativism (see Chapter 4).

"Up until [a few] years ago," wrote Orenstein in the late 1920s, "people here in Tel Aviv [did not pay particular attention] to the sea.

---

[44] Ibid., p. 128.
[45] From a documentary film, *Baruch Agadati*, Israel Broadcast Authority, Bet Ariela Dance Library, Tel Aviv.
[46] For a more nuanced study see Nicholas Rowe, "Dance and Political Credibility: The Appropriation of *Dabkeh* by Zionism, Pan-Arabism, and Palestinian Nationalism," *Middle East Journal* 65: 3 (2011): 363–380.

Hebrew Dance: Sculpting a New Jewish Body

Fig. 3.12 & 3.13 Zionist dancers created original modern dances by incorporating ethnic motifs from a variety of sources. Here, Baruch Agadati performs a dance based on Hasidic motifs (left) and a dance based on Arab motifs (right). Bat Sheva and Yitzhak Katz Archive, Information Center for Israeli Art, Israel Museum, Jerusalem.

... Lately, however, there are hundreds of young men and women who celebrate their bodies on the beach, in the sunlight, in the air and in the water."[47] Zionist dance practitioners wanted to capture this new sense of bodily freedom and give it symbolic form. "How does a camel dance?" joked the Austrian-born Orenstein after she moved to Palestine, and went on to create dances such as *The Waves*, in which she tried to capture her new Mediterranean environment and express it through movement.

Folk Dance

Zionist mythology is full of stories about pioneers bursting into song and dancing spontaneously into the late hours of the night, and images of those dance circles abound in Zionist iconography. Exaggerated or

[47] Aldor, *And How Does a Camel Dance?*, p. 55.

not, the stories testify to the great enthusiasm that animated the young men and women who came to the Land of Israel "to build it and be built by it," as they sang. At first settlers vented their energy and passion through dances they remembered from home, mostly in Eastern Europe. Later they expressed their joy in a more original way by dancing a circle dance called the Hora.

The Hora became hugely popular in the Yishuv (see Figure 3.14). As a large and simple circle dance that could go on and on, it became one of the most immediate ways to come together and celebrate the new Jewish community that had formed in Palestine. It was also one of the most recognized symbols of it. The exact provenance of the dance is not clear. It was probably based on similar circle dances that were common in the eastern parts of Europe, in Romania especially, where they were known by the same name, Hora, a derivation of the Greek Khoros, for a group or circle of performers. Hasidic circle dances could have been another influence, as was the Dabke or Debka, as it was called in Hebrew, a local Arab circle dance that captivated Jewish settlers,

Fig. 3.14 Agriculture students dancing the Hora, 1946. The circle and the dance steps were borrowed from Eastern European dances. The entwining of the arms by the dancers was adopted from a local Arab dance, the Dabke or Debka. National photo collection, Israel Government Press Office.

Hebrew Dance: Sculpting a New Jewish Body 97

who "might have known [the dances] once in the forgotten past and re-recognized them now," as one dancer mused.[48]

Circle dances were already part of life in the *moshavot*, but from the 1920s on they spread widely and became a popular pioneering pastime. The Hora had many variations, was frequently modified, and "became a permanent fixture of communal life," wrote Avigdor Hame'iri. The dance allowed young people "to free themselves from the bonds of exile, from their painful legacy of hatred, low self-esteem, submissiveness, mimicry, and prejudice." The Hora became an outlet for everything. "When we felt happy – Hora! When, God forbid, something bad happened – Hora! When in doubt – Hora! Hora is the essence of our vibrant life. ... Hora is our prayer."[49]

The Hora was only the first in a growing list of folk dances that were enthusiastically embraced by a society whose cultural traditions were still meager. Folk dancing, writes Nina Spiegel, was a socialistic art form par excellence that fit Zionism especially well: it was participatory, accessible, required no training, and provided a spiritual connection to land and people without being religious.[50] The new tradition also owed its popularity to passionate innovators and promoters such as Gurit Kadman (1897–1987), who established a national folk-dance festival in 1945. It was a huge success that attracted thousands of people from across the Yishuv. They came to celebrate their new nation by dancing, and to affirm it by watching dances performed on stage. "I am not sure if you could call it folk dancing," Kadman reflected about those early days. "They were only suggestions, hopes, the start of a folk dancing tradition" that would need time to solidify. "Many of the dances were obviously European, with few original numbers, Mizrahi for the most part."[51]

But if only a few of the dances were new, a reporter who covered the second festival two years later, in 1947, was overjoyed "to see the young generation that had grown up in the land, straight bodies, tall, flexible, filled with tension and expression. The joy of life is stirring

---

[48] Rowe, "Dance and Political Credibility," p. 366.
[49] Naomi Bahat-Ratson, "Is Hora an Israeli Dance?" *Mahol Israel* (1977), available at www.israeldance-diaries.co.il/wp-content/uploads/2018/10/ANNUAL1977_is_the_hora.pdf, pp. 9–15, at p. 10.
[50] Spiegel, *Embodying Hebrew Culture*, ch. 4 "Creating National Folk Dance," pp. 133–173.
[51] Gurit Kadman, *A Nation Dances* (עם רוקד), Schocken, 1969, pp. 17–18.

98 A *New Hebrew Body*

in them."[52] It was a crisp summary of the physical evolution that the diasporic Jewish body had undergone under the wholesome influence of a homeland, as Zionists would say. After Jews had hardened their bodies by working their land, after they toughened their spirit by fighting for it, they polished off the transformation with the grace and elegance of dance.

[52] Spiegel, *Embodying Hebrew Culture*, p. 159.

4 | *A New Hebrew Festival Calendar*

Darkness, darkness, go away!	בָּאנוּ חֹשֶׁךְ לְגָרֵשׁ.
We will burn you out today.	בְּיָדֵינוּ אוֹר וָאֵשׁ.
Each of us – a little light,	כָּל אֶחָד הוּא אוֹר קָטָן,
but together we are bright.	וְכֻלָּנוּ – אוֹר אֵיתָן.
Scram, O darkness, go, O black!	סוּרָה חֹשֶׁךְ! הָלְאָה שְׁחוֹר!
Scram, our light is back!	סוּרָה מִפְּנֵי הָאוֹר!

A popular children's song for Hanukkah by Sara Levi-Tanai from the 1940s
that contrasts the realms of darkness and light in striking ways.

Cultural innovations were all well and good; the problem was how to
consolidate them and make them last. Zionists met the challenge with
help from the Jewish festival calendar. They revised old Jewish festivals
and came up with completely new ones as part of an updated program
that enshrined their revolution in the spirit of Hebrew nationalism.[1]
And, since Jewish history is relatively long, they had a lot to work with.
At the opening of the Hebrew University in Jerusalem in 1925, the poet
Haim Nahman Bialik reminded those present that "modern nations
are not animated by religion anymore but by culture, a creative culture
based on a national heritage that should be reexamined and renewed."[2]

Educational institutions played a crucial role in the spread of new
Jewish festivals. This was true especially of kindergartens, where the
future generations of the envisioned Jewish state were first socialized.
It made the role of teachers more than usually important. Many educators were excited to shape the cultural curriculum of their new Hebrew

---

[1] A simple separation between religion and state was not really possible, perhaps
not even desired in the Jewish case. See Hizky Shoham, "The History of
Planting on Tu Bishvat" (מן העיר - ומן הכפר? על היווצרות הנטיעות הטקסיות בט"ו
בשבט), *Israel* 22 (2014): 21–44, at p. 25.

[2] Ya'acov Shavit, "Culture Work" (עבודת הקולטורא), in Yehuda Reinharz, Yosef
Shalmon, and Gideon Shimoni, eds., *Nationalism and Jewish Politics* (לאומיות
ופוליטיקה יהודית), Zalman Shazar, 1997, p. 141.

100   *A New Hebrew Festival Calendar*

society, and since the majority of them were women, this was a singular opportunity for many of them to contribute significantly to a cultural revolution that often betrayed the promises of equality it made them. Yemima Avidar-Tchernowitz (1909–1998) was one of those extraordinary teachers, whose popular book *My Kindergarten* (גן גני, 1947) introduced young children to the core Zionist festival calendar, shaped it, and circulated it.[3]

A quick look through the book's table of contents gives a clear picture of a national calendar that updated traditional Jewish festivals such as Passover, Hanukkah, and Purim, and introduced more original Zionist innovations, such as Arbor Day or Tu Bishvat, Shavu'ot (Pentecost), and Lag Ba'omer, which celebrated Jewish military prowess, the agricultural cycle, and the natural world of Palestine and its seasons. Toward the end of the book the editors inserted a short song that reminded readers why a book of this kind was needed. It is a duet between Jewish immigrants who arrive in the country and the community that welcomes them:

Song of the Jewish Immigrants (שיר העולים) by Levin Kipnis:

IMMIGRANTS:	COMMUNITY:
From far and away	Bless you one and all!
we came here to stay.	Bless you.
We escaped exile with fear,	
glad to be here!	
IMMIGRANTS:	COMMUNITY:
We were the first to go,	Bless you one and all!
but others will soon come in tow.	Bless you.
Exile is dark,	
our land, a bright spark!	
IMMIGRANTS:	COMMUNITY:
In exile we toiled for others,	Bless you one and all!
and worked not for our brothers.	Bless you.
Here we shall be free,	
to revive our land with glee.	

Some of the renewed Zionist holidays, such as Hanukkah and Purim, emphasized Jewish military power. Others, such as Passover, stressed the

---

[3] Yemima Avidar-Tchernowitz and Levin Kipnis, *My Kindergarten* (גן גני), facsimile ed., Oranit Publishing, 2011.

Celebrating Jewish Power 101

agrarian origin of Jewish culture. Context often determined the thematic boundaries between them. Purim was an urban festival; Passover was connected with the farming sector. Other holidays, such as Hanukkah or Shavu'ot, were popular in schools. Most of the festivals Zionists renewed were relatively minor ones in the traditional Jewish calendar. Some of them, such as Lag Ba'omer and Tu Bishvat, were completely new. This gave Zionists a good deal of creative freedom.

Festivals in the Yishuv were ceremonious affairs, some of them even sacramental. In the Diaspora, wrote shepherd-poet Matityahu Shellem, outside of a national context, Jews replaced their ancient ceremonies with humbler celebrations in the family circle.[4] The creation of a modern Jewish nation returned festivals to the public sphere, usually with an addition called מְסֶכֶת, a program of texts that were declaimed at the opening of festivals with a solemnity we would probably think bombastic today. The texts were meant to educate people and draw a new time map for the new national community. Declamations gave New Hebrews an opportunity to pause and reflect on the meaning of the national project they were engaged in, and ceremonies lent majesty to those moments.

Celebrating Jewish Power: Hanukkah, Purim, Lag Ba'omer

Zionists longed for power – physical power in particular. It wasn't a violent urge at first. When Nordau spoke about a muscular Judaism, he meant gym culture, replacing the sedentary habits of Jews with physical exercise and a love of nature. The desire for power was a desire for the recognition and respect it would bring from non-Jews. Militarism was absent from early Zionist thought, certainly from mainstream Zionist thinking, as it was from traditional Jewish culture. The rabbis had paid almost no attention to Jewish military heroes such as Judah Maccabee or Shimon Bar Kokhba, because they had little relevance for Jewish life in the Diaspora. Zionists wanted to change that, and used the festival calendar to introduce physical and then political power into the vocabulary of their new secular culture. Hanukkah was the first in a line of festivals that celebrated Jewish power even before the rise of Zionism.

---

[4] Ellah Zevulun and Dov Meisel, eds., *Matityahu Shellem: Kibbutz Festivals* (החג ביישוב הקיבוצי), Ramat Yohanan, 1984, pp. 14–5.

102   *A New Hebrew Festival Calendar*

It was followed by Purim and finalized by Lag Ba'omer, a completely
new addition to the festival calendar.

Hanukkah

Hanukkah commemorates the first Jewish war of independence, waged
by Judean rebels against the Seleucids in 164 BCE, and the establishment
of an independent Jewish kingdom under the Hasmonean kings following
its success. The book of Maccabees recounts that war and the rededication (*hanukkah* in Hebrew) of the Hebrew Temple in Jerusalem after
the Jewish victory. Chapter 4 in the first book of Maccabees chronicles
the rededication ceremony and the lighting of the temple menorah or
candelabra, which became a symbol of the event:

They burnt incense on the altar, and lighted the lamps on the candlestick to
shine light in the Temple. 49
    And they kept the dedication of the altar for eight days and offered burnt
offerings with gladness and offered the sacrifice of deliverance and praise. 54
    Moreover, Judas and his brothers with the whole congregation of Israel
ordained that the days of the dedication of the altar should be kept in their
season from year to year for eight days, from the five and twentieth day of
the month Kislev, with joy and gladness. 59

Since Jews in the Diaspora were seldom involved in politics before the
modern era, the national dimensions of Hanukkah gradually lost their
relevance. Until the end of the nineteenth century the festival was celebrated mainly by children, who marked it by lighting a menorah for
eight days and by playing parlor games. The festival rose in importance
during the Haskala, when it became a "Jewish Christmas" of sorts, a
convenient day for Jews who were not completely assimilated to mark
their distinct identity and still participate in the general European bourgeois culture – the festival was frequently referred to as a Maccabee
party or ball.
    Hanukkah owed its secular popularity to the social discomfort of
assimilated Jews, who were "a kind of superior proletariat," as Herzl
wrote in *Altneuland*. Jewish doctors and lawyers could not "simply
slip into public posts, like their Christian colleagues," Herzl observed.
If they did not want to become merchants, they had to improvise and
engage "in secret diseases and unlawful legal affairs." While many Jews

Celebrating Jewish Power 103

integrated fairly well into Christian society, barriers to their complete acceptance by non-Jews remained stubbornly in place. The Austro-Hungarian composer Gustav Mahler, for instance, felt it advantageous to convert to Catholicism before applying to head the Vienna Court Opera, the Hofoper.

The sense of social and cultural alienation must have been felt especially during the Christmas season, which became the highest point of the civic religious calendar in Europe by the end of the nineteenth century. Think about Charles Dickens' 1848 *A Christmas Carol*, or Thomas Mann's 1901 German epic *Buddenbrooks*, and the central place Christmas plays in those and similar novels that helped define the European middle class. Even after Christmas was commercialized as a bourgeois family festival, it retained Christian associations that were not comfortable for many Jews. Shall we call it a "Hanukkah Tree"? wondered Herzl, with a tinge of guilt perhaps, after Moritz Güdemann, a prominent Viennese rabbi, visited his home in December 1895 and was surprised to see that the Herzls had a decorated Christmas tree. The festival of Hanukkah solved that problem, and became an opportunity for secular Jews to get together during the Christmas season without feeling guilty about it. "After the guests ate and drank their fill," we read in Agnon's novel *A Simple Story*, "they began making merry, singing Passover songs whose lyrics they replaced with silly words." The organizers of the party are described as Zionists, and the festival is an excuse for an evening of drinking and card games.

Hanukkah had an additional benefit: it was a story about strong Jews, and Zionists loved it. Romantic ideas about honor were integral to national ideology and the military culture it encouraged. Both Herzl and his colleague Max Nordau frequently referred to honor and railed against the popular image of Jews as cowards. They urged their coreligionists to "toughen up" and become feisty and fearless, and to prove their mettle by the national standards of the day. Celebrating Hanukkah became a good opportunity to fight antisemitism, to remind the world of the Jewish heroic past and of its future potential. Bialik could not understand why the great book of Maccabees, as he put it, had not been incorporated into the books of the Hebrew Bible. "O children of the Maccabees," he concluded his 1899 poem "The Vanguard" (למתנדבים בעם), "Let the nation rise, let the people stand! / Rekindle the light, rekindle the light!" The first Hanukkah soirées in the German-speaking world emphasized the military heroism of Jews, and programs usually included speeches and music that celebrated it (see Figure 4.1).

Hanukkah and Zionism

The potent aspects of Hanukkah developed in the Yishuv into an open celebration of Jewish nationalism, and then militarism, after the conflict with the Arabs escalated. The festival became more didactic too, and, ironically, directed at children again. But if in the Diaspora children played diverting games and received candy, Yishuv children learned

Fig. 4.1 Illustration of Judah Maccabee by Tzvi Livni (Malevanchik) from a collection of stories for children, Ya'acov Hurgin, ed., *The Chain of Heroism* (שלשלת הגבורה), Tel Aviv, El-Hama'ayan, 1946. In the introduction Hurgin writes: "In these dark days for our people, this is a timely book that will foster in our children a sense of pride in their glorious past and a respect for the heroic acts of yore … and will discourage feelings of inferiority that the oppressive present may arouse in their fragile souls." Israel Museum, Illustration Library, courtesy of Ilana Gil.

Celebrating Jewish Power   105

about Jewish political history, held torchlit marches, sang heroic songs, and staged plays about the ancient Jewish wars for independence.

The knot between Hanukkah and nationalism was first tied by the principal of Rishon Letzion's high school – Yehuda Leib Matmon-Cohen, who later ran the Herzlia Gymnasium – who in 1905 organized a public torchlit march to commemorate the victory of the Maccabees. He was summarily fired, however, as a precaution against retaliation from the Turkish authorities, who were wary of such public displays of nationalism. But it was a small snag in Hanukkah's quick promotion to the Yishuv's most patriotic festival, an early Zionist Independence Day to which various national causes were routinely pinned. "We wanted to stress the heroic sides of Hanukkah," said Yemima Avidar-Tchernowitz, who encouraged kindergartens and schools to focus on Judah Maccabee and other ancient heroes.[5] Another teacher remembered the first celebrations of Hanukkah "as a huge festival ... the preparations lasted for weeks ... we would dance and sing in the streets for hours."[6] In the 1920s "there were marches all over Tel Aviv. It was an enormous event, candles everywhere, heaven on earth. [And] the children marching in the middle with the adults beside them holding torches, [with] singing, and [music] ... everything was so wonderfully Zionistic," that is, patriotic.[7]

Artists, composers, choreographers, writers, and poets were enlisted to help teachers shape the new Zionist festival calendar. There was a constant demand for original materials in Hebrew, remembered Levin Kipnis, songwriter and pedagogue extraordinaire. The Hebrew language war of 1913–1914 saw Kipnis and other educators at the forefront. "We convened the first [teachers'] seminar then ... and everyone was terribly excited about it. There weren't many of us at the time, but we were all [very committed to the Hebrew national idea] and so the first children's song I wrote was for Hanukkah."[8] Teachers were hungry for new materials, and were "always running after [poets], pleading with them to write something for their young charges" so they could use it

---

[5] Nillie Arieh-Sapir, "The Procession of Lights: Hanukkah as a National Festival in Tel Aviv, 1909–1936" (תהלוכת האור: חנוכה כחג לאומי בתל-אביב), *Katedra* 103 (2002): 131–150, at p. 136.

[6] Ibid., p. 137.

[7] Ibid., p. 141.

[8] Tsippi Fleischer, *Historical Development of the Hebrew Song*, 1964/2009, www.tsippifleischer.com/book/, vol. II, p. 387.

106   *A New Hebrew Festival Calendar*

to celebrate the festivals.[9] Their zeal must have been substantial because as early as 1933 the poet Nathan Alterman parodied it in his popular children's poem "A Great Big Miracle" (נס גדול היה פה).[10] The rhymes poke fun at the jingoism of the Hanukkah tradition that developed in the Yishuv by staging the heroic revolt of the Maccabees as a Zionist *Toy Story*, with dishes, rags, toys, and pets staging a mighty fight for Jewish independence.

Purim

The Purim festival as recounted in the book of Esther commemorates an unsuccessful plot to exterminate the Jews of Persia. The plot is hatched by the king's chief advisor, Haman, who feels disrespected by a Jew named Mordecai and decides to punish him by killing off all the kingdom's Jews on a day chosen by lot (*purim* means 'lots'). As it happens, the king's favorite concubine is Esther, Mordecai's niece. When Esther tells him about the plot to kill her people, the outraged king orders Haman's execution and promotes Mordecai to his position. However, since Haman had already incited the pogrom, the king permits the Jews to defend themselves, and they do so with great success. The festival of Purim marks their victory.

As in the Hanukkah story, the instruction to observe this victory is ordained not by God but by leaders of the community:

20 And Mordecai wrote these things, and sent letters unto all the Jews that were in all the provinces of the king Ahasuerus, near and far, 21 to fix the fourteenth day and the fifteenth day of the month of Adar, every single year, 22 the days when the Jews had rest from their enemies, and the month which was turned for them from sorrow to gladness, and from mourning into a good day; that they should make them days of feasting and gladness, and of sending portions of food to one to another, and gifts to the poor. (Esther 9:20–22)

If Hanukkah became a prominent festival prior to the rise of Zionism in Europe, Purim was the first modern Jewish festival to be revived in Palestine. It was an important part of early Yishuv culture, certainly

---

[9] Ibid.

[10] Nathan Alterman, *It Happened on Hanukkah or the Great Miracle* (זה היה בחנוכה או נס גדול היה פה), illustrations by Danny Kerman, Hakibbutz Hame'uhad, 2001.

Celebrating Jewish Power 107

the most visible part of it. But something peculiar happened to the festival in the Yishuv. While traditional celebrations of Purim emphasized Jewish power and celebrated it, Yishuv society underplayed it and chose to emphasize other aspects of the story instead. Observant Jews mark Purim by a public reading of the book of Esther in synagogue, a ritual that involves public gloating over the fall of the Jew-hating Haman and joy over the destruction of the Jews' enemies in the spirit of Esther 9:5: "Thus the Jews struck all their enemies with the stroke of the sword by slaughter and destruction, and did as they willed to those who hated them."

A decisive military victory of this kind should have appealed to Zionists. Instead, they emphasized the more carnivalesque sides of the occasion, its general merrymaking, drinking, and the tradition of the *Purimspiel*, the staging of shows based on the book of Esther. Perhaps it was due to the nature of the Jewish triumph in Esther, a surprising, last-minute victory that was negotiated by a VIP, a very bloody triumph – the Bible tells us of 800 people butchered in the city of Susa, and of 75,000 more casualties throughout the kingdom – and the distasteful gloating over it. Since the existence of Jewish communities in the Diaspora was often precarious, the Purim story was reassuring. It was comforting to fantasize about the influence of a clever Jewish intermediary, a last-minute escape from danger, a complete trouncing of their enemies, etc. But Zionists wanted to change this power dynamic, and used the festival to affirm the energy and the joy of their young national community. The costumes, floats, and slogans during Purim promoted the achievements of the Yishuv and put them on display. Almost from the start the Tel Aviv Purim carnival was sanctioned by the municipal authorities, who helped to organize it and led it.[11]

The Zionist overhaul of the festival began in Tel Aviv early in the 1900s with dance parties and masquerades organized by the dancer and dynamic cultural agent Baruch Agadati. Following the great popularity of Agadati's private Purim parties, they were quickly made public and received official sanction. In 1912 Tel Aviv had its first Purim carnival with a public procession and participants wearing costumes and masks, an annual event that became a venerable civic tradition in the Yishuv until budget problems and then World War II diminished it.

---

[11] For a photo of the Purim carnival procession in the early 1930s see https://commons.wikimedia.org/wiki/File:PikiWiki_Israel_47268_Tel_aviv.jpg.

In 1926 the Purim carnival – or Adloyada (from the Hebrew "to oblivion") a reference to the customary binge drinking – saw the addition of a beauty pageant, named Esther the Hebrew Queen after its biblical namesake. The objectifying criteria of the Zionist beauty contests tell us a lot about the values of their organizers, who wanted to select "the most beautiful and typical woman of Tel Aviv," as the daily *Doar Hayom* announced on January 29, 1926, someone who would represent the aesthetic side of the Yishuv and become the face of the new Hebrew nation that was being created in Palestine.

The first beauty queens to win the title between 1926 and 1929 represented the aesthetic values of their day. The politics of taste behind the selection of the first beauty queen in 1926 were obscured by the fact that, instead of the official contenders, an exceptionally attractive member of the audience, a woman named Lyla Tchertkov, was selected spontaneously by the audience. "She had gentle green eyes, and her black hair surrounded her head like a sparkling crown," reported *Doar Hayom* (see Figure 4.2).

Rekieta Chelouch, the 1927 queen, was selected for her Sephardi origin and her long roots in Palestine, which strengthened the Zionist claims of native connections (see Figure 4.3).

Fig. 4.2 Lyla Tchertkov, Tel Aviv Purim beauty pageant queen, 1926. Photo: A. Tchertkov Collection, Tel Aviv/National Library of Israel.

Fig. 4.3 Rekieta Chelouch, Tel Aviv Purim beauty pageant queen, 1927. Photo: National Library of Israel.

Fig. 4.4 Zipora Tzabari, Tel Aviv Purim beauty pageant queen, 1928. Photo: S. Korbman, the Museum of the History of Tel Aviv–Yafo Collection/ National Library of Israel.

The third and most well-known beauty queen was Zipora Tzabari, a shy milkmaid from a Yemeni family, who was discovered on one of her milk routes. Her dark complexion satisfied the Zionist pursuit of native Mediterranean, or "oriental," credentials, as they were called at the time (see Figure 4.4).

The fourth was Hannah Meyuhas-Polani, whose blonde hair and light skin represented the Ashkenazi community, as the papers put it (see

Fig. 4.5 Hannah Meyuhas-Polani, Tel Aviv Purim beauty pageant queen, 1929. Photo: National Library of Israel.

Figure 4.5). Taken together, they literally embodied the physical shape that the new Zionist society wished to take. The pageant acknowledged the diverse ethnic heritage of Jews – contestants wore ethnic costumes instead of swimsuits – and the hope that a native type would emerge by mixing them all.

Like other civic holidays that developed with the spread of nationalism, the festival of Purim had distinct commercial aspects.[12] But it was also the most visible and elaborate display of Zionist cultural inventiveness. Purim became hugely popular in the Yishuv and demonstrated the thirst for cultural invention and the creative energy of a secular Jewish society that emphasized life over learning. It was also the only urban festival of a culture that frowned on city life and encouraged farming. Nevertheless, the association of Purim with Tel Aviv, the so-called first Hebrew city, validated its credentials as a Zionist celebration.

[12] Hizky Shoham, "A Huge National Assemblage: Tel Aviv as a Pilgrimage Site in Purim Celebrations (1920–1935)," *Journal of Israeli History* 28: 1 (March 2009): 1–20.

Celebrating Jewish Power 111

Lag Ba'omer

The festival of Lag Ba'omer capped the Zionist celebration of Jewish power and political agency. Not surprisingly it was also one of two holidays that had no precedent in Jewish history – the other is Tu Bishvat or Arbor Day. The festival celebrates a Jewish strongman, Shimon Bar Kokhba, the leader of the failed Jewish rebellion against the Romans in the second century CE. Bar Kokhba presided over a spectacular political and military failure, a rebellion that brought death to half a million Jews and angered the Romans so much that they sold many of the surviving Jews into slavery and erased the name of Judea from their records, changing it to the province of Syria Palaestina. For much of Jewish history Bar Kokhba languished in a relative obscurity that many felt was well deserved. In the Middle Ages he was briefly revived by Spanish Jews as proof of the nation's military credentials. But it was Romantic Nationalism that made him into a Jewish King Arthur or William Tell, a national liberator whose name became the stuff of legends.[13]

The change was first suggested by a creative German Rabbi, Samuel Mayer, who in 1840 published a serial novel called *Bar Kokhba the Messiah King*.[14] In one of the more imaginative moments in the novel the Jewish leader meets a fierce lion, overcomes the beast, and tames it. It was a simplistic literary device that reworked the Samson story, but it was readily embraced by German Jews eager for "manly" credentials. Bar Kokhba soon joined Judah Maccabee as a paragon of Jewish heraldry and the namesake of Jewish sports clubs and youth movements throughout Europe. The fanatical general also inspired Nordau to tell delegates to the Second Zionist Congress that, "for the first time since the desperate war of the great Bar Kokhba, we can finally understand the terrible damage that 1800 years of exile have done to us."[15]

The rising popularity of Bar Kokhba and his heroic appeal called for commemoration, and in the early 1900s it was fixed for LG Ba'omer, the thirty-third day of the Omer period (the numerical value of the letters L and G in the Hebrew alphabet is 33; Omer refers to ancient

---

[13] For a 1905 statue of Bar Kokhba by the artist Enrico Glicenstein see www.nli.org.il/he/archives/NNL_ARCHIVE_AL997009633120605171/ NLI#$FL170200444.

[14] Sara Turel, "Bar Kokhba, Creating a Myth," in *Bar Kokhba: Historical Memory and the Myth of Heroism* (בר כוכבא: הבנייתו של מיתוס), Land of Israel Museum, 2016, p. 13.

[15] Ibid., p. 15.

112   *A New Hebrew Festival Calendar*

farming dates that marked different harvests). The date was associated with old traditions of mourning over the failed rebellion, which end on that day and are marked by expressions of joy. At some point they included outings to the countryside and games of different kinds, including archery. Another custom that developed separately in Palestine around that day included lighting candles, torches, or fires in honor of Galilean rabbis connected with the ancient rebellion. In the 1920s Zionists combined these disparate traditions to create a new festival and another day that celebrated Jewish strength and the struggle for national independence.

"I believe we need to connect the story of Bar Kokhba to the situation in the Galilee today," wrote Rachel Yana'it Ben-Zvi in the early 1900s. She was referring to the security problems at Zionist farms that were attacked by neighboring Arabs. "I decided to put together a pamphlet that will give people a better picture of the leader of the rebellion against the Romans, not just one for school children. I wonder if he was anything like Ezekiel, was he as short as him? Maybe he was more like Alexander Zaïd, a man of few words ... or like Mendeleh Portugali, tall and cheerful?" Ezekiel, Alexander, and Mendeleh were friends of Yana'it Ben-Zvi who worked as watchmen in Jewish settlements in the Galilee. Like many Zionists she conflated present and past. When she handed out the pamphlet to people who came for the more traditional fire-lighting Lag Ba'omer celebrations in the Galilee, they were confused at first. "How is [Bar Kokhba] connected to Lag Ba'omer?" someone asked.[16]

But by the 1920s the connection was clear to all, and the new festival became a big hit in the Yishuv. In kindergarten, children declaimed a rousing song about the general's meeting with the lion:

> Bar Kokhva,[17] as you know,
> was a brave bro.
> He climbed the lion,
> And rode it to Zion,
> Over valleys and hill,
> Shouting freedom with thrill.
> The nation all clapped,
> Our hero is back!
> He's back!

[16] Yana'it Ben-Zvi, *We Are Immigrating to Israel*, (אנו עולים) pp. 103–104.
[17] The colloquial Israeli pronunciation is Kochva.

Celebrating the Jewish Return to the Land   113

Teenagers loved the lion tamer too and spent the day playing with makeshift bows and arrows in his honor. At night they lit bonfires and gathered around them, bonding as a nation in the making, a nation of strong Jewish men, who in the words of 2 Samuel 1:17, "teach the children of Judea archery." Literally.[18]

Celebrating the Jewish Return to the Land: Passover, Shavu'ot, Sukkot, Omer, Tu Bishvat

The Zionist desire for physical agency was complemented by the wish for a return to the land in literal and symbolic ways. This figment of European Romantic Nationalism was actually inscribed in the festival calendar of Jews, who began their national life as a pastoral people, after all, and whose ancient festivals focused on farming. Indeed, one of the greatest feats of the rabbis after the fall of Bar Kokhba was to replace the centrality of the land in the Israelite cult with a focus on text. It changed Jews from an agricultural community to a textual or imagined community. One of the greatest feats Zionists managed was to swing that pendulum back by retrofitting existing festivals, by resurrecting extinct festivals, and by inventing completely new festivals in the spirit of modern nationalism that turned Jews into a political community again.

Passover: From a Family Festival to an Agricultural Feast

Passover, *pesach* in Hebrew, is one of the most important festivals in the traditional Jewish calendar. It is a national foundation story that describes the exodus of the Israelites from captivity in Egypt and their re-formation as an independent nation on their way back to their ancestral land, the Land of Israel.[19] It is the first of three major holidays in the Bible that mandated pilgrimage to Jerusalem. With the destruction of the Temple in the first century CE and the eventual growth of substantial Jewish communities outside Palestine, annual trips to Jerusalem became moot. Instead, an alternative festival tradition developed for Passover

---

[18] For a photo of Lag Ba'omer on Kibbutz Migdal Oz in 1932 see www.nli.org.il/ he/archives/NNL_ARCHIVE_AL997009696834505171/NLI#$FL5532637.

[19] For a discussion of Passover as a myth invented by the sixth-century BCE Judean king Josiah see Elon Gilad, *The Secret History of Judaism* (ההיסטוריה הסודית של היהדות), Am Oved, 2023, pp. 29–35, as well as Jacob L. Wright, *Why the Bible Began*, Cambridge University Press, 2023.

114   *A New Hebrew Festival Calendar*

that was eventually centered around the family. At some time in the Middle Ages the tradition became rich enough to be compiled into a miscellany or instructional reader. Named the Passover Haggadah, it was a compendium of stories, homilies, benedictions, prayers, and ritual poems that retell the exodus from Egypt as a kind of revenge story in which the terrible punishment God visits on the Egyptians becomes a projection of the Jews' wish to avenge themselves on their persecutors. Vengeance was initially directed at crusading Christians, but ultimately became a wish to take revenge on any persecutor of Jews, at any time. While the reading of the Haggadah during the ritual meal transformed the family into a symbolic nation that reenacted its past on an annual basis, the vengeful aspects of the celebration perpetuated a Jewish sense of victimhood.

Because Passover was such a major Jewish festival, the ability to modify it significantly was limited, but it wasn't necessary because the festival already spoke about national birth. Zionists simply emphasized the historical parallels between the exodus from Egypt and the settlement of Canaan and their own national project. These changes were not unusual, in fact, and followed an old tradition. Official bibliographies list thousands of different *haggadot* that were created throughout history in Jewish communities around the world. The basic order or *seder* of the festival is identical in all of them, although many readers include added materials that reflect local traditions. Zionists did the same, and the changes they made were telling. They minimized the sense of persecution and victimhood and emphasized instead the agricultural roots of the festival and their connection to the land.

Not surprisingly, the kibbutz movement contributed some of the most significant changes to the Passover celebration under Zionism and, in the tradition of the genre, produced a variety of *haggadot*. Common to all of them was a shift from a revenge story and a reliance on God to a story of national rebirth and an independent life on the nation's ancestral soil. The fact that the contents of the Haggadah were amenable to change as a matter of tradition lessened the force of the new additions. At the same time, because the celebration of Passover on kibbutzim retained many of its traditional elements – including a festive meal that involved the entire kibbutz community as a symbolic family – its ideological rewriting stood out in contrast. It was another example of the Zionist fondness for filling old vessels with new wine.

The changes were not obvious, or even coherent, at first. An early Passover on Kibbutz Bet Alfa was held in the mountains nearby. As

Celebrating the Jewish Return to the Land 115

celebrants seated themselves on one side of a small canyon, "several other members stood on a rock on the opposite side and recounted the life of Moses through song and dance." One of the dancers remembered how terrified she was that one of the performers might fall off the rock during the performance.[20] Not everyone liked it. "The difference between the majesty of the Passover seder at my father's house [in Eastern Europe] and our first frivolous attempts at it was very painful to me," recalled a member of another kibbutz. "I would lock myself up in my room and long not just for my parents' home ... but for a more meaningful secular existence."[21]

In time, the kibbutz Haggadah took on a distinct form through changes to the text, the artwork, and especially the music, all of which emphasized a particular Hebrew nationalism. Thanksgivings to God were replaced with poems about the agricultural cycle and the beauty of the land, and rabbinic homilies about the exodus were replaced with biblical citations about it. References to the persecution of Jews were counterbalanced with an emphasis on Zionist defiance, especially during the 1940s. Finally, traditional songs in praise of God – "Ehad mi Yode'a," "Had Gadya," and "Dayeynu" – were often replaced with poems or proclamations of a more nationalistic type.

Music played an important part in the kibbutz *seder*, as in the exemplary Haggadah of Kibbutz Yagur. It was composed by Yehuda Sharet (1901–1979), an accomplished folk musician, who wrote a rich festival program of original music, texts, and staged agricultural rituals that became one of his most celebrated works. In many ways the Yagur Haggadah was a Jewish passion play that replaced the passion of Christ with the passion of the exodus from Egypt, which it staged before the whole community as a public profession of its core beliefs.

The 1947 edition of the Yagur Haggadah replaced the traditional blessing that opens the *seder* with a dramatic proclamation about the spring harvest. SPRING, reads the first page, which goes on to announce the first harvest of the year:

> The field in its sheaves is ready for harvest.
> Each sheaf heavy with grains.
> Is the sun setting? Asks the reaper.
> Yea – replies the congregation.

[20] Yoram Goren, *Fields Dressed in Dance* (שדות לבשו מחול), Ramat Yohanan, 1984, p. 33.
[21] Zevulun and Misel, eds., *Kibbutz Festivals*, p. 98.

116   *A New Hebrew Festival Calendar*

> Shall I use this sickle to harvest?
> Yea – replies the congregation.
> Shall I harvest this field? He asks again.
> Yea – replies the congregation.

The exchange is based on a Mishnaic text – this was unusual for kibbutz festivals, which preferred the more "genuine" Hebrew Bible – about an ancient Jewish cultic ritual which was adapted here to the new Jewish life on the land. It also refers to the kibbutz community by the traditional Jewish term, "congregation." Old and new are mixed here together, the ancient roots of the festival with Zionist innovations.

Haggadot on kibbutzim often replaced traditional references to God with more nationalist materials, such as Bialik's grand poem "The Last Mortals of the Desert" (מתי מדבר אחרונים), which emphasizes Jewish self-sufficiency and independence: "No! We shall not eat stale bread, partridge or manna from heaven," it asserts. Instead, Zionists declare their intention to eat "the fruits of their labor." Likewise, the hard labor that Adam and Eve are sentenced to after their ejection from Eden is embraced in kibbutz *haggadot* as a blessing, not a curse.

Agricultural rituals became integral parts of the Passover passion play on kibbutzim that emphasized connection to the land. Before the text above was read, a column of children carrying bundles of sheaves would enter the dining hall, pass before the community, lift the bundles up, and then lay them down as the choir declaimed: "What are these bundles of sheaves in your hands? It is the blessing of the earth and of labor / sheaves of a new crop."

The kibbutz *seder* was much more performative than the intimate family meals of traditional *seder*s. It was probably inevitable given the size of the community. Still, the combination was unique and telling. On the eve of Passover, the entire kibbutz sat together to eat as one big family and celebrated the nation's renewal in grand fashion. "From time to time I had to get outside and wipe my eyes," recalled the participant who had been upset by the first feeble attempts to celebrate the festival. He was deeply moved by the meaningful changes that had been made to it since. For some, the experience of renewal was sensual, and they remembered "the smell of cooking food, of wine, of freshly cut flowers … [that] drifted through the kibbutz [on the eve of the holiday], mixed with the smell of freshly cut hay, of cow dung and of tree blossom."[22] If the simulation of

---

[22] Ibid., pp. 150–151.

Celebrating the Jewish Return to the Land 117

Torah study within the family circle was a medieval innovation of the traditional *seder*, as Hizky Shoham showed, the kibbutz *seder* became a passion[ate] [dis]play of a community of Zionist believers.[23]

Shavu'ot (Pentecost)

Shavu'ot, or the Feast of Weeks, was renewed in ways that should be familiar by now: an ancient Jewish festival that received a Zionist update according to the ideals of Romantic Nationalism. Shavu'ot completes the cycle of spring festivals that begins with Passover. The name refers to the seven weeks of the Omer period between the end of spring and beginning of summer and the Temple offerings connected with it. Again, the festival lost much of its significance after the destruction of the Temple. Instead, traditions that associated Shavu'ot with the law-giving event at Sinai developed and emphasized the study of scripture. Zionists did away with those traditions and revived the ancient farming roots of a festival that was celebrated mainly by children in the Yishuv.

The festival received a significant boost in the early 1930s, when it began to be hosted by the city of Haifa in an attempt to compete with Tel Aviv and its popular Purim festival. For one of the first celebrations of the festival, in June 1930, the farmers of the plains and valleys around Haifa were invited to display and celebrate the fruits of their labor. "Thousands of people came to see the children of Haifa and [Kibbutz] Yagur, who brought the fruits of their harvest and other products from factories in the area. An orchestra played music, and the Haifa school choir sang Hebrew songs."[24]

Two years later the city issued the following announcement "to the residents of Hadar-Hacarmel!" in Haifa, which read: "Popular celebrations are planned in the city over the next few days. The celebration of the 'First Fruits' will attract many guests from around Haifa, from the valley, from Samaria, and from the country at large and will be held in [the neighborhood of] Hadar-Hacarmel."

---

[23] Hizky Shoham, "The Jewish Family: Passover," in *Israel Celebrates: Jewish Holidays and Civic Culture in Israel*, Brill, 2017, pp. 20–63. For a photo of a Passover *seder* on Kibbutz Gan Shmuel see https://commons.wikimedia.org/wiki/File:PikiWiki_Israel_1542_Kibbutz_Gan-Shmuel_sk1-_10_ _גן-שמואל-סדר 1947_הפסח.jpg.

[24] Yair Safran and Tamir Goren, "Shavu'ot Celebrations in Haifa" (חגיגת שבועות בחיפה), *Haifa Historical Society Bulletin* (בטאון העמותה לתולדות חיפה) 16 (December 2018): 25–27.

118   *A New Hebrew Festival Calendar*

"Popular" and "planned" are not complementary. The prediction about guest numbers is speculative as well. Both disclose the engineering aspects of cultural innovation in the Yishuv and the energy behind it. The announcement instructs the public that "the days of the festival and the popular celebrations that will follow will symbolize the gladness of the Hebrew nation on its soil during the feast of the first fruit." Residents are also told that they "should feel very lucky to have the good fortune to host the festival in [their] neighborhood." They are asked to "appreciate the project that the [voluntary] festival committee took upon itself" and "help by beautifying the houses and the streets." The note concludes with an enthusiastic injunction that uses language from the Purim story: "Let there be gladness and light during the [upcoming festival] in the Hebrew city of Haifa!"[25]

Shavu'ot provided a good opportunity for a community that wished to become politically independent and economically self-sufficient, and put great emphasis on realizing both through a physical and spiritual connection to the soil. The occasion stressed these values and displayed the skill of Jewish laborers and the potential of the land to flow with "milk and honey." In 1932 the Haifa celebrations were extended to include

an artistic program of theater, athletic shows, dance concerts and balls. The next day saw a concert by local choirs and a morning show for children. The high point of the day was a festive procession with samples of produce, that ended at the technical school, the Technion, where the produce was ceremoniously received by various officials with the ancient Temple benediction, "Brothers, welcome in peace."

Two years later, in 1934, the festival had become a hopping success. The papers reported that Haifa was "teeming with people ... and that the organizers expected 25,000 participants."[26]

Like many festivals that lost their religious context in modern times, and not just in Jewish culture, Shavu'ot was celebrated mainly by children and became a staple of the festival calendar in kindergartens and schools. The focus on children was an opportunity to extend the agricultural display of plenty to fruits of the womb, the future

[25] From a poster titled "To the Residents of Hadar Hacarmel" (אל תושבי הדר הכרמל), National Library of Israel.
[26] For a photo of the 1932 Shavu'ot procession on Herzl Street, Haifa, see https://he.wikipedia.org/wiki/ 1928_,חיפה_-_הכרמל_בהדר_שבועות_תהלוכת:קובץ.jpg.

Celebrating the Jewish Return to the Land   119

generations of the Yishuv, as in the words of this 1933 song, written
by Pinchas Elad and composed by David Zehavi: "Our barns are full
of grain and our wineries flow with wine. / Our homes are teeming
with babies / and our cattle are fruitful." But the song that came to
represent the festival even better was the 1929 hit "With Baskets on our
Shoulders" (סלינו על כתפינו), written by Levin Kipnis and composed
by Yedidya Admon:

> With baskets on our shoulders,
> garlands on our heads,
> we come from all the country's corners,
> our harvest here to spread.
>
> From Judea, from Samaria,
> from the valley, from Galilee—
> make way for us,
> the harvest we amassed,
> bang the drum, play the flute![27]

Sukkot

The festival of Sukkot, also called Tabernacles, belongs to the harvest
cycle too. But since the festival has a secondary historical and non-
agricultural significance – to commemorate the wandering of the
Israelites in the desert – it continued to be celebrated in the Jewish
Diaspora. As a result, and since both Omer and Shavu'ot sated the
Zionist appetite for the pastoral, Sukkot was not renewed in ways that
were significantly different from its celebration in the Jewish Diaspora.

Omer

The Omer festival was the most elaborate Zionist cultural creation, a
high example of Zionist tastes and sensibilities. *Omer*, which literally
means a bundle of sheaves in Hebrew as well as a measurement, most
often refers to the sheaf offering in biblical times that marked the

---

[27] In a 1931 photo from a Shavu'ot program in Tel Aviv, schoolchildren
wear garlands of flowers and leaves, a staple of the festival's finery. Baskets
with produce can be seen on the ground on the right. See www.israelhayom
.com/2023/05/25/kkl-jnf-unveils-photos-of-shavuot-festivities-in-british-
mandate-era/.

120 *A New Hebrew Festival Calendar*

beginning of the Omer period, the fifty days that separate spring and summer. On the second day of Passover, offerings from the year's first harvest were brought to the Jerusalem Temple for a public ceremony of thanksgiving. The first part of the ancient custom, which opened the Yagur Haggadah, took place out in a field, where representatives from the Temple would harvest bundles of sheaves and then deliver them to Jerusalem. The second part took place in the Temple, where the priests would thresh the sheaves, roast the grains, grind them, mix them with oil and incense, and place the concoction on the altar. This cultic ritual disappeared together with the Temple in 68 CE. In the 1940s, almost two thousand years later, it was revived in the spirit of nationalism by two prolific cultural entrepreneurs, Matityahu Shellem (1904–1975) and Leah Bergstein (1902–1989), both from Kibbutz Ramat Yohanan.[28]

Shellem and Bergstein came to Palestine in the early 1920s and became two of the most creative contributors to the festival tradition that thrived on kibbutzim, Shellem as a songwriter and Bergstein as a dancer and choreographer. They were dynamic collaborators who created several original festivals, such as the Shearing Festival (חג הגז) and the Water Festival (חג המים). The first was a romantic celebration of sheep-shearing inspired by biblical sources. The second was based on an ancient rain ritual. Both were short-lived, whereas the Omer continues to be celebrated, or rather performed, today.

Sporadic attempts to revive the Omer ceremony began in the 1920s before Shellem and Bergstein gave it a lasting shape. An early account from Kibbutz Ein Harod that brings to mind a community of farmers somewhere in Eastern Europe describes how "the sun was still high in the sky when all work has stopped. A solemn hush fell." After the bell announced the beginning of the ceremony, people began marching down to the field. "The reapers led the way, carrying gleaming scythes over their shoulders. They were followed by the gathering women, carrying pitchforks and rakes and adorned with flowers." The rest of the community followed behind.[29]

Shellem took part in one of those early celebrations and felt deeply moved by it. The symbolic recreation of a Jewish harvest for the first

---

[28] An initial attempt to reintroduce the ancient ritual into the Yishuv's festival cycle was made in Kibbutz Ein Harod in the late 1930s by the composer and kibbutz member Shalom Postolsky (1893–1949). But Postolsky's version of the Omer was partial and gained little traction until the idea was fully developed and instituted by Shellem and Bergstein.

[29] Zevulun and Meisel, eds., *Kibbutz Festivals*, p. 170.

Celebrating the Jewish Return to the Land 121

time in 2,000 years was a spiritual experience for him.[30] A few years later he created a fuller version of the festival for his kibbutz – not an easy task, as he confessed. Sources on the ancient ritual were few, their meaning was not clear, the celebrants and their faith were different, and farming had also changed; such challenges were common in Zionist cultural innovations. "The first thing I did was to go to [Jewish] sources to find out about the Omer," said Shellem. "I also consulted scholars at the university … and read the rabbis."[31] What became clear to him "is that [the Omer] was not just a religious ceremony, but a Hebrew spring festival that was conditioned by the life and customs of a nation of farmers."[32]

By the end of 1943 Shellem had finished writing the festival program. He asked Bergstein to add a number of dances to it, and the two brewed a rich concoction made up of Bible, farm work, and references to nature. "This Omer celebration is a legacy from our fathers before they were exiled from their land," proclaims an announcer at the opening of a ceremony staged in the middle of a wheat field as a reenactment of God's old promise that the people of Israel would inherit the land.

The Zionist festival was fortified with elements from the local Bedouin culture. In the early 1920s Shellem worked side by side with Arab laborers. "It wasn't very easy to communicate with them, but I tried my best because I was … fascinated by their music." Later he worked with Bedouin "who would sing at work" and dance the Debka, an Eastern Mediterranean line dance.[33] Bergstein was also captivated by the dance, which she saw for the first time at a Bedouin wedding. As she was watching a line of dancing men, "a magnificent woman burst out of the tent carrying a heavy sword, faced the men, and began to dance."[34] Bergstein was deeply struck by it and felt immediately drawn to a folk culture she saw as rooted in the soil and attuned to nature. She turned her experience into a short, powerful dance, a rousing number Shellem called "Sing Forth" (הֵן יְרוֹנֵן), which paraphrases Isaiah 16:10: "Sing forth, proclaim and announce / may the State of Israel / blossom and multiply and go forth / on the soil of Israel," an ironic paraphrase, given the Arabic source of the dance.

---

[30] Ibid., p. 59.
[31] Fleischer, *Historical Development*, p. 369.
[32] Goren, *Fields Dressed in Dance*, p. 63. For a performance see www.youtube .com/watch?v=iC1xjyBpSKk&t=2297s.
[33] Fleischer, *Historical Development*, p. 363.
[34] Zevulun and Meisel, eds., *Kibbutz Festivals*, p. 34.

122   *A New Hebrew Festival Calendar*

Finally, in his popular song "A Stalk in the Field" (שבולת בשדה),
Shellem celebrated his love for the land, for its nature, and for the rustic
landscapes his generation created:

> A stalk in the field
> bent in the wind
> heavy with grains
> In the sweeping mountains
> the day is coming to an end
> the sun is all orange and gold.

The dancers of this Zionist pastoral begin with sweeping movements
that simulate stalks swaying in the wind. Bergstein thought of it as
"the dance of the lumbering farmers" and tried to cast inexperienced
dancers, usually men, whose awkwardness, she believed, represented
working people who were unaccustomed to the cultural refinement of
dancing.[35] She was meticulous indeed.

Special outfits completed the theatrical celebration. Bergstein designed
long dresses that reflected older traditions and made the dancers look
impressive as they moved about the stage, slowed by garments that
swayed dramatically in the wind. She chose a priestly white and embellished it with elements she borrowed from other traditions: Greek,
Arabic, Eastern European, and Indian. She was completely honest about
it. "There is no point pretending we're natives," she said, "so let's celebrate our multiple belongings."[36] She also designed an ornament she
dubbed "ear curls," short, knotted ropes that hung over the heads of
female dancers to invoke lambs' ears. The inspiration for it came from
a pastoral poem by Shellem.

But if Bergstein had no illusions about being a native, her cultural
engineering project appears to have been more successful than she
imagined. As one of her young disciples confessed, the Omer was a
transportive experience.

I remember how once, after dancing at the Omer, I walked back home wearing
the dress Leah designed and thought about the clothes people wore in the past.
… I suddenly felt that it was not [just] me walking there but that [with me
were] thousands, millions of young women like me, Israeli, Jewish, who [used

---

[35] Ibid., p. 67.
[36] Goren, *Fields Dressed in Dance*, p. 120.

Celebrating the Jewish Return to the Land

to] live on this soil. With every step I took, I felt as if millions of other women were walking with me. I had a feeling that I was not living in the present but in history ... a feeling that grew from a sense of continuity. ... Something in the dance I [had] just performed made me a part of this landscape.[37]

The Omer was an immediate success, and the annual celebration in Ramat Yohanan and other communities attracted hundreds of guests from around the country (see Figure 4.6). But its remit remained confined to a small number of kibbutzim. It was not surprising, given the specifically agricultural nature of the festival. Even in biblical times the ritual was performative, a symbolic gesture by a community of anxious farmers. Zionists modified the symbolism, but not by much.

Fig. 4.6 The Omer festival in Kibbutz Ramat Yohanan, 1940s. Ramat Yohanan Archive, Pikiwiki.

Tu Bishvat

Tu Bishvat, like Lag Ba'omer, was a radically new festival. As Hizky Shoham pointed out, it was the Zionist version of an American holiday, Arbor Day, dedicated to the romance of nature as a cure for the ills

---

[37] Ibid., p. 72.

Fig. 4.7 Students from an agricultural school in Nahalal with produce they grew and brought to the festival celebration in Haifa, 1932. Central Zionist Archive.

of urban society.[38] The day was usually marked by planting trees, and Zionists grafted it onto the fifteenth day of the month of Shevat (t+u (טו) = 15), an ancient administrative date connected to agricultural taxation. In the Jewish Diaspora the original date lost its relevance and was replaced with a vague sense of appreciation for nature. People ate dried fruit on that day, and children received time off from school. Toward the end of the nineteenth century it became more closely associated with the renewal of Jewish life in Palestine. In 1894 the first suggestion to link Arbor Day with Tu Bishvat was made in the Hebrew journal *Hatzfira*, which claimed the festival was a Jewish invention to begin with, as Shoham notes: "Our forefathers marked the festival in the past with much ado and named it the Rosh Hashana of Trees (Arbor Day)."[39]

---

[38] Hizky Shoham, "The History of Planting on Tu Bishvat," in *Israel Celebrates*.
[39] Ibid., p. 30.

Celebrating the Jewish Return to the Land 125

The fiction was probably not necessary to convince Zionists, who were happy for any reason to commune with nature and get close to the soil. Tree-planting initiatives were common among the Jewish settlers of Palestine long before then, but they were not officially associated with a date until 1906, when the Hebrew Teachers' Union suggested it. A year later 300 students from the Mikveh Yisrael School held the first official tree-planting ceremony, with an extensive program of readings and songs.

Tu Bishvat, like other invented Zionist holidays, was observed primarily in educational institutions (see Figure 4.7). The program often included a procession of children who marched to a planting area with saplings in their hands, singing the "Planters' Song," with lyrics by Itzhak Shenhar and music by Yedidya Admon:

> Here come the planters:
> With a song in our hearts and a hoe in our hands.
> We come from all corners of the land,
> from near, from afar –
> On Tu Bishvat!
> On Tu Bishvat!
>
> What are you here for?
> We're here to prep the soil,
> to dig holes with toil,
> the earth to roil,
> On Tu Bishvat!
> On Tu Bishvat!
>
> What shall you plant?
> A tree in every hole,
> so that a forest grows tall,
> and covers our doleful land over all –
> On Tu Bishvat!
> On Tu Bishvat!

Arbor Day provided Zionists with a wonderful opportunity to mark their restorative ideology officially and turn it into a festival that was quickly added to the Zionist festival calendar. During the Yishuv period and the early decades of statehood it was a prominent date that was not always limited to one day or to Palestine/Israel. Tree planting became a powerful acculturation device that had obvious practical and symbolic

126　　　　　　　　　　　　　　*A New Hebrew Festival Calendar*

qualities. The planning of new forests was announced with great fanfare in the Hebrew press and was often connected to an event or a cause. The planting itself usually involved an official ceremony, and the greening agenda extended to Jewish communities around the world, who were invited to contribute to it and support the national Jewish project.

All societies draw lines between disconnected events in their history and create illusions of continuity or topographies of the past, as the sociologist Evyatar Zerubavel calls them.[40] These traditions of remembering, which began in the Hebrew Bible, played an important part in the renewal of the Jewish festival calendar in the Yishuv. Festivals do this especially well because their repetition year after year allows societies to emphasize historical connections and revise their stories of origin by creating unique emotional maps. The Zionist festival calendar did it especially well.

---

[40] Evyatar Zerubavel, *Time Maps: Collective Memory and the Social Shape of the Past*, University of Chicago Press, 2003. See also Orit Baskin, "Hanukkah according to the *Book of Festivals*" (חג חנוכה על פי ספר המועדים), *Zmanin* 61 (1997): 38–50.

5 | New Hebrew Aesthetics

Christians often thought of Jews as ugly people who dressed differently, spoke their own ugly language, ate unfamiliar food, and smelled bad. This perception of Jews persisted in the modern era and became part of antisemitism, which singled Jews out as vulgar parvenus who lacked "good [German/French/English] taste" (see Figure 5.1). One of the first tasks Zionists turned to, then, was an aesthetic regeneration, as they called it, that would bring beauty back into Jewish life and make it attractive. The question was, how?

It was a bias that preoccupied Herzl and his contemporaries, who dedicated the Fifth Zionist Congress in 1901 to disproving it. Organizers of the congress mounted an exhibition of works by various Jewish artists – illustrations, paintings, sculptures – that were meant to showcase Jewish artistic genius and aesthetic sensibilities. The commissioned works revolved around Jewish themes and, in general, depicted two extremes, the illustrious Jewish past in ancient times and the pathetic state of Jews in the present (see Figure 5.2). Later, Zionists would regard the entire period of Jewish life outside the Land of Israel, from the loss of sovereignty in the second century CE to the establishment of the Yishuv in Palestine, as "non-history," a black hole.

The call for new Jewish aesthetic standards brought up the question of art in traditional Jewish culture more generally. It was a lively debate at the time. People like the poet Mordechai Tzvi Maneh challenged Jewish intellectuals "to raise the love of beauty in the hearts of Jewish youth" to "sweeten our lives and give us a taste of heaven on earth."[1] Others, such as Ahad Ha'am, spoke against such mimicry and called for a more original modern Jewish culture based on what he vaguely termed Jewish ethics.

---

[1] Mordechai Tzvi Maneh, "General and Jewish Aspects of the Art of Painting" (חכמת הציור בכלל ובין בני עמינו בפרט), available at https://benyehuda.org/read/5376.

Fig. 5.1 Theodor Herzl, who was very serious about changing the perception of Jews as unattractive, imposed a strict dress code of black tie for the opening of the First Zionist Congress in Basel in 1897. "For the ceremonial opening session," read the delegate cards, "black party dress and white tie are mandatory." Many delegates resented the demand, including Herzl's right-hand man, Max Nordau. Representatives from Eastern Europe were especially anxious. Many of them were not familiar with these conventions, and some could barely afford the dress. But Herzl insisted. It was an opportunity to show the world that Jews were a civilized people too: dignified, respectable, aesthetic – or, in other words, white. Image of the Second Zionist Congress, Basel 1898. Kevin Viner, Elevator Digital, Toronto, the David Matlow Herzl and Zionism Collection, www.herzlcollection.com.

The argument, not new by then, focused on the tension between Jewish particularism and a wish to assimilate into the greater European culture, to be "human and Hebrew" at one and the same time, as author and pundit Micha Yosef Berdichevsky put it, and unite general knowledge with Jewish heritage.[2] When the Zionist intellectual Nahum Sokolow visited the celebrated Dutch painter Jozef Israëls, he marveled

---

[2] Micha Yosef Berdichevsky, "At the Crossroad, an Open Letter to Ahad Ha'am" (על פרשת דרכים מכתב גלוי לאחד העם), *Hashiloach* 1 (1896) (התרנ"ז): 154–159.

New Hebrew Aesthetics

Fig. 5.2 One of the artists featured in the Fifth Congress was Ephraim Moses Lilien (1874–1925). His elegant *Jugendstil* illustrations embodied the aesthetic call of Zionism, a complement to a cultural and political revolution that would put Jews on par with other modern Europeans. The drawing shows a group of beautiful men whose Jewish beards, Greek bodies, and wings – one of them is clearly Theodor Herzl – reveal some of the deepest desires of Zionists and gives their political agenda a distinct aesthetic form.

at his ability to capture the inner soul of the subjects he painted, "even the sea," by dint of his Jewish heritage. "Do Jews paint differently from Gentiles?" replied the old master, mystified by the essentialism of his visitor. "How exactly is an ocean Jewish?" he wondered.[3]

For Zionists the answer to this question was obvious. Without a place of their own, they claimed, a territory where they would develop an authentic national culture, Jews would not be able to develop a distinct aesthetic sense. None of them could define the nature of Jewish art, although all agreed how to achieve it, by creating a national space where Jewish heritage could be reengaged in a secular context. Speaking at the 1901 "art congress," Martin Buber reminded delegates that Jewish artists do not necessarily create Jewish art. A national art, he said, requires a national soil and a national community. In time, both

[3] Nahum Sokolow and Jozef Israëls. https://benyehuda.org/read/5354. Published in *Hatzfira*, October 22, 1915 (ידי בחשון תרע"א).

130

New Hebrew Aesthetics

would nurture artists who would internalize the spirit of the new Hebrew nation and give it aesthetic expression, as he and others thought they should. Jewish art would be the Jews' sentimental education, declared Buber, who suggested that since art and truth go together, "Jewish art will give voice to our Zionist essence. ... By looking at it, we will know ourselves."[4] It was an open conversation about the role of (Jewish) art in the service of (Jewish) national life that laid bare the civic theology behind a utopian aesthetics, a relationship that Zionists cultivated enthusiastically, sometimes openly, at other times less so.[5]

The call for cultural regeneration seems vague and even naïve today. Real art is not created by committees. But it highlights the very premise of culture, any culture, as a process of formation. Many of the Jewish leaders and intellectuals who concerned themselves with the Jewish Problem at the time came up with various ways to ease the tension between Jewish tradition and modernity. The exact nature of these suggestions was often unclear even to those who proposed them. Art in its most abstract sense was an important part of these cultural wake-up calls, not just because of its symbolic value, but also because it was suggestive without being too specific and expressed the inchoate nature of the calls themselves.

National Hebrew Art in Palestine

As the pragmatists they were, Zionists decided to nudge the Jewish muse, and in 1906, five years after the 1901 congress, they established an arts and crafts academy in Jerusalem under the direction of the energetic artist and activist Boris Schatz (1866–1932). Ephraim Moses Lilien designed the seal of the Bezalel School of Arts and Crafts, as it was called. His design celebrated the school's namesake, the biblical craftsman Bezalel ben Uri, chief decorator of the Israelite tabernacle in the wilderness. The crest shows two of Ben Uri's creations, the Ark of the Covenant and the tablets of the Ten Commandments. It was yet another reference to the ancient Israelite past so beloved of Zionists, who ignored the religious significance of the symbols and stressed instead the skill it took to make them, an emphasis on craft rather than art that distinguished the school at first.

---

[4] Sara Chinsky, *Kingdom of the Meek* (מלכות ענווי ארץ), Hakibbutz Hame'uhad, 2015, p. 73.

[5] Ibid., p. 22.

National Hebrew Art in Palestine 131

Bezalel made a big splash in the small Jewish community in Palestine, but its success in engineering a new Hebrew aesthetics was hotly debated, probably because of the early focus on crafts. Not everyone was happy about commercializing an art school, which focused on producing artifacts for export during its first phase – the school closed down in 1929 and reopened as a more conventional art school in 1935. Director Schatz, however, was open about it and proud of it. "The first department that is planned," announced the Jerusalem newspaper *Hashkafa* on December 26, 1905, "is a weaving workshop for expensive rugs" that "will provide employment and a stable source of income for local Jews." The rugs would surely appeal "to the thousands of tourists who come to Palestine every year" and would "have a big market abroad," especially in the USA, "where several big stores have already shown an interest in the merchandise, provided it is of high quality." Woodworking, metalworking, and needlepoint were also planned. "By working together," concluded the paper, "the Jewish artisans and their teachers will gradually develop a sense of beauty that will turn their craft into art." Indeed, the first art classes at Bezalel served the production of crafts. Drawing classes were held in the evenings and were open to "any crafter who would like to hone their drafting skills and become better at their job."

The philanthropic nature of Bezalel did not add to its stature as an academy of art either. Schatz was eager to hire unemployed Jews and make them more productive, as Zionists put it. Most of those workers were women and Yemenis, who were instructed how to manufacture rugs, silverwork, ceramics, and woodwork in a distinctive style. The idea was to replace a Christian and European visual dictionary with references that would be more Jewish, would reflect Palestine more closely, and would eventually become part of a uniquely Jewish visual subconscious.[6]

The Bezalel style, as it came to be known, was a collection of visual cues that drew on Jewish folkloric traditions, on the Jewish past and Jewish mythology, on the geography and ethnography of Palestine, and on Zionist politics, as a 1920s Hanukkah menorah illustrates (see Figure 5.3). The winged lions on either side of the candelabra motif refer to Assyrian art as well as to the Lions of Judah. But their posture and symmetry also suggest the cherubim on the Ark of the Covenant. The temple imagery is reinforced by the colonnade at the bottom and

[6] Ibid., p. 78.

Fig. 5.3 Hanukkah menorah or candelabra, Bezalel, 1920s. Jewish Museum/Art Resource/Scala, Florence.

by the two iconic columns on the sides – the columns have names in the Bible, Yachin and Bo'az – that create a tableau of the inner sanctum of the Jerusalem Temple. Small circles above the columns show local flora, and Hanukkah benedictions above and below add a more familiar Jewish touch. The words "Bezalel, Jerusalem" at the top give Zionist credentials to the object.

The weaving workshop created a similar mixture of Judeo-Zionist images and produced ornamental rugs that featured the image of Herzl, iconic sites from around Palestine, such as the tomb of Rachel the matriarch near the town of Bethlehem, or the Tower of David in Jerusalem. Rugs were usually framed by interlocking stars of David with the word "Zion" woven in the middle, and Hebrew verses from the Bible would often be included, as well as flowers that reflected the local flora, which were collected in the school's small museum to inspire domestic (read: authentic) design.[7]

---

[7] Reuven Gafni, ed., "A Temple in the Wilderness" (מקדש במדבר), *Et-mol* 186 (Spring 2006): 23–24.

National Hebrew Art in Palestine   133

"I have an important idea, and you will help me realize it," Schatz told zoologist Yisrael Aharoni, soon after Bezalel was established. "As you know," he explained, weavers everywhere "decorate their carpets with the lovely birds and butterflies of their countries." He suggested doing the same. A zoologist shouldn't have too much difficulty in breeding attractive butterflies "so that our artists can draw them and other birds and glorify our carpets with them."[8] The Bezalel museum – it later became the Israel Museum – was soon filled with dried flowers, stuffed animals, archaeological findings, and various artworks Schatz had collected. It was all meant to shape the new visual dictionary he envisioned.

The museum epitomized the greater ambition of the Bezalel project to create a cosmology of objects that would be defined and categorized as Hebrew.[9] Not everyone was impressed with the doctrine. Painter Reuven Rubin, a renowned graduate of the school, saw the museum as "a filthy stable ... the most revolting collection one could imagine ... a caricature ... covered ... with smears of the impotents who make Jewish art ... I am disgusted by them."[10] But the invented style of Bezalel was, arguably, among the most innovative initiatives of Boris Schatz, who envisioned a Hebrew room in Jewish homes around the world with handsome collections of Jewish traditional ritual objects – Passover plates, scent boxes, Hanukkah menorahs – redesigned in the distinctive style of Bezalel, which often blended the organic forms of *Jugendstil* with elements borrowed from various folk traditions, such as that of the Yemenis, Romantic National imagery, and themes and verses from the Hebrew Bible.

Following John Ruskin, Schatz believed that beauty should have a political purpose, and he measured the value of modern art by its ability to serve the Jewish national ideology. Crafts could communicate it more clearly than paintings or sculptures because they were more concrete and required little interpretation, especially familiar ritual objects. It was a modernistic idea that, in typical Zionist fashion, tried to turn religion into art, a neat solution for creating a new Hebrew folk culture from scratch. The riches of the Jewish religious tradition were reworked in

---

[8] Y. Aharoni, "Reminiscences of a Hebrew Zoologist" (זיכרונות זואולוג עברי), in Nurit Cohen, *Schatz's Bezalel 1906–1929* (בצלאל של שץ), exhibition catalogue, Israel Museum, 1983, p. 319.

[9] Chinsky, *Kingdom of the Meek*, p. 127.

[10] Dalia Manor, *Art in Zion: The Genesis of Modern National Art in Jewish Palestine*, Taylor & Francis, 2005, p. 91.

134 *New Hebrew Aesthetics*

the Bezalel workshops and redistributed as objets d'art that blended elements from the Hebrew Bible, Palestine, and Zionism.

It was a conspicuous orientalism that played on the negative image of Jews as orientals in Europe and, in the spirit of Zionism again, turned it to advantage. First, by stressing the ancient Jewish connection to the Eastern Mediterranean. Second, through a production process that employed "exotic" Jewish workers, mostly women and Yemenis, whose poverty and traditional background validated the products they manufactured as folklore, even though few of them were designed by them. Yemenis were frequently featured as the Jewish folk of Palestine whose primordial culture was the ancient kernel from which the new Hebrew nation would spring.

It was pure invention, of course. Yemeni Jews had arrived in Palestine in the 1880s, and although they had a rich silversmithing tradition, little of it was used in Bezalel, where Ashkenazi masters dictated the style. "Make it in the following way," wrote Shmuel Persov, who was in charge of filigree design at the school: "form two circles into one. Make a small ring of thin dotted wire in the middle ... produce three meters of this, and we can later decide if we want to make more of it."[11] But since Yemenis were the only Middle Eastern Jews who took part in the formation of Zionism as a community, and since they looked so different from local Jews – "When we arrived in Jerusalem in 1881," said Rabbi Shlomo Kassar, "no one believed we were Jewish ... because we were brown ... we looked like Arabs"[12] – they were often exoticized by Eastern European Zionists, who, ironically, were themselves exoticized by German Jews in Europe.

The synthetic style of Bezalel was ridiculed as manneristic, old-fashioned, and irrelevant already by 1923.[13] The forced attempt to merge (European) modernity with (Jewish) mythology was seen as too prescriptive, and a few years later, in 1929, the academy closed. The closure was welcomed by local artists who had felt constrained by Bezalel. But ideology continued to exercise a strong influence on art in the Yishuv and on the different forms it took. It was manifest in the local

---

[11] Gideon Ofrat, "The Bezalel Colony in Ben-Shemen, 1910–1913" (מושבת בצלאל בבן שמן), *Katedra* 29 (July 1981): 123–164, at p. 147.

[12] Rabbi Shlomo Kassar in Nitza Droyan, *The First Yemeni Immigrants 1882–1914* (חלוצי העליה מתימן), Zalman Shazar, 1982, p. 15.

[13] Gil Weissblai, *The Revival of Hebrew: Book Art in Weimar Germany* (קב ונקי), Carmel, 2019, p. 133; Avigdor Hameiri, *Doar Hayom*, December 14, 1923.

Painting in Hebrew

modernistic school of painting and sculpture that flourished after the school was closed, in the drawing styles that developed in the Yishuv, in photography, in graphic design, in book design and calligraphy, and even in font design and book illumination, all of which were shaped by Zionist ideology.

Painting in Hebrew

Two versions of the town of Tiberias and the Sea of Galilee come close to capturing a transformative moment in the evolution of Zionist art from its formative beginning in a tourist poster by Ze'ev Raban (1890–1970) to a more conventional European Modernism in the oil painting by Nahum Gutman (1898–1980) (see Figures 5.4 and 5.5). Raban was a leading teacher at Bezalel and one of the main creative forces behind the school's distinctive style, which straddled the blurred line between

Fig. 5.4 Ze'ev Raban, *Come to Palestine*, 1929, Poster for the Society for the Promotion of Travel in the Holy Land, Lithograph H: 99 X W: 64 cm. Israel Museum, Jerusalem. B02.0801. Photo Elie Posner, Israel Museum, Jerusalem.

Fig. 5.5 Nahum Gutman, *Tiberias*, 1926. Nahum Gutman Museum, Israel.

craft and art. This tourist poster is not very different from his other decorative work. It is a neat orientalist image of a Palestine where the Hebrew Bible and local Arab culture are brought together harmoniously. Gutman's painting reflects the local landscape more ruggedly through movement and light that show the dry hills and the humble character of Tiberias as a small mountain village. The impression of reality is more personal and follows modern artistic conventions, where the politics of art – unlike those of Bezalel – are less direct and presented as spontaneous, unique, and individual.

Gutman was part of the so-called Modernist school that turned away from the manifest orientalism of Bezalel and chose more updated ways to handle it. His work points to Western artistic influences that softened the blatant exoticism of Bezalel by giving it more modern figurations, such as Primitivism. Artists like Gutman, who rejected Schatz's vision, were committed Zionists, but they showed their commitment in different ways. Few painters depicted the drastic transformation that the Zionist movement made to Palestinian space by industrializing farming, rerouting waterways, and dressing the land with "concrete and cement," as described by the poet Nathan Alterman in his early 1930s love poem to the Land of Israel, "Morning Song," which charts a total spatial makeover:

Painting in Hebrew 137

> From the slopes of Lebanon to the Dead Sea,
> We'll criss-cross you with ploughs.
> We'll plant and build you,
> We will make you beautiful.
>
> We'll dress you with concrete and cement,
> and carpet you with gardens ...
>
> We'll build a road through your desert,
> We'll drain your swamps ...[14]

Not many artists appear to have noticed this makeover, as a visitor to a 1926 exhibition of contemporary art in Tel Aviv noted, complaining that the works "have nothing to do with labor and laborers in this land."[15] Unlike the clearer passion of modern Hebrew literature and poetry, visual artists showed their revolutionary commitment in other ways and were less direct about articulating a new cultural identity.

Instead, some artists used more traditional Jewish motifs to show their fealty to the Zionist cause, as in a 1925 painting by Reuven Rubin (1893–1974). Viewed from west to east, the Old City of Jerusalem on the left is small and dark, pitted against the bigger and brighter hills above it to the right. The blackened rocks below the city look charred, and the roads around it appear to strangle it. Against this crammed and oppressive image of the holy city, the empty hills above it to the east glow with bright light. There are no traces of the Zionist project in the picture, but the potential for it is there. It is implied by the dramatic conflict between the Old City below, dark and depressing, and the space above, empty and full of light, dotted by neat gardens of green trees, close to the heavens and ready to be impregnated with new meaning (see Figure 5.6).

The desire to create an authentic Hebrew identity and gain direct access to the land, either through dead remains such as ruins or through living remains such as "biblical" Yemenis or native Arabs, was shared by the early Bezalel school and the modernists, although in very different ways, as Dalia Manor and Yael Gil'at note.[16] Was it the kind of identity

---

[14] Nathan Alterman, *Popular Songs* (פזמונים ושירי זמר), Hakibbutz Hame'uhad, vol. 2, 1979.

[15] Manor, *Art in Zion*, p. 171.

[16] Ibid., p. 185. Yael Gil'at, *Yemeni Art and the Creation of National Visual Culture in Israel* (צורפות בכור היתוך: אמנויות יהודי תימן והתהוותה של התרבות החזותית הלאומית בישראל, 1882–1967), Ben-Gurion University Press, 2009, p. 155.

Fig. 5.6 Reuven Rubin, *Jerusalem*, 1925, oil on canvas, Rubin Museum collection, Tel Aviv.

Buber, Schatz, Sokolow, and some of the other Zionists from the 1901 congress had in mind? Let's put aside our intellectualism and sophistry, Buber told his listeners, and create art that will allow Jews to express themselves fully, independently, and truthfully. Let Jewish art teach the nation about itself.

The road to authenticity, whatever it means and however defined, was long. Some works by Modernists such as Siona Tagger, one of few female artists at the time, nudged it along with the random snapshots it took of life in the Yishuv, as in her iconic 1928 painting of Tel Aviv, titled simply *The Water Tower and Clock in Rothschild Boulevard*.[17] As the cultural capital of the Yishuv and a city designed as an urban Zionist utopia, Tel Aviv was more frequently painted than labor and laborers. However, the partial view of it in Tagger's work underplayed any kind of ideological grandstanding, even if its prosaic nature was

[17] For a photo see https://lib.ta.cet.ac.il/pages/item.asp?item=18879.

Sculpting in Hebrew: Canaanism 139

meant to stress the opposite, to signify the success of a revolution that created the setting for such mundane views in such a short time.

Sculpting in Hebrew: Canaanism

The boldest expression of Modernism in the Yishuv was offered by a local Primitivist movement that flourished for a short time in the 1940s and a bit beyond. Disparagingly dubbed Canaanism at first, it was a local expression of wider trends in Western art at the time. Like all Primitivists, Canaanites used pre-industrial society as a retroactive telescope that allowed them to imagine a primordial past, often as a basis for what they promoted as a purer or more genuine national culture.[18] For Canaanites this meant a protest against Zionist politics and the kind of sentimental use of biblical tropes that characterized Bezalel. The romance of the Canaanites stretched far back to an ancient Middle Eastern universe they considered nobler even than the Hebrew Bible, with its petty "diasporic" politics of patriarchs, kings, and prophets.

The beginning of Canaanism is usually attributed to Yitzhak Danziger (1916–1977) and his 1939 statue *Nimrod*, a striking Primitivist figure: the falcon on the lad's shoulder is pharaonic, the boyish look recalls Greek sculptures of adolescent boys known as *kouroi*, the wide and flat nose is Polynesian, and the slender and sensual body brings to mind ancient Indian sculpting conventions (see Figure 5.7).

Uncircumcised and standing at about a meter tall, the handsome statute captivated people in the small Yishuv. When it was first displayed in the window of the Israel Gallery on Ben Yehuda street in Tel Aviv, "young women would press their lips to the glass and kiss the statue," recalled Danziger's older sister, Hava Magnes.[19]

Danziger spoke lovingly about "the grainy feel, the sandy essence of the stone and its red hue" which he used for making the statue. The alleged origin of the stone in Petra, the ancient Nabatean city carved in stone, was an attraction too. "I tried to bring together matter and spirit," he explained, "to create an emotional and material

---

[18] Chinsky, *Kingdom of the Meek*, p. 63.
[19] Neri Livneh, "The Legend of Danziger" (אגדת דנציגר), *Haaretz online*, February 19, 2002, available at www.haaretz.co.il/misc/2002-02-19/ty-article/0000017f-e1e7-df7c-a5ff-e3ff80320000.

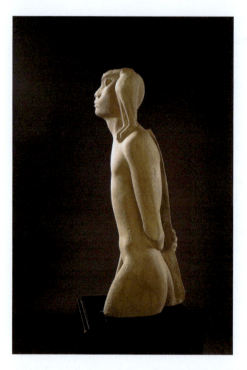

Fig. 5.7 Itzhak Danziger, *Nimrod*. Courtesy of Nurit Reches Danziger and the Israel Museum, Jerusalem.

completeness of a hunter, a falcon, a sandstone, Petra and the Nabateans, a meeting of a heroic myth with [Palestine] and the sandy desert rock."[20]

Canaanism presented New Hebraism with a revolutionary aesthetics that resonated far beyond a vague, brief movement. Against the tragedy of World War II, the Canaanites offered a radical position that took the central tenets of Zionism to their logical extreme. "Forget the Jewish diaspora and its pathetically passive so-called heroism," the Canaanites wrote in their 1943 *A Call to Hebrew Youth*: "shake it off," "clear the fog of the Jewish diaspora that stands between you, your country, and your past." Instead, "let the glory of the Hebrew era shine for you" and welcome "the ancient and intense world of our great ancestors, the people of this land since then" in all its glory and reality.

---

[20] Gideon Ofrat, "Nimrod, the Whole Story" (נמרוד: כל הסיפור), in *Gid'on Ofrat's Storeroom* (המחסן של גדעון עפרת), June 1, 2011, https://gideonofrat .wordpress.com/2011/06/01/נמרוד-כל-הסיפור/.

Sculpting in Hebrew: Canaanism 141

Elements from ancient Middle Eastern art had been used in Bezalel before that – some artists created entire works in the spirit of ancient Mesopotamia, such as Abraham Melnikov's *Roaring Lion* statue, made in the early 1930s as a monument for fallen Hebrew soldiers. But with the Canaanites, with the audacious connections they made to an imagined Israelite past, Hebrew irredentism received its boldest visual expression. "Danziger and I were complete romantics," recalled the sculptor Kosso Skorohod, who later changed his last name to Eloul, an Akkadian word for harvest and the name of a Hebrew summer month. "Exoticism was everything for us. ... We looked for the past in the bible of the present [*sic*]. ... I visited archeological sites whenever I could," and the more remote and biblical, the better. "I imagined myself as a Nabatean ... who shaped clay into forms that would one day mean the world to us, Young Hebrews." Egyptians and Assyrians? "They were too refined. The crude simplicity of the Canaanites spoke to us much more," Eloul confessed.[21]

Many of these energetic attempts to create an original Hebrew art, whether at Bezalel or by Canaanites, were at first considered forced, artificial, and orientalist. "Paint a pioneer, a camel, a donkey, or an Arab village and, voila! you have a native Hebrew artist," quipped the painter H. Glicksberg in 1933.[22] Most Jewish artists in the Yishuv ignored Arab Palestine and developed instead a Continental Modernism that appealed to them as Europeans, or European wannabes. Bezalel initiated that discourse, first by prescribing a distinct national aesthetics, and second by upholding art as a European cultural ideal that filtered the local environment and made it more meaningful to Zionist settlers. Zalman Shazar, who became Israel's third president, admitted that the familiar lens of modern art helped him and other immigrants from Russia accept the alienating environment of the Middle East and "fall in love once more with the homeland and its landscapes."[23]

Landscape, climate, and especially light were mentioned by artists again and again as markers of an elusive sense of place that eventually

---

[21] Kosso Eloul in conversation with Tamar Manor-Friedman, "Kosso Eloul 1920–1995," *Gid'on Ofrat's Storeroom*, October 18, 2019, https://gideonofrat.wordpress.com/2019/10/18/1995-1920-קוסו-אלול/

[22] Gila Ballas, "Who Are We, Really? East vs. West in Early Israeli Art" (מי אנחנו בעצם? מזרח מול מערב באמנות הישראלית בעשור הראשון למדינת ישראל), *Iton 77*: 230 (1999): 24–29.

[23] Dalia Manor, "Imagined Homeland: Landscape Painting in Palestine in the 1920s," *Nations and Nationalism* 9: 4 (2003): 533–554, at p. 551.

142   *New Hebrew Aesthetics*

became part of a visual vocabulary that eased some of the difficulties
of acculturation. "Every country has a unique light that gives it a
unique color," wrote Y. Kopalivitz in a 1928 art review that called on
local Jewish artists to pay more attention to it. "In the Land of Israel,"
he advised, "we have neither the operatic blue of Italy nor the sugar-
whiteness of its houses. ... Light here blends the colors more evenly; it is
more serious than Italian light, spiritual in nature," a fitting background
to the cradle of monotheism, he concluded complacently.[24]

In the early 1980s the Israeli sculptor Yigal Tumarkin was asked
about his artistic sense of place. He replied with the truism that good
art is local even when it uses international vocabulary to express itself.
Except that in the context of the Zionist cultural revolution it was
more truth than truism. "I can't create without a soil, without a sense
of place, without affinity to tangible things like a Jerusalem of Stone,
[like] light, sea, desert, olive trees, and grapevines or a more spiritual
sense of hope."[25] This obvious observation about any kind of local
art echoed the prophecy Buber had made eighty years earlier when he
spoke about the natural connection between place and art, between
the establishment of a Jewish national community and the distinct art
it would naturally inspire.

Drawing in Hebrew

Drawing tells the story slightly differently, and perhaps more clearly,
because illustrations are crisper and less layered than paintings or sculptures, especially those for children. Zionists were consumed with their
children, the first native generation of the future Jewish state, and paid
great attention to books that instructed their young. Again, this was
not unique to Zionism. In Europe, illustrated children's books became
common tools of acculturation from the nineteenth century on. The
tales of the Brothers Grimm in Germany, *Mother Goose* in Britain,
Charles Perrault in France, Alexander Afanasyev in Russia, and Hans
Christian Andersen in Denmark: nation after nation produced compi-
lations of so-called fairytales that socialized children and taught them

---

[24] Y. Kopalivitz, "Mera'ava: The Seventh Artists' Exhibition in Jerusalem"
(מַרְאָוָה: תערוכת האמנים השביעית), *Ktuvim*, May 3, 1928.
[25] Ballas, "Who Are we, Really?" p. 28.

Drawing in Hebrew 143

about their national myths of origin and other local particulars. Early twentieth-century innovations in printing enriched the visual impact of those works and enabled the production of magnificent children's books, such as Me'ir Gur-Aryeh's 1925 illustrated Zionist tales, *Elijah the Prophet*.

The book was a collection of Zionist stories celebrating the Land of Israel and its new Jewish community. The obvious idealism of the tales, where Bible, Talmud, and Zionism combine to create distinct Hebrew myths of origin, is matched by an equally rich visual style, a dazzling display of Zionist orientalism à la Bezalel. The only difference between the illustrations of Gur-Aryeh and other Bezalel products was their high production value and an intensity that highlighted the Central European materiality of the imagery. The difference became more obvious in illustrations for children because those needed to convey ideas and tell a story simply and clearly, unlike more independent works of art. But if some of the magnificent illustrations for children in Europe reflected a rich and developed society, the lush visuals in Gur-Aryeh's book clashed with the reality of a small, fledgling national community.

The challenge lay in matching form to content. German Jews went through a similar search when faced with some of the pressures that gave rise to Zionism, except that in Germany assimilated Jews chose a cultural revival instead of a national one – a revival that relied on Eastern European Jewish sources and was later stimulated by the rise of Nazism. The wealthy businessman Salman Schocken encouraged his coreligionists "to go back to their roots," take traditional Judaism out of the ghetto, and bring about a cultural renaissance. "Let's entrust our tradition to the hands of poets and writers" instead of rabbis, he said, and helped to establish a Jewish cultural committee that oversaw the process.[26]

But turning religious tradition into art was no easier in Germany than it was in Palestine, even if the German Jewish community enjoyed a broader artistic context, attracted more artists, and had more money to support it. The spectacular failure of ספר האותיות, *The Book of Letters*,

---

[26] Ada Vardi, "The German Illustrated Book, 1900–1933," in Marit ben Yisrael and Ada Vardi, eds., *Book of Tom* (ספר תום), Asia Publishing/Mineged, 2022, p. 189.

144   *New Hebrew Aesthetics*

highlights the complexity of the challenge. In 1919 Schocken invited two rising artists, the illustrator Tom Siedmann-Freud and the Hebrew writer S. Y. Agnon, to collaborate on an illustrated book that introduced the Hebrew alphabet to children. Siedmann-Freud was commissioned to draw the letters of the alphabet, and Agnon was asked to write short rhymes for each of them, a simple enough project that was eventually abandoned because of the difficulties it met with. Each of the artists failed in instructive ways. Siedmann-Freud's avant-garde art, steeped in the aesthetics of German Gothic and Christian Romanticism, "had no Hebraic spirit at all," as Bialik said elsewhere.[27] Agnon's art reflected the traditional Jewish Rabbinic world. When the two worlds met on the pages of the book, they clashed, or, as Agnon drily put it, it felt like having "to fit a foot for a shoe" instead of the other way around.[28] Even after both provided clarifying notes, Siedmann-Freud on her illustrations and Agnon on his verses, the book was shelved, along with plans for a Jewish version of a Brothers Grimm anthology.

It turned out that growing Semitic roots to order was not very realistic, as Boris Schatz and artists such as Gur-Aryeh realized when their visual vocabulary became progressively less relevant. The Hebrew culture that was forming in Palestine called for something entirely different, for new aesthetic notions that would capture "the charm of children's life [here in Palestine], the freedom they enjoy, their spirited nature ... their new stories and the Hebrew fun they have," as one reader observed in 1910.[29]

It was a formidable challenge that was exacerbated by the strong influence of Europe, especially on artists who grew up there, like the German graphic designer and illustrator Fritz Ruschkewitz. Although he changed his name to Peretz after immigrating to Palestine, Ruschkewitz's work remained deeply connected to his former home, as in a 1939 children's travelogue that he illustrated entitled *To Children's Land* (לארץ הילדים) (see Figures 5.8 and 5.9).[30]

---

[27] Marit ben Shaul, "Illustrations of our Own" (ציורים משלנו, על הספר הגנוז של ביאליק ותום), in ibid., n. 58.

[28] Nehama ben Aderet, "On Agnon's Book of Letters" (אני קטן ושר לילדים קטנים, על ספר האותיות מאת ש"י עגנון), *Agnon Research Journal* (כתב עת לחקר יצירת עגנון) 1 (2011), at p. 1.

[29] Quoted in Ayala Gordon, "Hebrew Illustrations" (איורים עבריים), in *Hebrew Illustrations: The Hebrew Illustrated Book in the International Era, 1900–1925* (הספר העברי המאויר לילדים העידן הבינלאומי, 1900-1925), Nahum Gutman Museum, 2005, p. 51.

[30] Nir Feldman, "Peretz Ruschkewitz, the Yekke Illustrator" (פרץ רושקביץ המאייר הייקה), *Et-mol* 258 (2018). The booklet is housed at the Israel Museum, Illustration Library, Youth Section.

Drawing in Hebrew 145

Fig. 5.8 Few children in the Yishuv had the inclination or the means to go on the kind of recreational trips abroad described in this middle-class travelogue, written by Anda Pinkerfeld and illustrated by Ruschkewitz. Moreover, save for a cactus on the right and a small palm on the left, it would be hard to tell that we are no longer in Europe. Israel Museum, Illustration Library, Youth Section.

Fig. 5.9 During their journey the children visit iconic pioneering sites, a kibbutz, a construction site, and finally make it to Tel Aviv. The details are all correct: the modernistic buildings of Tel Aviv, the palm trees, the cypresses, and even the uniformed traffic controller with his Ottoman fur hat. But like Ruschkewitz himself, perhaps, the boy in the picture, driving a car, wearing a jacket and cap, and smoking a pipe, belongs much more in London or Berlin than in Tel Aviv. Israel Museum, Illustration Library, Youth Section.

146   *New Hebrew Aesthetics*

The evolutionary jump in the formation of a distinct local style of illustration can be linked, as is usual with such changes, to a particular artist and the circumstances that shaped their art. The artist was Nahum Gutman again, and the circumstances were the sparse conditions and ideological asceticism of Yishuv life. Both likely inspired Gutman's airy minimalism, an early version of what Sara Breitberg-Semel later called דלוּת החוֹמר, literally "want of material," impoverished art, or Arte Povera, as Italian artists dubbed it a bit later and for similar reasons.

Gutman's light touch was enthusiastically embraced by the public and the local art world alike, probably because the style was both sketchy and cheerful without being too colorful or seductive like Ruschkewitz's illustrations. It was a good fit for the fledgling and optimistic Yishuv community, as in a sketch of early Tel Aviv (see Figure 5.10). The empty spaces between the few flimsy houses on the sands of what later became the hub of Jewish life in Palestine are filled with swirling footprints (left by excited settlers?). A convoy of donkeys at the bottom, fluttering in as light as butterflies, carry heavy sacks of sand for the buildings that will soon crowd the empty space and make a more permanent mark on the dunes. There is no visual symbolism here, no references to an aesthetic tradition, only a scant materiality that marked Gutman's work and that of other illustrators who followed him.

Gutman immigrated to Palestine with his parents in 1905 at the age of seven and grew up in Tel Aviv. He began his studies at Bezalel and completed them in France, where he was likely influenced by contemporary artists such as Matisse and Dufy. But unlike the French artists, according to the illustrator Yirmi Pinkus, Gutman's lines are fewer, airier, and often not entirely closed, reflecting the elemental state of the Yishuv as a work in progress.[31] Light returns here as a central motif of the new Jewish life in Palestine.

After Gutman began to work for the new children's supplement of the leading daily *Davar* in the early 1930s, his lean style became

---

[31] Personal interview, Tel Aviv, November 6, 2022.

Drawing in Hebrew

Fig. 5.10 Nahum Gutman, *The Beginning of Tel Aviv*. Gutman Museum, Tel Aviv.

a new standard, a dynamic minimalism that was picked up by other illustrators, such as Aryeh Navon and Rut Schloss. The breezy figures were no doubt shaped by material and logistical considerations – budgets, publication deadlines – but to the minds of many they

148 New Hebrew Aesthetics

visualized the essence of a new, no-frills Hebrewism, where children are happy, playful, and energetic, they don't cry much, and they are not anxious.[32]

Hebrew Photography

But it was photography, more than any other art form, that gave Zionism its iconic shape and spread it at home and abroad. Like other nationalists, Zionists recognized the power of pictures early on. "You may well ask yourselves what photography has to do with our national revival," wrote Yaakov Zerubavel in 1912, "and yet I tell you that there is nothing more useful for our revival than photography."[33]

"Photographic exhibitions cost little and produce nice results," wrote another Zionist functionary a few years later in 1920, "and we should organize them in many countries."[34] A 1929 letter to the Jewish National Fund urged administrators to get with the times: follow Soviet Russia, where politics is communicated through photographs, and do the same for Zionism.[35] "Please hire me," wrote the pioneering film-maker Yaacov Ben-Dov in passionate letters he sent to Jewish agencies in 1931. "The conditions of our movement today ... demand a firm response from us. I can help," he wrote. "Commission me to make a series of photographs of construction workers, farmers, builders. ... There is good reason to take such photos ... and a great demand for them ... they will strengthen our hearts and lift our spirits and shine the light of our truth on the path leading to Zion."[36]

Photography was enlisted in the service of Zionism much more than any other art form, and for obvious reasons. First, it was immediate and accessible – a genuine record of the real world rather than a manipulation of it, as most people thought of it at the time. A more significant

---

[32] Muki Tzur, "To Educate a Thinking Reader" (לגדל קורא חושב), from a museum catalogue, Davar Supplement for Children, דבר לילדים), curated by Monica Lavie, Nahum Gutman Museum of Art, 2015, p. 108.

[33] Ya'acov Zerubavel (signed as Sagi Nahor), "Flutterings" (רפרופים), Ha'ahdut (האחדות) 1912 (ידי בניסן תרע"ב שנה שלישית), no. 25–26, at p. 19.

[34] Yosef Gal-Ezer, Keren Hayesod, 1920.

[35] From an unsigned letter to the JNF, November 12, 1929, quoted in Rona Sela, Photography in Palestine (הצילום בפלסטין/ארץ ישראל בשנות השלושים והארבעים), Hakibbutz Hame'uhad and Herzlia Art Museum, 2000, p. 40.

[36] From two different letters of 1931, in ibid., pp. 44–45.

Hebrew Photography 149

reason was economic. Camera equipment and the picture-production process were expensive, and since the distribution of photos relied on a number of agents, most photographers worked with sponsors, underwriters who made specific demands. "I want to establish a photographic agency in Palestine" and use it to show the face of Zionism around the world, wrote Nachman Shifrin in 1933. Shifrin owned one of the biggest photo-distribution agencies in Berlin at the time. "Has the world press seen what life on a kibbutz is really like?" he asked, "has it seen the hard and long work of Jewish farmers, the bravery of our pioneering men and women?"[37]

A number of photographers produced more independent work – ethnographic, artistic, personal – but the majority worked in the service of Zionist organizations and cast members of the Yishuv as extras in a grand national opera. Given the nature of the medium and of Palestine, it was not surprising. Before the Zionist era, Palestinian photographers engaged in their own politics when they took pictures of archaeological sites and cast locals and tourists in the role of biblical figures to promote tourism to the Holy Land: "Native outfits for customers," read an advertisement that hung in the window of the Jerusalem studio of Joseph Toumayan, a local Armenian photographer.[38] And when the Palestinian photographer Khalil Raad developed his ethnographic portfolio, his images of a rooted and traditional Palestine were very different from the modernistic pictures of the land that Zionists curated.

Zionist organizations used photography on a larger and more intensive scale by employing professionals such as the Hungarian photographer Zoltan Kluger (1896–1977), who became a Zionist house photographer by accident. When events in Europe forced Kluger to extend his 1933 visit to Palestine indefinitely, the compelling pictures he began to take in the Yishuv soon turned him into an important designer of the Zionist "look" (see Figures 5.11 and 5.12). Kluger worked for Nachman Shifrin and various Zionist organizations

---

[37] Letter to Leo Herman, general secretary of the United Israel Appeal, July 23, 1933, in Rana Oren and Guy Raz, *Zoltan Kluger: Head Photographer 1933–1958* (1933-1958 זולטן קלוגר צלם ראשי), exhibition catalogue, Eretz Israel Museum, 2008, p. 10.

[38] Guy Raz, *Photographers of Palestine / Eretz Israel* (צלמי הארץ מראשית ימי הצילום ועד היום), exhibition catalogue, Hakibbutz Hame'uhad, 2003, p. 31.

and produced some of his best art as a news photographer in their service. In his sponsored trips across Palestine he focused primarily on those parts that showcased the Zionist settlement project in all its glory, including aerial photography – Kluger had served as an aerial photographer in the Austro-Hungarian air force during World War I – photos that extended the domain of Zionism to the sky and highlighted its proportions as a grand modern epic.

Kluger was a talented practitioner of the art and its modernistic aesthetics, a style that played into the self-perception of Zionists as revolutionaries, members of an anti-traditional movement that was aligned with industrial development and technological innovation. Like most of the Jewish photographers in the Yishuv he was trained in Europe and informed by contemporary trends, mostly German, such as photojournalism and New Objectivity, a clean, dynamic snapshot technique that aimed at capturing "objective" action. Soviet Russia was another source of influence, especially the manipulation of social reality. But Kluger, who was known for his motto "better staged well

Fig. 5.11 Zoltan Kluger, *Workers Coming Home after Work in the Fields, Hefer Valley*. National Photo Collection of Israel, Government Press Office, Wikimedia.

Fig. 5.12 Zoltan Kluger, *Youth Aliyah Members from Germany Dancing the Hora in Kibbutz Ein Harod*. National Photo Collection of Israel, Government Press Office, Wikimedia.

than photographed badly," was not always happy with his assignments. "I can't breathe," Shifrin remembered him saying; "I'm dying here, I make no progress, I have no time to keep up with other photographers in the world. People here are dying of malaria, they languish in poverty, they are exhausted and gloomy, and I have to take pictures of them smiling." Unlike Ben-Dov, Kluger was "tired of taking pictures of cheerful pioneers."[39]

But there were photographers who still managed to do it, to capture the modernistic essence of Zionism in a more personal or artistic way, as it is often called. The avant-garde photographer Helmar Lerski was one of them. Lerski (1871–1956) was a special case, a unique artist, who had established his credentials before coming in the early 1930s to Palestine, where he made his signature industrial portraits of Yishuv members (see Figure 5.13) and created the iconic pioneering film *Avodah* (Labor). "It was not very difficult for me to create those pictures," Lerski

---

[39] Nahman Shifrin, quoted in Oren and Raz, eds., *Zoltan Kluger*, p. 26.

Fig. 5.13 Helmar Lerski, *Jemenit, aus der Reihe: Jüdische Köpfe / Araber und Juden, 1931–1935* (Yemeni, from the series: Jewish Heads / Arabs and Jews). Silver Gelatin Print. Estate Helmar Lerski, Museum Folkwang, Essen.

said in 1944, because "my work reflects the emotional reaction I had to everything I saw in Palestine when I first arrived."[40]

The first photographic exhibition at the Tel Aviv Museum in 1943 was made possible thanks to Lerski's artistic cachet. Called למשק ולנשק (roughly translated as "Farmers and Soldiers"), the exhibition was a retrospective of photographs commissioned by the National Fund in previous years. It was naked Zionist propaganda, and everyone knew it, which is why the museum objected to displaying the pictures in the first place. In the end, it was המצב (the Situation), as Israelis came to refer to their perpetual state of emergency, that tipped the scales, on condition that only pictures of the highest quality were selected. It was a convenient evasion, of course, though Lerski, for one, had no problems with it. Like Walter Benjamin, he believed that good art had the potential to reveal the moral value of ideology, or, as he put it, "the thought that one of my friends abroad will see my contribution to the Jewish war effort in Palestine gives me great satisfaction."[41]

[40] Sela, *Photography in Palestine*, p. 48.
[41] Ibid., pp. 6, 230.

Hebrew Graphics

Graphic design joined other arts in propagating Zionist ideology through a variety of products designers were commissioned to create, from political posters, advertisements, book jackets, and fonts to more esoteric projects, such as an illustrated botanical dictionary of local flora. As with many of the Zionist cultural innovations, Germany was influential here too, especially after the rise of Nazism pushed many Jewish artists to Palestine, where they found work at Bezalel in architecture, landscape design, book design, dance, and music.

Attention to graphics began at Bezalel, where the study and practice of decorative art was part of the school's curriculum as early as Schatz's days. But when the artist and typographer Yosef Bodko became the director of the New Bezalel in 1936, design became even more important as a way to promote Jewish cultural regeneration.[42] In fact, the discipline was called practical design rather than graphic design at the time, a name that speaks for itself. "Practical design is not created for its own sake," explained a magazine article in 1943. "It is an artistic way to communicate with the public in order to convey specific messages: commercial, cultural or communal." Graphics "are efficient means for circulating new ideas," and the role of designers "is to explain to buyers what the seller wants."[43] The writer goes on to specify how: be a proficient illustrator with a good sense for color, understand the needs of consumers, and know the psychology of the target audience. These fundamentals of advertising were used in the service of Zionist ideology.

The expansion of the Yishuv and its economy during World War II professionalized the practice and used the art more directly to promote commerce and ideology, often together. This was the story of the brothers Gabriel and Maxim Shamir, formerly Sheftelowitz, who moved to Palestine in 1935 and began to ply their trade with flare and savvy (see Figure 5.14). They were also prolific, which made their work iconic, a graphic complement to Kluger's photographic work. Working within the pared down, simple, and forceful modernism that turned away from embellishment after World War I, the Shamir

---

[42] Hezi Ami'or, *Elly Gross Retrospective* (עלי גרוס, אותיות ועיטורים: מלאכת הספר של עלי גרוס), exhibition catalogue, copy by Gil Weissblei, Sifriya Le'umit, 2012, p. 14.

[43] *9 in the Evening* (ב ערב 9), February 18, 1943, unsigned.

Fig. 5.14 In these ads for cigarettes, the Shamir brothers used the brand's name, Dugma, meaning example or model in Hebrew, for national socialization. The three boxes from right to left read: A Model Soldier, A Model Secretary, A Model Driver. They appeared separately in the daily *Haaretz* on December 28, 1948, November 12, 1948, and January 4, 1949.

brothers designed posters and other official signs – their studio designed the state's seal and some of the first banknotes – on which they often employed conspicuous Zionist tropes: iconic landscapes, pioneering imagery, and soldiers.

The Shamir brothers, like Kluger and other Yishuv artists, were products of their time and their countries of origin. From a design perspective their Zionist art was similar to contemporary political art in other countries, mainly in Europe, the USA, and Japan. It was marked by sharp, modern forms, strong colors, simple and often angular fonts, and images of intent and earnest-looking people. Initially the Shamir brothers were informed by a modern European aesthetic that came across in the elemental look of their work, such as that of the Hungarian Israeli designer Pesach Ir-Shay (István Irsai, 1896–1968). Later, as their world was plunged into a second big war, Soviet sensibilities became more visible in the emphasis on youth, on community, and on heroism.[44]

---

[44] Examples of Ir-Shay's work are available online; see, e.g., https://onegshabbat .blogspot.com/2015/03/blog-post_25.html. Old and new are contrasted in this symbolic and almost abstract modern poster. The round shape and thorns of the cactus on the left are a reminder of the wild and inhospitable nature of

Hebrew Fonts 155

The differences were in the local context and the Hebrew language, of course. This is not meant as a slight but as a reminder of the cultural sources and the nature of the Zionist cultural revolution. The new content and context of these images were revolutionary for Jewish history and Jewish culture. People like Gutman, Lerski, and Ir-Shay matched form to content in more original ways, but most filled borrowed vessels with new wine, which was, after all, the goal of a revolution that called on Jews "to be like all other nations."

Hebrew Fonts

Fonts that displayed the spirit of New Hebraism soon followed graphics. Once again, the cultural context was European – more British in this case, as in the work of Edward Johnston (1872–1944), an Arts and Crafts typologist and calligrapher who drew inspiration from Old English and Latin manuscripts in the spirit of folk nationalism. This may have been the reason behind Johnston's popularity in Germany, where he taught for a while in the early 1910s, and where he may have influenced artists who later moved to Palestine. But Johnston is just an example of wider contemporary trends.

Fonts received a lot of attention in industrial economies at the beginning of the twentieth century. In part, this was due to the spread of mass communication and the rise in literacy. Both called for new letter shapes that would keep up with printing technologies and with the need to quickly process a growing number and variety of reading materials. But the industrialization of printing also inspired a countertrend that sought to revive older and slower writing traditions, as practiced by Johnston; a trend that thought of older scripts as symbols of the nation's soul.

Hebrew was swept up in this trend too, although modernizing its fonts was complicated by the antiquity of the language and by some of the hallowed traditions of writing it. Hebrew scribes were often bound by font shape and by writing regulations. And while printing was less encumbered, early printers still felt constrained by them, even secular printers such as the German Rafael Frank (1867–1920), who came

Palestine, which Zionism has tamed and turned into a modern and orderly universe, represented by the angular lines of the houses and trees of the new settlement on the right, awash in green.

156   *New Hebrew Aesthetics*

up with the Frank-Ruhl design, one of the first modern Hebrew fonts (see Figure 5.15). "Changing a Hebrew font," he wrote, "is complicated and requires consulting the *Shulkhan Arukh*," an important halakhic text.[45] The historical and typographical details that occupied Frank guided Zionist designers too. Some designers, like the hardened modernist Pesach Ir-Shay, put the past behind them and focused on geometry alone. Others, such as Elly Gross, had a more romantic approach that incorporated graphic elements from older Hebrew traditions.

When Ir-Shay published his first poster, people were scandalized by the modern shape of the letters he designed and thought of him as a "lunatic who defied Jewish tradition and dared to defile the [holy Hebrew] letters with his secular hands." But after the poet Bialik encouraged him to carry on with his work, he "felt that Hebrew print has received a new meaning, and that Hebrew has become a living language." "We all felt the need for change at that time," he recalled, "for a new form that will distinguish between the letters of scripture and the letters we use daily."[46] Ir-Shay named the font Haim, after Haim Nahman Bialik (see Figure 5.16).

As a font, Haim became widely used for newspaper headlines and obituaries that relied on the power and bluntness of the thick block letters. Ironically, it is often used in Jewish religious fatwas or pashkevils, plastered broadsides that rely on the crude visual power of a simple

אבגדה

Fig. 5.15 In 1924 the new Hebrew font Frank-Ruhl was introduced to the public in the Berthold Printing Press catalogue. Frank based his new design on a fifteenth-century prototype, known as the Bomberg type, after the Venetian printer Daniel Bomberg. He evened out line width, minimized curves, and replaced all embellishments by finishing the tops of all letters with a uniform tip.

---

[45] Rafael Frank, *On Printing Letters and Fonts* (על אותיות דפוס וגופנים), p. 10, available at www.tau.ac.il/~stoledo/fonts/frank-hebrew.pdf. Translation of the German original by Moshe Yarden, in *Halishka letipografia ivrit* blog, available at https://yaronimus.wordpress.com/.

[46] Pesach Ir-Shay, "The Creation of the First Hebrew Letter" (כך נוצרה האות העברית הראשונה), in *Halishka letipografia ivrit* blog, available at https://yaronimus.wordpress.com/2015/01/16/ פסח-עיר-שי-כך-נוצרה-האות-העברית-המודרנ/.

אבגדהוזחטיכלמנסעפצקרשת
אבגדהוזחטיכלמנסעפצקרשת

Fig. 5.16 Haim font, designed by Pesach Ir-Shay

and unsentimental font that shows no graphic trace of older Hebrew writing traditions.

Elly Gross (1921–2014), on the other hand, was more attuned to the romance of Hebrew nationalism. "Before designing letters," she wrote, "I always studied archaeological findings and old manuscripts because I wanted to preserve the unique character of Hebrew letters" (see Figure 5.17). "I was careful not to allow Latin script to influence my work," said Gross, who grew up in Vienna, came to Palestine with her parents at the age of eighteen, and studied graphics at Bezalel. The department put its students through a demanding curriculum of Hebrew revivalist history. For her qualifying examination, Gross was given four days to "produce at least six pages with several types of Ashkenazi script, including a [book] jacket."[47] The idea was to educate a new cadre of designers by giving them a solid foundation in the history of Hebrew scripts to enable them to use it as a basis for creating something new, a promise Gross fulfilled. During her productive career she produced an impressive portfolio that ran the gamut of Hebrew calligraphic traditions.

Hebrew Book Illumination

A more esoteric project, which shows the realm of Zionist cultural imagination, was a plan for an illustrated encyclopedia of local flora with a special mention of biblical plants. The project was the brain-child of the botanist and educator Ephraim Rubinowitz-Hare'uveni (1881–1953), who was the inspiration behind the botanical drawing classes at Bezalel. "I must tell you that I found a great sense of beauty and art in your work," Schatz wrote to Rubinowitz-Hare'uveni and his

[47] Gil Weissblei, ed., *Elly Gross: Letters and Ornamentations* (עלי גרוס: אותיות ועיטורים: מלאכת הספר של עלי גרוס), exhibition catalogue, National Library of Israel, 2012, p. 24.

Fig. 5.17 For this 1944 jacket of a book on ancient Israelite economic history, Gross drew inspiration from a first-century CE Hebrew script found in the Dead Sea Scrolls. National Library of Israel.

wife, Hannah, after he visited the small botanical museum they had set up in their home. "Your work will be very useful to artists. I was greatly inspired by it."[48] At one point the couple drew up detailed plans for a "historical garden where a collection of plants mentioned in the Bible and in the Talmud would be on display," a garden imbued with "the spirit and good sense of the prophets and sages."[49]

The concept behind the couple's projects was a desire to do away with the separation between science and religion and join them together in the spirit of Zionism. "My heart tells me that you have chosen a true path," Bialik wrote to them after he too visited their home museum. "You approach our plants not as strangers, but as old friends ... in joining together the plant world with the world of our ancient literature you are renewing the covenant between the nation and its flora," he added earnestly.[50]

---

[48] Tamar Manor-Friedman, ed., *The Song of the Grass: Shmuel Haruvi's Paintings* (שירת העשבים, ציורי שמואל חרובי), exhibition catalogue, Israel Museum, 2006, p. 10.
[49] Ibid., p. 30.
[50] Ibid., p. 31.

Hebrew Book Illumination

The Rubinowitz-Hare'uvenis commissioned a friend, the landscape painter Shumuel Haruvi (1897–1965), to produce a series of watercolor studies. Haruvi was educated in the old Bezalel, where he learned to style local flora into decorative shapes. However, the naturalist watercolors he created for the encyclopedic project could not have been more different. And although the reference book never materialized, Haruvi's flowers remain a graceful visual index of the Palestinian natural world and a testament to the Zionist attempt to domesticate it (see Figure 5.18).

Fig. 5.18 Shmuel Haruvi, *Sage*, 1923. The botanist Ephraim Rubinowitz-Hare'uveni believed that the sage plant was the inspiration behind the design of the Temple menorah or candelabra. He planned to give it a prominent place in the garden of historical plants he and his wife, Hannah, designed. In the 1960s a modified version of the garden became part of a national park, Ne'ot Kdumim (ancient pastures). From *The Botanist's Brush: Shmuel Haruvi's Drawings for the Hareuveni Floral Treasury of the Land of Israel*, Israel Museum, Jerusalem, 2006, courtesy of Ziva Seidler.

160 New Hebrew Aesthetics

Or, in Zionist parlance, a symbol of the Jewish aesthetic regeneration, which the drawings exemplified.

In the end, all of these artistic works and artifacts became Hebrew not because of the quality of the light in Palestine, not because of Jewish history, and not because of Jewish ethics, which Zionists dreamed of visualizing somehow. What made art "Hebrew" was the prosaic fact that it was created by Hebrews – that is, by a community of artists who were distinguished by a set of characteristics we call "national." And if the art itself was not unusual, the community that created it was formed in unusual ways that were reflected in its art.

6 | *New Hebrew Sounds*

On April 4, 1928 the Hebrew daily *Davar* published this agitated piece:

It's nice to stroll on the beach in the moonlight at night with a group of friends ... and sing together ... [except] what do we sing? Would a Russian peasant ask the same question? ... Would a German woman wait to be asked [what music to play?] ... And what about us? I often get together with people who want to sing together but soon give up because they can't find a song familiar to all. Someone would start a Hasidic [tune] or a folksong but would then stop because no one else knows the music. ... [And then] all of a sudden, everyone would break into a stirring Russian number ... but the sounds would soon die down, lost between the flat-roofed houses. ... It's nice to stroll with friends in the moonlight. But something is missing. There is no singing. No sound.[1]

Coming up with a new Jewish music was a colossal challenge. The first problem was the category itself. What is "Jewish music" or any kind of so-called national music? Does ethnicity have a sound? If Jewish communities around the world developed different musical traditions throughout history, in the Yishuv many of these traditions came together in ways that eventually created all sorts of connections among them. Some of those connections were made by ideology, others happened more naturally. In time, this complex process created "Jewish," or "Hebrew," or later "Israeli" music in the same way we think of music as Brazilian, Japanese, or British. Philip Bohlman calls this an ontological moment, a moment in which a body of music is given meaning for a religious, social, or political purpose.[2] This chapter looks at the ontological moment of the creation of a "Hebrew" music.

Nathan Shaham dedicated an entire novel to this moment, his 1987 *The Rosendorf Quartet*, about members of a string quartet, refugees

---

[1] Quoted in Jehoash Hirshberg, *Music in the Jewish Community of Palestine, 1880–1948: A Social History*, Clarendon Press, 1995, p. 92.

[2] Philip V. Bohlman, "Ontologies of Jewish Music," in Joshua S. Walden, ed., *The Cambridge Companion to Jewish Music*, Cambridge University Press, 2015, pp. 11–26.

162   *New Hebrew Sounds*

from Nazi Germany, whose stormy relations mirror the national fervor of the late 1930s, the rise of Nazism, the efforts to build a Jewish state in Palestine, and the challenges of creating culture under these trying conditions. At one point in the novel members of the quartet travel to perform at a remote kibbutz, where they meet Rudi, a classically trained musician from Germany. When he is not picking oranges, Rudi composes music – music that brings together European and local traditions to create a "native" Hebrew sound, as he puts it. "Every year, during the vacation he received from the kibbutz," he tells the surprised quartet members, "he toured the towns and villages of Eretz Israel and visited synagogues and mosques, writing down Yemenite, Bukharan, Spanish, Caucasian, and Arab tunes. His hope was to familiarize himself with these eastern melodies long enough to be able to discover their 'ancient Hebrew roots' that would 'make his music grow'."[3]

It was a romantic notion imported from Europe, where the high emotional resonance of music played a big role in the cultural politics of modern nationalism. Think of national anthems and the history of classical or art music in the nineteenth century. It's full of such stories, especially in the relatively newer nations of Eastern Europe, where Zionism resonated deeply. One example, Bedřich Smetana's cycle of symphonic poems, *Ma Vlast* (my country), has a special connection to Zionism. The second poem in the patriotic cycle about Czech history and folk culture, named *Vltava* after Bohemia's biggest river, is based on an old folk tune that eventually found its way into the Israeli national anthem, "Hatikvah," as well.[4]

The absence of any kind of "native" Hebrew music worried Zionists. "How sad," wrote the musician Joachim Stutschewsky, "that even our national anthem is based on a Czech tune."[5] This is one of the ironies in *The Rosendorf Quartet*, in which Rudi tries to come up with new Hebrew music based on Arab traditions. But it was exactly what Zionist musicians tried to do. Their greatest wish was to bring together Western

---

[3] Nathan Shaham, *The Rosendorf Quartet* (רביעיית רוזנדורף), Am Oved, 1984, p. 138.

[4] Edwin Seroussi, "Hatikva: Conceptions, Receptions and Reflections," *Yuval Online* 9 (2015), available at https://jewish-music.huji.ac.il/en/yuval/22482. Hirshberg, *Music in the Jewish Community of Palestine*, p. 92.

[5] Joachim Stutschewsky, "Our Songs" (שירנו), *Haaretz*, July 6, 1939.

Inventing Folk Music   163

and Eastern music and create a new local Hebrew *melos* of folk music
and of concert or art music.

Inventing Folk Music

The Jews who began to settle Palestine toward the end of the nineteenth
century drew on various musical traditions. Some of their early songs
originated in the clubs of the Hibbat Zion (Love of Zion) movement that
predated Zionism. It was mostly an Eastern European repertoire with
a few original labor songs that were composed in Palestine, usually by
wedding a Yiddish or Slavic tune to a few short lines in simple Hebrew. It
was a marriage of convenience: the familiar tune helped the newcomers
memorize the unfamiliar Hebrew words.[6] A selection of nine of those
songs was published in 1895 with the lyrics only. Printers in Palestine
were not set up to print notes yet, so the names of familiar tunes were
added below song titles to guide singers. "Sing after the familiar tune,"
read the text under the title of "Hatikvah" on page 6 of the 1895 booklet,
in the hope that most readers would know the reference. In his review
of the songbook, Eliezer Ben-Yehuda wrote that although "some of
[the tunes] have been borrowed from other nations, the Hebrew lyrics
give the music a noble air."[7] It was an encouraging step, although the
songbook was too patchy and too random to satisfy serious Zionists.

In fact, Joel Engel (1868–1927) came close to a useful definition of
Jewish folk music. On November 30, 1900 he gave a memorable lecture
in Moscow, in which he claimed that Eastern European Jewish music is
distinguished by its particular emphases on borrowed elements, "distinctive vocal intonations ... nuances of pitch, timbre, and instrumentation,"
which he termed "the modal harmonic system."[8] He demonstrated it
on a Yiddish song called "How Does One Sing?" (,ווי זינגט דער חסידל
דער ציגוינערל, דער איבאנקע, How do a Hassid, a Gypsie and an Ivan

---

[6] Yaffa Berlowitz, "From the Songs of Hibbat Zion to Motherland Songs: The
Songs of the First Aliyah as a Foundation of Israeli Song" (משירת חיבת ציון
לשירת מולדת, הזמר בעלייה הראשונה כמסד לזמר הישראלי), *Bikoret Ufarshanut*
44, special issue: *The Hebrew Song, Poetics, History, Music, Culture* (הזמר
העברי: פואטיקה, היסטוריה, מוסיקה, תרבות), ed. Tamar Wolf-Monsohn, Bar-Ilan
University, 2012, pp. 13–59.
[7] David Assaf, *Oneg Shabbat* blog (עונג שבת), December 8, 2017, available at
https://onegshabbat.blogspot.com/2017/12/blog-post_25.html.
[8] James Loeffler, *The Most Musical Nation: Jews and Culture in the Late Russian
Empire*, Yale University Press, 2010, p. 68.

164   *New Hebrew Sounds*

Sing), in which a Jew, a Romany, and a Russian sing the same tune with different intonations that mark their respective cultures. It was an inspired presentation that drew a standing ovation, but it was still not good enough for Zionists, who looked for something altogether new that would put a distance between them and Eastern Europe.

"The land of Israel sings to us, but our diasporic soul is unable yet to understand those sounds, to make sense of them," wrote someone named Michael in the newsletter of Kibbutz Usha in 1937. "Let's listen to the natural sounds of our renewing homeland ... and make it into a permanent hymn."[9] The poet Yehuda Karni advised musically minded Zionists on how to achieve it. After arriving in the country, he wrote, keep quiet for a while, try and free yourself from the soundscape of the Diaspora and tune in to local sounds instead. "The wild cry at an Arab wedding [in Palestine] is more important for the future of Hebrew art than imported European tunes. The same is true of the dances of our road builders. They are more important than modern foreign dances," he wrote, encouraging readers to learn from non-Ashkenazi / European traditions.[10]

The Music of the Orient

Work on a more original Jewish or Hebrew musical tradition was aided by ethnographic trends in turn-of-the-century Europe. Those arrived in the Yishuv in 1907 with the ethnomusicologist Abraham Zvi Idelsohn (1892–1938), who came ready to prove the existence of a distinct Jewish musical tradition that spanned time and space. Like other Jewish musicians of his generation Idelsohn was a Romantic Nationalist, and like many of them he bought into the racial discourse that usually went with it. In the world of music the discourse was shadowed by Richard Wagner's famous antisemitic tract *Judaism in Music*, which created a stir toward the end of the nineteenth century. Although serious musicians dismissed Wagner's bizarre claim that Jews are congenitally incapable of composing truly artistic music, it had a peculiar resonance in the Jewish world. As odd as the assertion was, it led some Jewish musicians to try and disprove Wagner by internalizing his racial essentialism, not unlike the Zionist call for a muscular Judaism.

[9] *Hedei Usha*, September 9, 1937, p. 2.
[10] Hirshberg, *Music in the Jewish Community of Palestine*, p. 254.

The Music of the Orient

Idelsohn came to Jerusalem to find what he called the racial peculiarities of Jewish music, which were obscured by the social conditions Jews lived in, he argued. "Once we remove [the] exilic form" of Jewish music and "purify [it] from the filth of its prison, the temporary abode of its host nation ... we would stand in full awe" of its original, biblical beauty. Jewish music, he wrote, has "no relation to European music, and what is more, it cannot tolerate European melody, harmony and theory."[11] To find that origin and connect the Zionist present with its biblical past, Idelsohn embarked on ambitious ethnographic research into the musical traditions of Jewish communities. "During the fifteen years I lived in Jerusalem," he wrote in a biographical sketch toward the end of his life, "I collected the synagogue music of all the known Jewish communities, including Yemenis, Babylonians, Persians, Aleppans, Dagestanis, Bukharans, Sephardis, Moroccans and various Ashkenazi and Hasidic communities. To deepen my understanding of eastern music I also collected music from Arabs, Turks, and Persians." If there was indeed a common origin to Jewish music, Idelsohn expected these diverse traditions to prove it. Such common elements, he wrote, "would be the sparks of the nation's soul – the original music of the Hebrews."[12]

One happy outcome of Idelsohn's extensive research was that, in time, it became a valuable history of different Jewish musical traditions, which

Fig. 6.1 Idelsohn suggested that musical notes be written from right to left, like Hebrew, as in this rendition of the first notes of "Hatikvah," which became Israel's national anthem. *Sefer Hashirim* (The Book of Songs), Berlin, Hevrat Ha'ezra Liyhudei Germania, 1912, National Library of Israel.

---

[11] Assaf Shelleg, *Jewish Contiguities and the Soundtrack of Israeli History*, Cambridge University Press, 2014, p. 22.
[12] Idelsohn, Abraham Zvi, "My Life" (חיי), *Yuval* 5 (1986), available at https://jewish-music.huji.ac.il/index.php/en/yuval/22924.

166

he carefully recorded, transcribed, and then published in ten volumes between 1914 and 1933. Driven by the same desire, Idelsohn founded an Institute for Jewish Music to promote musical nationalism through a live archive, a library of local musical traditions, and a program of concerts that would showcase them. "Ye Hebrew musicians, singers, cantors, and instrumentalists!" he wrote in an official announcement in 1910, "though you be small in your own eyes, you bear the spirit [of old Israel]! ... Heirs to the Levite singers ... arise ... come ye together in one place, unite into one great choir; and the [Western] Ashkenazi Jew shall not be put above the Persian, or the Sephardi above the Polish or the Yemeni above the Babylonian."[13]

In the summer of 1910 Idelsohn organized a concert that demonstrated the kind of cross-fertilization he had in mind. Three different choirs, Ashkenazi, Yemeni, and Syrian (Aleppan), numbering seventy singers in total, "sang together and in alteration, each group in its own style, and it all combined into a pleasant harmony," wrote Itamar Ben-Avi in his review of the concert.[14] But the Institute for Jewish Music did not survive long. It met with resistance from local Jewish religious groups, it was plagued with financial troubles, and it suffered from Idelsohn's penchant for independent work. The closure freed Idelsohn to work on his important music ethnography, which, ironically, disproved his own musical essentialism. Rather than reflecting Wagner's polemic in reverse, Idelsohn's ethnography proved the diversity and richness of the music Jews made.

It was a very challenging diversity, as singer Bracha Zefira found during her long career as one of the first and most successful native Hebrew musicians. Born to a Yemeni family in Jerusalem in 1911, Zefira was orphaned young and grew up in a succession of foster families – Yemeni, Sephardi, and Persian – where she learned a variety of musical traditions. Her education at a Zionist boarding school brought her into the orbit of Zionism and set the trajectory of her career as a popular singer in the 1930s and 1940s.

Zefira epitomized the saying about the right person in the right place at the right time. As a Yemeni she belonged to a community that was considered exotic then. Having arrived in Palestine in the 1880s, the Yemenis were less insular and less embedded in the old Jewish

---

[13] Unattributed translation, ibid.
[14] Hirshberg, *Music in the Jewish Community of Palestine*, p. 17.

The Music of the Orient 167

communities of Palestine, which they initially joined. Having no parents, she was also less bound to the community of her birth. Her education at a Zionist boarding school loosened those connections even more and exposed her to Western music. The absence of a traditional family influence probably made it easier for her to join various artistic initiatives in the Yishuv at the age of sixteen. Finally, her trip to Germany in the late 1920s to further her music education, and her marriage to the Russian-Jewish composer and pianist Nahum Nardi, led to a fruitful collaboration and several concert tours across Europe, the United States, Egypt, and Palestine.

Zefira took advantage of her unique position to become a dynamic cultural agent, a mediator between East and West and between liturgical and popular music and art music.[15] She handled the tension by modifying Eastern melodies and making them more appealing to Western ears, as in her adaptation of Bialik's love poem "Between the Tigris and Euphrates" (בין נהר פרת ונהר חידקל), where she took the music of a popular Arabic love song and modified it to fit Bialik's poem with piano accompaniments by Nardi.[16] She adapted the tune for Western ears by turning the modulations of the original Arabic performance into a series of operatic trills that were accompanied by corresponding piano embellishments.

But Zefira's attempts to create a native Hebrew school of music were not as successful as she had hoped. It was not only that her familiarity with both Eastern and Western musical traditions was unique, even if her access to them was not always direct. The fact that she was primarily a performer and not a composer limited her legacy. Musical notes stay; musical performances do not. Moreover, most of the composers Zefira worked with came from Europe, and their capacity to adopt unfamiliar melodies was limited, even if they wished to do so. It was easier and probably more comforting to adapt music that reminded the majority of immigrants of their homes in Eastern Europe.

---

[15] Gila Flam, "Bracha Zefira, a Case Study of Acculturation in Israeli Song," *Asian Music* 17: 2: *Music in the Ethnic Communities of Israel* (Spring–Summer 1986): 108–125.

[16] For information on the song and its adaptation history see the Internet music archive *Zemereshet*, at www.zemereshet.co.il/m/song.asp?id=332. See also an ethnographic recording, *A Concert and Interview with Bracha Zefira*, interview with Avner Bahat, Kfar Masaryk, 1964 (קונצרט של ברכה צפירה וראיון עמה), National Library of Israel, available at www.nli.org.il/he/items/NNL_MUSIC_AL990038949440205171/NLI.

168   *New Hebrew Sounds*

An Original Hebrew Folk Sound

Until the popularity of Mizrahi music in the 1980s, the influence of non-European musical traditions on Hebrew popular songs was limited, certainly in comparison to the influence they had on art music.[17] There were a number of reasons for it, including the growing political tension between Jews and Arabs, but demographics played the biggest role.

The majority of Zionist settlers came from the eastern parts of Europe, and many of the melodies they knew and loved came with them. Russian folk songs were favorites, not only because of cultural connections, but also because of ideological sympathies. Zionists admired the Russian socialist counterculture, especially the Narodniks, the nationalist folk movement that predated socialism and inspired it. The Narodniks, who had an anti-Czarist agenda, believed in "going to the people" as a way to promote a more egalitarian society based on peasant communal structures.

It was precisely the kind of Romantic Nationalism that attracted Zionists. There was only one problem: The closest Jewish folk culture or "people" Zionists could "go to" were the traditional Jewish communities of Eastern Europe. But since Zionists rejected that life as old-fashioned and irrelevant, Russian folk culture became a substitute for it. Many of the cultural innovations in the Yishuv were "made in Russia," from the social structure of kibbutz communities to early Zionist fashion. Music was another one. Some of the first Hebrew folk songs were imported from Russia and then translated into Hebrew or rewritten anew. The Israeli online music archive *Zemereshet* groups Israeli folk songs in categories of origin: Yiddish, 216 songs; Russian, 141 songs; Hasidic, 125 songs (Masorti or Ashkenazi traditional, 53); Yemeni, 41 songs; Sephardi, 40 songs; Arabic, 18 songs; Bukharan, 11 songs.

One of the first pioneering songs, "Hurry, Brothers" (חושו אחים, חושו) from the early 1880s, was based on a Slovenian song that became popular throughout Eastern Europe at the time.[18] The writer Yechiel Pinnes replaced the patriotic Russian words with a rousing Hebrew version and introduced it at the end of a Passover banquet in Jerusalem in 1883. It was an instant hit. Years later one of the guests who had

---

[17] Mizrahi, meaning "eastern" in Hebrew, designates non-Ashkenazi or non-European origin (Ashkenaz is an old Hebrew word for Germany), usually from North Africa or the Middle East.

[18] For early recordings of the song see www.zemereshet.co.il/m/song.asp?id=354.

An Original Hebrew Folk Sound   169

been present that night recalled how twenty young men left the party
singing the song loudly in the streets of the city. "Our hearts were
aglow, and our souls were astir," he wrote. "One of the more excitable
fellows threw his hat to the ground ... and shouted: 'O Land of Israel!
For nearly two thousand years you haven't heard Hebrew spoken. We
have now returned to revive you and to embrace your soil'."[19]

Russian version		Hebrew version	
Мы дружно на врагов,	We are together against enemies	חוּשׁוּ, אַחִים, חוּשׁוּ	Hurry, brothers, hurry,
На бой, друзья, спешим,	We are in a hurry to fight, friends,	נָרִימָה פְּעָמֵינוּ	Let's pick up our pace.
За родину, за славу,	For the homeland, for glory,	טוּשׁוּ, אַחִים, טוּשׁוּ	Fly, brothers, fly
За честь мы постоим!	We will stand for honor!	אֶל אֶרֶץ הוֹרָתֵנוּ	to our ancestral land.

A later song from 1920, "The Sky has Darkened" (קדרו פני השמיים),
commemorated the death of Joseph Trumpeldor, an early Zionist martyr.
The Hebrew version is based on a contemporary Russian song, "Among
Dense Forests," Среди лесов дремучих, which honors the death of a
popular robber, a Russian Robin Hood of sorts. The song had several
Russian versions and is likely based on an earlier German song on a
similar theme.[20] In the Hebrew version the name of the Russian robber
was changed to that of the Zionist hero with a few place names added
to place it in Palestine.

Yiddish and Hasidic music was even more popular, despite the Zionist
disdain of both. But that should not be surprising, given that the majority
of settlers came from traditional Jewish homes in the Yiddish-speaking
Pale of Settlement, and given the emotional resonance of music. In the
words of an old Aramaic saying, knowledge acquired in childhood is not
easily forgotten (גרסא דינקותא, אינה משתכחא). The early pioneering hit

[19] David Assaf, *Oneg Shabbat* blog (עונג שבת), March 17, 2017, available at
http://onegshabbat.blogspot.com/2017/03/blog-post_89.html.
[20] For recordings see https://www.zemereshet.co.il/m/song.asp?id=1665.

170   *New Hebrew Sounds*

"Hava Nagila," probably the most widely recognized Israeli folk song of all time, was based on a Hasidic tune from Idelsohn's ethnographic collection. In 1918 Idelsohn and his students captured the high spirits in the Yishuv following the Balfour Declaration by adding a few words to it: "Let us cheer and rejoice / let us sing / wake, brothers, with a joyous heart." In typical Hasidic fashion, the lines are repeated over and over again as a kind of mantra that rouses the singers to ecstasy. Based on Isaiah 25:9, "Let us cheer and rejoice in the salvation of the Lord," the words of the Zionist song deliberately omit the name of God.[21]

As the poet Yaacov Orland put it, songs in the Yishuv were created by happenstance. What he meant was that songs were often written in real time as a response to all kinds of events. "As I was leading my horses back from the field one evening," wrote the composer Shalom Postolsky, "a fellow came over and told me" that a member of a neighboring kibbutz "wrote a new [harvest] song and is looking for someone who could set it to music, preferably someone familiar with field work." I was happy to oblige.[22]

But if circumstance and ideology suggested the words, music was harder to come up with, especially original music that would sound indigenous. And since no one could define that sound with clarity, folk songs in the Yishuv reflected a variety of influences that became more difficult to identify with time. The composer and educator Immanuel Amiran used to tell his students that if they thought a song sounded Russian, they should discard it. If it sounded Arabic, Hungarian, German, or like the song of any other people, they should have nothing to do with it because it was not an Israeli song. But if they found a song that sounded like nothing they had ever heard before, that would be an Israeli folksong.[23]

Most of the composers who tried to create that sound searched for different musical elements to add to their Yiddish and Slavic repertories.

---

[21] Idelsohn's original notes for "Hava Nagila" at the National Library of Israel, available at https://blog.nli.org.il/en/hava_nagila/. For an early recording of the song see www.zemereshet.co.il/m/song.asp?id=1271.

[22] In a letter to Yisrael Shalita, September 18, 1949. Yisrael Shalita file, Felicja Blumental Music Archive, Israel.

[23] Efrat Barth, "Wine from an Ancient Vineyard in an Old Bottle: The Original Songs of Immanuel Amiran" (סוגת שיריו המקוריים של – יין מכרם עתיק בקנקן ישן עמנואל עמירן), *Iyunim bitkumat yisrael* 8, special issue: *Music in Israel* (מוזיקה בישראל), ed. Michael Wolpe, Gideon Katz, and Tuvia Friling, Ben-Gurion University Press (2014): 362–376, at p. 362.

An Original Hebrew Folk Sound   171

Some of them included experimentation with older European liturgical music believed to go all the way back to the Jerusalem Temple. "There is no doubt that music from the temple in Jerusalem was transferred to the early Christian church by new Christians," wrote Mordechai Golinkin, founder of the Palestine Opera. It was only later, he continued, "that the Gregorians tried to erase all musical traces of their Jerusalem origins."[24] While it was impossible to prove such claims, some composers experimented with the Dorian or Doric mode, associated with ancient Greek harmony. Daniel Sambursky (1909–1977) used it in his music for Nathan Alterman's 1934 love song for the land, "Song of the Valley" (שיר העמק).[25]

Rest to the weary
Peace to the toiler.
A pale night falls
on the Jezreel Valley.
Dew below and moon above,
From Bet Alfa to Nahalal.*

A night like all nights.
Hush in Jezreel.
Sleep, beautiful valley,
we guard you well.

The sea of wheat ripples,
the sound of the herd rings.
This is my land and its fields,
this is the Jezreel Valley.
Bless my country, praise it,
from Bet Alfa to Nahalal.

---

* Names of kibbutzim

Mental images like these come up again and again in many of the folk songs that were written at the time. The idea behind them was to stress

---

[24] Mordechai Golinkin, *From the Temples of Japheth to the Tents of Shem* (מהיכלי יפת אל אהלי שם), Golinkin Memorial Committee, 1948, p. 171.
[25] Nathan Alterman, *Popular Songs* (פזמונים ושירי זמר), Hakibbutz Hame'uhad, vol. 2, 1979. For a recording of the song see https://www.zemereshet.co.il/m/song.asp?id=161.

172   *New Hebrew Sounds*

the Jewish connection to the land, through agricultural work, glowing
descriptions of the land, and biblical associations, which here relate to
the Jezreel Valley as the site of several biblical battles. The last stanza of
the song stresses these sinister connections and the need for the settlers
to stand on guard:

> Darkness on Mount Gilboa.
> A horse gallops in the shadows.
> A piercing cry flies high
> above the fields of Jezreel.
> Who fired a shot, who fell,
> between Bet Alfa and Nahalal?

Thinking back on his first years in Palestine, the musician Menashe
Ravina (1899–1968) recalled the new Palestinian soundscape that so
charmed Jewish immigrants from Europe, and which Karni referred to
earlier: snatches of Arabic song in the distance, the braying of donkeys,
unfamiliar prayers of local Jews. Zionist composers readily associated
such sounds with the biblical past and tried to set it to music. None of
it was connected to King David or King Solomon, Ravina confessed
about a cultural atavism that was common at the time.[26] In "Song of
the Valley" Sambursky tried to break loose from "the dictatorship
of the old [European] tonal system" via old church hymns and their
alleged connection to ancient Hebrew music.[27] Whether it was indigenous or not, it was a far cry from an earlier song by the same name, a
1928 number written by Kadish Yehuda Leib Silman to the music of
Beethoven's *Ode to Joy*.[28]

Other attempts, which focused on the Palestinian present, were
just as romantic and included music that sprang from the landscape
and climate of Palestine, as their composers asserted. Yedidya Admon
(1894–1982), for instance, said that the oriental elements in his popular
song "The Camel Song" (שיר הגמל, 1927) were intuitive, inspired by
the local Eastern Mediterranean environment:

---

[26] Efrat Barth, "The Meeting of Early Hebrew Songs with the East" (מפגשם של
מלחיני הזמר העברי המוקדם עם המזרח), *Iyunim bitkumat yisrael* 8, special issue:
Music in Israel (מוזיקה בישראל), ed. Michael Wolpe, Gideon Katz, and Tuvia
Friling, Ben-Gurion University Press (2014): 326-343, at p. 330.

[27] Shai Burstyn, "Inventing Musical Traditions: The Case of the Hebrew (Folk)
Song," *Orbis Musicae* 13 (2003): 127–136, at p. 131.

[28] For a recording see www.zemereshet.co.il/m/song.asp?id=672.

An Original Hebrew Folk Sound

173

Camel, my camel, camel, my camel,	גָּמָל גַּמְלִי, גָּמָל גַּמְלִי,
You are my mate in [transporting] sand.	חָבֵר אַתָּה לִי בְּזֵיפְזִיף.
How goodly are thy tents, O Jacob, thy	מַה טוֹבוּ אֹהָלֶיךָ יַעֲקֹב, מִשְׁכְּנוֹתֶיךָ
dwellings, O Israel! (Numbers 24:5)	יִשְׂרָאֵל.
Camel, my camel, camel, my camel,	גָּמָל גַּמְלִי, גָּמָל גַּמְלִי,
You are my mate in [transporting] sand.	חָבֵר אַתָּה לִי בְּזֵיפְזִיף.
Behold a people that riseth up as a great lion, and as a young lion doth it lift itself up. (Numbers 23:24)	הֶן עָם כְּלָבִיא יָקוּם וְכַאֲרִי יִתְנַשָּׂא.

The words bind the Mediterranean countryside – camels, sand – together with the dynamic spirit of Labor Zionism. Both were part of the Zionist project: sand for construction, camels for carrying it. The speaker addresses the camel as a fellow worker in this modernistic project, which he then sets against the ancient Israelite past and its national connotations.

Admon used the oriental aspect of the song by keeping it very simple, with short, repetitive melodic motifs that bring to mind the monotonous trudge of a camel.[29] What we have here, wrote the composer Alexander Boscovich a few decades later, is an example of New Hebrew secular liturgy. Boscovich celebrated what he termed a primitive simplicity. To his mind it was an ingenious expression of the monotony of the Near Eastern landscape that liberated Israeli music from the more layered Eastern European diasporic traditions.[30]

Other experiments included attempts to graft local Near Eastern musical elements onto the European musical stratum, Jewish as well as Arabic. Matityahu Shellem's shepherding song "A Lamb and a Kid" (שה וגדי) was based on an Ashkenazi Sabbath tune, "God Provideth" (צור משלו אכלנו), which Shellem embellished with oriental trills that mimic the sound of a Bedouin flute.

Writing in 1946 in what was intended to be a summative collection, the editors of a three-volume anthology of Hebrew folk songs noted the care they took "to include a variety of Jewish musical traditions, especially eastern Jewish music, which until recently was overlooked," but was nevertheless foundational for the new music of the Land of Israel.

---

[29] Burstyn, "Inventing Musical Traditions," pp. 130–131.

[30] Alexander Boscovich, "The Problems of Israeli Original Music" (בעיות המוסיקה המקורית בישראל), *Orlogin* 9 (1953): 280–294, at p. 287. For early recordings see www.zemereshet.co.il/m/song.asp?id=5020.

174   *New Hebrew Sounds*

"Eastern Jewish music is so important," they told readers, "because its character suits the landscape of Israel and because the sound of its Hebrew is precise and correct."[31] Such programmatic pronouncements were not especially accurate or useful. To this very day, admitted the composer David Zehavi in 1964, it's impossible to say what an original Israeli song is.[32] Eventually, of course, it was the very search for a native music that created it.

Composers

Music historian Jehoash Hirshberg tells us that, from the beginning of the twentieth century until the establishment of Israel halfway through it, some 4,000 folk songs were composed in the Yishuv, almost 1,000 per decade. About a thousand of those were in wide circulation. Of the nearly 200 people who composed those songs, roughly a third were teachers in kindergartens and schools, and another third were kibbutz members. That only one-third of composers were professional musicians says a lot about the ideological commitment of Yishuv society.

It was not surprising that many of these accidental composers belonged to two communities that were at the vanguard of Zionist culture. While teachers labored to devise a new curriculum that would reflect the cultural ambitions of the Yishuv, kibbutz members were eager to display the agricultural values of Zionism and its new holiday tradition. But since the traditional Jewish repertory contained no such songs, they were often written ad hoc by creative members of the Yishuv.

A common creation story involves teacher-composers such as Daniel Sambursky, who were regularly called on to supply new songs for their young charges. In 1932, two weeks after Sambursky arrived in Palestine from Germany, he became a teacher in a Ramat Gan school. Save for a few festival songs, he remembered, there were very few songs for children. Sambursky promptly sat down to write some. Another dynamic composer, Nahum Nardi, received regular requests from kindergarten teachers eager to expand their repertoire. Nardi obliged by writing songs that became household names, including "The Little Rabbit" (השפן הקטן) and "Happy New Year" (שנה טובה).

---

[31] Quoted in Nathan Shachar, "The *Eretz-Israeli* Song 1920–1950" (השיר הארץ-ישראלי בשנים 1920–1950 היבטים מוסיקליים וסוציומוזיקליים), PhD thesis, Hebrew University, 1989, p. 120.

[32] Fleischer, *Historical Development*, p. 320.

Composers

175

The new life on the land was a rich creative source as well, especially on kibbutzim. Shepherd-poet Matityahu Shellem recounts a traumatic experience that inspired one of his well-known songs, "At Dawn" (עם צאת החמה). One morning in the late 1920s he was tending his flock when one of his sheep, which had apparently eaten a poisonous plant, began to shake violently and then collapsed and died. "I felt depressed. Some of the Bedouin shepherds who were tending their own flocks in the vicinity mocked me for taking such bad care of my sheep … I comforted myself by pouring my grief into a new poem": "At dawn / an innocent sheep / out to pasture / suddenly died / alarmed, the shepherd threw [down] his flute / and mourned his lovely sheep."[33]

By 1948 there were 217 shepherding songs circulating in the Yishuv. The occupation itself was negligible, but it had a high symbolic value for Zionists, representing the modern Jewish re-connection to the ancient land. The songs mentioned specific geographies with biblical connotations, the bond between the shepherds and their sheep, the sound of sheep's bells and the shepherd's flute, often an Arabic tune.

Other song writers admitted that the exuberance of the pioneering experience prompted them quite literally to burst into song. Moshe Bick, who came to Palestine in 1921, was inspired to compose the hit "We Shall Build our Land" (נבנה ארצנו) following his work in road construction. "Everyone felt that it was their duty … to contribute to the struggle and the vision of the Yishuv. That's what made me think of the words to a song" that promises to "build our motherland" because it is "decreed by blood and history," to put an end to the "festering bondage" of Jews, and that calls on the "fire of freedom" to lead the Jewish people "to march boldly toward freedom."[34]

"I never stopped to think what or how I write," said another composer, Marc Lavry (1903–1967). "We felt an urge to experiment, to write buoyant, hopeful songs, because the Jewish folksongs [in Eastern Europe] were sad, written in a minor key. … In Palestine, everything was different, people were different, and we wanted upbeat songs about

---

[33] Ibid., p. 371. On shepherding songs see Michal Sadan, "Following the Sheep" (בעקבות הצאן), *Iyunim bitkumat yisrael* 8, special issue: *Music in Israel* (מוזיקה בישראל), ed. Michael Wolpe, Gideon Katz, and Tuvia Friling, Ben-Gurion University Press (2014): 295–325. For a recording see www.zemereshet.co.il/m/song.asp?id=1238.

[34] Fleischer, *Historical Development*, p. 306. For early recordings, see www.zemereshet.co.il/m/song.asp?id=117.

176   *New Hebrew Sounds*

labor and the new country [we came to]."[35] Indeed, it would be difficult to imagine a more extravagant song than the pioneering favorite "Our Barns Are Full of Grain." Composed by David Zehavi to lyrics by Pinhas Elad, the song conveys the high spirits of the pioneers, who wanted to express the immensity of the pioneering project and their joy at its success: "Our barns are full of grain and our wineries brim with wine / our homes are teeming with babies / and our cattle are fruitful / What else will you ask of us, motherland / that we have not given you yet?"[36]

When Yisrael Shalita (1906–1982) collected information for a comprehensive encyclopedia of Jewish music he was putting together in the 1940s he wrote to Yishuv composers asking them to specify those elements that gave their music a distinctly Jewish character. It was an essentialist question that exercised many people at the time. Shalita simply focused it on music. Perhaps he meant the Jewish *melos*, as Stutschewsky and other composers referred to it at the time, using the ancient Greek word for melody.[37] The dutiful replies Shalita received were almost identical and repeated much of what has been mentioned above about Jewish music as a mixture of old Jewish musical traditions.

Yariv Ezrahi divided the songs he composed into three groups. The first were Slavic songs. The second were Eastern European and Jewish, "although not diasporic and weepy in nature," he added. The third group was his favorite, "songs that are more biblical and Semitic in nature and that I wrote intuitively, without a guiding western hand," he noted.[38] Abel Ehrlich wrote to say that "every Hebrew text [of mine] strengthened my connections to the roots of Hebrew culture and empowered me, as if I was not composing by myself; with me were my ancestors, my people, the kings and the prophets as well as my contemporaries."[39] A. U. Boscovich described how the guttural letters of the Hebrew language "inspired me to write music for bassoon and viola,

---

[35] Fleischer, *Historical Development*, p. 330.

[36] For recordings see www.zemereshet.co.il/m/song.asp?id=578.

[37] "The various emotions [the Jewish *melos*] arouses and the layered history it carries," as well as "the variations of Jewish rhythm and its harmonies, must be placed at the center of every musical composition," Stutschewsky wrote expansively: Joachim Stutschewsky, "Jewish and *Eretz-Israeli* Music" (מוזיקה יהודית וישראלית), *Davar*, June 12, 1939.

[38] Yariv Ezrahi, letter, July 18, 1949, Y. Shalita file, Felicja Blumental Music Archive, Israel.

[39] Abel Ehrlich, letter, August 6, 1969, ibid.

Circulation and Inculcation   177

two instruments that are quintessentially made for expressing [Hebrew]
tonality." He also instructed drummers to use their fingers rather than
sticks to "channel their [Hebrew] vitality" more directly in imitation
of the "expert agility of eastern drummers."[40]

But not everyone complied. The celebrated songster Yehuda Sharet
wrote back wryly:

[Kibbutz] Yagur, 3.7.1949

To my associate Y. Shalita, greetings.

I beg your forgiveness for not replying earlier.

I am really sorry, but I am not used to such requests. After mulling it over, I
am unable to provide you with an answer. I am confident, however, that no
one will be the worse for it. And since I doubt an answer is even possible, I
am not going to worry about it too much.

Food for thought: Are all composers made of the same cloth? They may be
united by the language of music, which they use in their works, but they are
made of different stuff and in different ways. Each one of them is distinct.
Some may oblige and answer your question while others may not.

I never meant to disrupt your work, and I am sure my tardiness did not affect
it in any way.

....

Apologetically yours,
Yehuda Sharet[41]

Circulation and Inculcation

Writing music was one thing. Getting that music out to people was
another matter altogether, something individual composers could not
manage or sustain on a large scale, no matter how enthusiastic they were.
Effective distribution needed coordinated efforts that connected songs

[40] A. U. Boscovitch, letter, March 9, 1948, ibid.
[41] Yehuda Sharet, letter, July 3, 1949, ibid.

178 New Hebrew Sounds

with singers. Zionist organizations served that purpose by supporting the mass production of songbooks and by coordinating sing-alongs and public performances.

Songbooks were a popular way of spreading the ideas of Zionism and imagining a community of singers, even if music was secondary to ideology at first. In 1900 a festive edition of songs was prepared for the Fourth Zionist Congress in London and included a selection of texts that spanned Jewish history, from the Bible through medieval Spanish poetry to more contemporary hymns. It was part of a larger program that called on art to demonstrate the genius of Jews and their viability as a modern nation. A year later an exhibition of Jewish visual art, organized at the Fifth Zionist Congress in Basel, was designed with the same goal in mind.

In the following decades handier songbooks were published in the Yishuv with increasing frequency. They served the same purpose as church hymnals, providing the words and music for a growing body of folk songs and imparting ideological messages through emotional identification and the creation of a community of spirit.[42] "Musical education," wrote Binyamin Omer in the 1940s, "has an important role in providing an emotional foundation for national and socialist belief, in deepening the link with the soil, with the homeland, and with the working class, here and abroad."[43]

Musical education posed a serious challenge that required guidance and organization by professional musicians. "Yishuv members are a diverse bunch," wrote Menashe Ravina in 1927, "and it will be a long time before we become a more cohesive community" with common musical and other traditions. Ravina's advice was to organize public singing events modeled after those in Germany. During a trip he made to a folk music festival in Frankfurt in 1927, Ravina was deeply impressed by an assembly of about two thousand people who came together to learn five folk songs under the direction of Fritz Jöde. "If only we could replicate this in the Yishuv," he wrote, "and teach the immigrants from

---

[42] Yael Reshef, *The Early Hebrew Folksong* (הזמר העברי בראשיתו), Mossad Bialik, 2004; Shai Burstyn, "Totalitarian Tendencies in Music Education: The Israeli Case," available at https://bazhum.muzhp.pl/media/files/Musicology_ Today/Musicology_Today-r2010-t7/Musicology_Today-r2010-t7-s212-225/ Musicology_Today-r2010-t7-s212-225.pdf.

[43] See Burstyn, "Totalitarian Tendencies," p. 220.

Circulation and Inculcation 179

Europe Yemeni and Arabic songs," it would surely go a long way toward creating a Hebrew music tradition.[44]

For a fledgling national community with few entertainment venues, songbooks were very useful. Singalongs, like folk dancing, did not require infrastructure or complex organization. They were also open to all, a fitting socialist pastime that had redeeming national values. They instill "unity, discipline, and a social aesthetic," wrote the Revisionist leader Zeev Jabotinsky, in a preface to a 1939 songbook.[45] Songbooks provided another important service by familiarizing new immigrants with the Hebrew language, expanding their vocabulary, and teaching them correct pronunciation.

At first singalongs were fairly spontaneous events, and in the small settlements of the early Yishuv they gave the young and lonely settlers an immediate sense of community. But when the number and makeup of Jewish immigrants began to grow from the 1930s onward, centrally organized singalongs and prescriptive songbooks became more common. Finally, in 1946, a definitive collection of folk songs was published in a three-volume *Book of Songs and Melodies* (ספר שירים ומנגינות). It was a popular work that circulated widely and canonized a repertoire of songs that were eventually called songs of the motherland (שירי מולדת), the name Zionists gave to the various folk songs that were written in the Yishuv.

Songbooks were one of many devices that helped to spread popular Hebrew music and educate the public about it. Musical ambassadors were another, people like composer Emanuel Zamir (1925–1962), "who travelled from one festival to another, from one musical group to another, from village to moshav to kibbutz to immigrant camp. Nowhere was too remote for spreading [the gospel] of Hebrew song," wrote Shalita about one member of a Zionist host of self-motivated cultural activists.[46]

Zionist musical education was effective in the main, though some of it bewildered Mordechai Levitas (1914–1997), who was struck by the absence of soprano voices in the choirs he trained in the 1950s (see Figure 6.2). "Teachers claimed that the voices of Israeli children are different from children's voices elsewhere and lack the soprano register," he wrote incredulously. They said it was due to the hot climate and the

---

[44] *Davar*, December 20, 1927, p. 8.
[45] Quoted in Shachar, "The *Eretz-Israeli* Song," p. 103.
[46] Y. Shalita, notes on Emanuel Zamir, Y. Shalita file, Felicja Blumental Music Archive, Israel.

Fig. 6.2 Song instruction at Kibbutz Gan Shmuel, 1945. Photo: Pikiwiki.

guttural letters of the Hebrew language. Levitas thought it ridiculous. The real reason behind the "ugly and declamatory" singing in the Yishuv, he explained, was "the pioneering spirit, the spirit of heroism, and the fight against the British and other ideologies, which led to very loud singing that was best achieved through lower registers." Teachers were not instructing their students in music but in politics, he wrote. "Singing was silenced, and politics was installed instead."[47]

The politics of Hebrew music was all-consuming, and some of it stretched the limited capacities of the Yishuv. The earnest attempt to establish an opera company in Palestine was one example. Another was an ambitious program of biblical oratorios that, it was hoped, would add cultural gravitas to the fledgling Zionist project and ensure it Western, middle-class respectability.

The Palestine Opera was the darling project of Mordechai Golinkin (1875–1963), an energetic musician who gave up a successful conducting career in Russia to bring opera to Zion. Following an encouraging campaign to support the cause, Golinkin arrived in Palestine in 1923 and immediately went to work. The project attracted a lot of attention

[47] Y. Shalita, notes on Mordechai Levitas, ibid.

Circulation and Inculcation   181

at first, locally and abroad. But conditions on the ground were trying. For the first performance, Verdi's *La Traviata*, "the only opera we could stage with local talent," wrote Golinkin, he cobbled together a small orchestra of music students from a local school and a patchy group of singers. The libretto was translated into Hebrew, of course, and "everyone felt elated" and burned "with patriotic zeal."[48]

The first performances of the Palestine Opera were a great success indeed. People came to see the same show more than once, and performances around the Yishuv were well attended by European immigrants, who still longed for the culture they had left behind. In one of the shows in Haifa, remembered Golinkin, "the manager came to ask me what he should do about a young pioneer, who trekked on foot all the way from her kibbutz but had no money for a ticket. 'I can't turn her away,' he said; 'she is big, strong, and very insistent.' I immediately told him to let her in and make sure she gets a good seat. It's for people like her that opera was made, I explained."[49] But in 1927, after three eventful years, the opera company all but closed. The project was probably too big for the small Yishuv and too bourgeois to attract support from its socialist establishment.

Operas were performed in Hebrew as a matter of principle. This included both a classical repertoire and original materials, which did not work so well. Four Hebrew operas were written in the Yishuv or inspired by it, two biblical and two pioneer operas. Idelsohn completed his *Jephtah* in 1912, an ethnomusical work based on his own research, but he never managed to stage it in full. In 1921 the Russian-Jewish composer Mikhail Gnessin began a short work based on Eastern European Jewish motifs which he called *The Youth of Abraham*, but he never published it.[50] Jacob Weinberg combined Arabic labor songs with traditional Eastern European Jewish tunes in a work aptly titled *The Pioneers*. The opera was performed in Palestine in 1925 and, after winning a composition prize in Philadelphia a year later, it was staged a few more times in the USA and in Berlin shortly before the Nazis rose to power. The most successful work was Marc Lavry's kibbutz opera *Dan the Guard*. Mixing Mediterranean elements with Hasidic music and a libretto that pressed all the right Zionist buttons, the opera got

[48] Golinkin, *From the Temples of Japheth*, p. 119.
[49] Ibid., pp. 121–122.
[50] The score was rediscovered by Rita Flomenboim, who organized a small performance of it at Levinsky College in Israel in 2007.

182 New Hebrew Sounds

more traction than the other works and, after its 1945 Tel Aviv premier, it toured the Yishuv as well.[51]

Biblical oratorios were simpler to stage and were performed with more regularity under the dynamic direction of Fordhaus Ben-Tzissy (1896–1979). In 1939 Ben-Tzissy explained to readers of *Haaretz* that, since "most oratorios are based on the Hebrew Bible, they are a wonderful way to bring together the Bible as the source and foundation of [Jewish] existence with the blessings of refined music."[52] He went on to make an explicit connection between the escalating conflict with the Arabs and the staging of Handel's oratorio *Samson*, that "legendary Hebrew warrior who fights bravely for his people's freedom." Ben-Tzissy took liberties with the words and with the order of scenes and made them fit contemporary Zionist politics.[53] Since Handel's libretto "does injustice to the biblical source we were forced to change it and resurrect old glories … [we purged the text of foreign elements to] reflect our time and place more accurately," he wrote. Taking advantage of the Christian cachet of the Hebrew Bible and claiming Jewish ownership of it at the same time was a common Zionist practice. In a review of Ben-Tzissy's rendition of Haydn's *Creation*, the *Palestine Post* noted that "Haydn would probably have been delighted to hear his oratorio performed in the language of the Bible, though one is not sure what he might have thought of the [rearrangement of] some of the sections so as to maintain the Biblical sequence."[54]

Creating Hebrew Art Music

Many of the composers who wrote folk songs composed art music as well, although the challenges they faced in writing longer works were different. Writing folk songs was limited by the need to come up with

---

[51] The opera had a small academic revival in 2015 when parts of it were performed at the Israel National Library. See Assaf Shelleg, "From Be'er Sheva to Dan" (מבאר שבע ועד דן, לכבס הכל לבן), *Haaretz* online, May 24, 2015, available at www.haaretz.co.il/literature/study/2015-05-24/ty-article/.premium/0000017f-e2d3-df7c-a5ff-e2fb3b280000?utm_source=App_Share&utm_medium=iOS_Native&print=true.

[52] Fordhaus Ben-Tzissy, "On Shimshon" (לקראת הצגת שמשון), *Haaretz*, February 23, 1939, Fordhaus File, Felicja Blumental Music Archive, Israel.

[53] The practice itself is not new, of course. Stage performances of plays, operas, and oratorio librettos were, and still are, rewritten to suit changing agendas.

[54] C. [Fordhaus Ben-Tzissy], "The *Creation* in Hebrew," *Palestine Post*, March 1, 1942.

Creating Hebrew Art Music   183

catchy tunes. Art musicians had greater room for experiments. Even if the source materials were often similar, such as Eastern music and Jewish liturgical music, concert music facilitated a longer and more contemplative integration of these elements. The challenges had intriguing results.

By offering an opportunity to create a genuinely new Hebrew musical style, Zionism was uniquely positioned to soothe what musicologist Assaf Shelleg has called "the scarred concepts of musical Judaism." European Jewish composers who wished to integrate national elements into their music had a problem. What musical sources could they draw on if they wanted to stress their Jewish identity? National-Romantic composers such as Grieg, Tchaikovsky, and Smetana could claim affinity with the folk traditions in their countries in the name of nationalism. But which folk would a French or German-Jewish composer invoke? Some of those composers looked to the more traditional Jewish communities in the eastern parts of the continent. But since they were far removed from them in almost every sense, the attempts were often seen as artificial, denying both past and future, especially in the context of Wagner's slander.[55]

On the face of it, attempts to do something similar in Palestine, to create a "native" Hebrew art music by incorporating the Eastern musical traditions of Jews and non-Jews alike, seemed even more absurd. After all, Yemenis, Bukharans, and Arabs were even more removed from European composers like Rudi in *The Rosendorf Quartet*. The difference was in the words "past" and "future." Under the shadow of nationalism in Europe, both the past and the future of Jews seemed problematic at the time. In the Land of Israel, however, these ideas could be recontextualized, as Idelsohn suggested earlier, invoking the need to write historical plays and set them to music, theatricals that display the nation's past glory and bring back a vision of its past life on its ancestral soil. If Jews were to create such works about their own history and perform them in their ancestral land, they would gain a completely different meaning from the kind of biblical spectacles that had been common in Europe at least since Handel.

In some ways it was simpler to write new art music than new folk music. If Jewish folk music in Europe was not widely recognized, the Jewish middle classes were much more familiar with art music, as practitioners and as listeners. It was no surprise, then, that Jewish immigrants to Palestine tried to recreate a European musical milieu

---

[55] Shelleg, *Jewish Contiguities*, p. 16.

184   *New Hebrew Sounds*

shortly after their arrival. Several agricultural villages organized small orchestras soon after they were founded in the late 1800s. The plan for a music school in Jerusalem in 1910 and the opening of another one in Jaffa in the same year were the beginnings of what became a widespread musical education system later. As noted above, there was a Hebrew opera house in Tel Aviv between 1923 and 1927, and when tens of thousands of middle-class immigrants fled the nationalist wave in Europe prior to World War II in the 1930s, they swelled the ranks of the local bourgeoisie and brought with them musicians in search of employment and patrons eager to resume old cultural habits. Finally, the establishment of the Palestine Symphony Orchestra in 1936, which later became the Israel Philharmonic, crowned the attempts to recreate European middle-class musical culture on the eastern shores of the Mediterranean.

But these conditions posed two challenges for art musicians in search of new and original sounds they could call Hebrew. On the one hand, they wanted to satisfy public demand as well as their own sense of home by continuing a musical tradition they loved and cherished. At the same time, they were pressured by what Shelleg calls the "high voltage of Zionist rhetoric" and an expectation that they would write music that would ring "the bells and whistles of the Zionist project."[56] It was a tall order that few could meet and a frustration that our fictional literary composer, Rudi, admitted when he confessed to a skeptical inner voice which told him that "there is something artificial about a man whose soul is made of Schubert and Brahms but whose passion for Persian melodies" leaves him cold.[57]

Verdina Shlonsky (1905–1990) would have agreed with Rudi whole-heartedly. She was one of the only composers who resisted this trend at the time. Rather than chase an elusive idea of questionable merit, Shlonsky thought that a unique Hebrew or *Eretz-Israeli* sound should be a modernist project, not an embarrassing scheme to create some kind of orientalist Disneyland, as we would put it today. Her own Romanticism was different. She wanted to create a contemporary Jewish sound by reformulating Jewish devotional music. "Guided by religious melodies, folk songs, and the national dance [Hora]," she wrote in 1942, "the

---

[56] Ibid., pp. 80, 4.
[57] Shaham, *The Rosendorf Quartet*, p. 138.

Creating Hebrew Art Music 185

Jewish composer may unhesitatingly venture toward the creation of Jewish music."[58]

Late in her life Shlonsky was asked to reflect on the early search for an original Hebrew sound in Palestine. "All of this hysteria in search of style," she replied. "Yes, I call it hysteria! I looked for a way out when I saw that the whole thing became a power [struggle], like a [political] party ... There was a feeling that composers sought assurance in their writing: how to write? I didn't ask [myself] this question. I asked, what sort of person am I, why do I write and not how to write." And no, "I don't know what orientalism is," she said with irritation and defiance; "Tell me, what is it? Hummus?"[59]

But Shlonsky was not only a female composer – a rarity at the time – she was also woefully untrendy, a cosmopolitan artist at the height of a Jewish national revival. Most of the real-life composers who inspired Rudi's literary image continued to look for their Persian melodies, so to speak. The idea was to infuse what were essentially European musical forms with more local traditions, to express the eastern Mediterranean environment as well as the traditions of various Jewish communities to create a new Hebraic national sound. Among the most dynamic and articulate of these musicians was Alexander Uriah Boscovich (1907–1964), who eventually labeled such music Mediterranean.

Boscovich's penchant for mixing music and ideology began before he came to Palestine with a project he was involved with in his hometown of Culj in Transylvania, in the mid-1930s: an ethnographic expedition to remote Jewish villages in the Carpathian Mountains to collect and transcribe Jewish folk songs. This late iteration of a European National Romantic practice, modeled after the earlier work of Bartók and Kodály, had two important outcomes for Boscovich. It resulted in his first important compositional work, *Chansons populaires juives*, an arrangement of the Jewish folksongs he collected, and his first programmatic essay, *The Problem of Jewish Music*.[60] Based on his ethnographic experience, Boscovich planned to expand the project to the rest of Europe. But in 1938, he was unexpectedly invited to attend the premier of his

[58] Ronit Seter, "Verdina Shlonsky: The First Lady of Israeli Music," *Min-Ad: Israel Studies in Musicology Online* 7 (2007): 2007–2008.
[59] Oded Assaf, "Electronit hi lo savla" interview in *Ha'ir*, March 2, 1990, p. 70.
[60] Hirshberg, *Music in the Jewish Community of Palestine*, p. 161.

186   *New Hebrew Sounds*

Chansons by the Palestine Orchestra, a performance that saved his life, as he liked to say.[61]

In Palestine Boscovich continued his work on the connections between Jewish identity and sound. He thought it crucial to develop new musical sensibilities that would express the Palestinian locality with its sights and sounds, which were very different from those of Europe. Like Karni before him, he called on Hebrew composers to become attuned to the Eastern Mediterranean with its deserts, bare mountains, sands, harsh sun, and the hard sounds of its Semitic languages. At the same time, he was wary of superficial musical unions between East and West and warned against such exoticism, calling it a loveless and improper match.[62]

And yet, Boscovich was not free of the essentialism of his age. He too encouraged Israeli composers to turn their impressions of Palestine into transcendental works that would resonate with the memories of an ancient nation that was being reborn on its ancestral soil. The task of the Zionist composer, he wrote, was to find a way to convey the dramatic tension between a dormant East and the dynamism of the Jewish settlement project, to channel the subconscious memories that Eastern music arouses in Jewish composers and use them to "mend the historic continuity of the Hebrews" by coming up with a new Semitic sound that would express the Jewish reconnection to its cultural cradle.[63]

It would be inadvisable, he cautioned, to try and combine sounds that are fundamentally alien to one another. The disharmony of Eastern music, an "airier, expansive" music that rings faintly "with a Semitic sense of the desert," does not suit the piano, for instance, that harmonious and "most domestic of European musical instruments ... which communicates with the outside through a parlor's window."[64] It would be better, Boscovich wrote, to replace the piano with local instruments such as the oud or the rebab. His suggestion was to reboot the Jewish

---

[61] Alexander Boscovich, "The Jewish Suite" (הסוויטה היהודית), *Duchan* 3 (1963): 47–51, at p. 49.

[62] Boscovich, "The Problem of Israeli Original Music," p. 290.

[63] Ibid., pp. 289–290.

[64] Ibid., p. 292. See also Jehoash Hirshberg, "Alexander U. Boscovich and the Quest for an Israeli National Musical Style," in Ezra Mendelson, ed., *Modern Jews and their Musical Agendas*, Oxford University Press, 1993.

Creating Hebrew Art Music   187

musical genius, so to speak, and write for it a new software made from local materials that would shape Israeli music more organically.

This approach and the music it would create was later labeled Mediterraneanism, perhaps as a way to ease the abruptness of immigration and soften the culture shock of life in the Middle East. After all, the Mediterranean Sea connected Europe and Palestine, and to invoke it meant maintaining some of these connections. It was a psychological exercise that was applied to other cultural areas, a telltale sign of the tension that inhered in Zionism between West and East.[65]

There is more than a little irony in the fact that Jews, who were seen as oriental in Europe and labeled impostors trying to pass as white by antisemites, were later accused of appropriating Eastern musical traditions when they internalized that bias and moved to Palestine. Idelsohn, for example, went as far as describing Europe as a "prison" and its influence on Jewish music as "filth." It was a violent reaction to Wagner and his like, which, initially, acted as a powerful engine of innovation. In fact, attempts by Jewish composers at what has been called auto-exoticism began in Europe long before they came to Palestine.

The celebrated Israeli composer Paul Ben-Haim (born Frankenburger) began his musical journey to the East in his native Germany. Long before his migration to Palestine in 1933, he experimented with various elements that he hoped would make his music sound more Jewish. He borrowed motifs from archaic European music as well as from the music of Eastern European Jews. It was part of a wider German-Jewish trend at the time of presenting Judaism – or, rather, Jewishness – not just as a religion but as a culture, rooted in the Semitic East. Calls to "return to the pure and ancient Jewish music" in order to be reacquainted with the "expressive monotony of the tones and melodies of the old East" were not infrequent in the German Jewish press in the first decades of the twentieth century.[66] The growing racial discourse in Germany pushed Jews toward such quests, but they were also pulled by their own search for an identity which religion could no longer provide.

Years later Ben-Haim reflected that if life in Palestine was completely new to him, the musical challenges he encountered upon arrival were not. "Eastern Jewish melodies, especially Yemeni music, was already

[65] Noam Ben-Zeev, *An Israeli Tune: Report on the Sounds of a Transformed Nation* (מנגינה ישראלית), Hakibbutz Hame'uhad, 2009, p. 20.

[66] Alice Jacob-Loewenson, "Zur alten und neuen liturgische Musik," *Jüdische Rundschau*, no. 76/77, September 28, 1928, p. 546.

ingrained in me," he said. As mentioned earlier, the belief that archaic Christian music – Gregorian chants, for instance – originated in the Near East, perhaps going as far back as the priestly singing in the Jerusalem Temple, was not uncommon at the time. In Germany this kind of historical calisthenics allowed Jews to react to German musical nationalism by reinterpreting their ancient connections to the Land of Israel through a distinctly Western musical vocabulary. In Palestine it became a convenient way to create a symbolic bridge between selective antiquity and the Zionist present, "a newfound national allegory built upon a romanticized idea," according to Shelleg.[67] Ben-Haim had used it in his oratorio *Yoram*, which he composed in Germany between 1931 and 1933, shortly before he left. After moving to Palestine, Ben-Haim became a skilled practitioner of this style.

And there was another irony still. Attempts to "ring the bells and whistles of Zionism" led many art composers to the devotional music of Eastern Jews. This was partly because religious works, unlike other kinds of local music, certainly Arabic music, used the Hebrew Bible and other old Jewish sources. The ancient provenance of these texts emphasized the nation's origin, which transcended the nagging paradoxes of modern Jewish nationalism. The irony, however, was that such references undermined the strong secular spirit of early Zionism. Consider, for example, the 1940 *Motets* for an all-male choir by Mordecai Seter, who based some of the music on Babylonian, Samaritan, and Bukharan Jewish liturgical traditions. Shelleg explains that, while the music of the work avoids exoticism, the biblical texts in the *Motets* lend religious undertones to the Zionist narrative of redemption that they chart.[68]

The *Motets* begin with Psalm 137, "By the streams of Babylon, there we sat and wept, as we remembered Zion," and end with Psalm 144, which calls on God, not man, to "rescue me, and deliver me out of many waters, out of the hand of foreigners." And although the final part of the *Motets* stops halfway through Psalm 144, the diligent reader will find that the psalm concludes with proclamations about the peace and prosperity that God will provide, announcing that our "garners are full," our "sheep increase by thousands," our "oxen are well laden." We have met a similar pioneer song before, paraphrasing these very

---

[67] Assaf Shelleg, "Israeli Art Music: A Reintroduction," *Israel Studies* 17: 3 (2012): 119–149, at p. 129.

[68] Assaf Shelleg, "Imploding Signifiers: Exilic Jewish Cultures in Art Music in Israel, 1966–1970," *Hebrew Studies* 60 (2019): 255–292, at p. 259.

Creating Hebrew Art Music 189

verses by proclaiming, "Our barns are full of grain and our wineries brim with wine / our homes are teeming with babies / and our cattle are fruitful." If the pioneers celebrated their own agency, Seter reintroduced God into the mix, a gesture that proves ever more prescient with the passage of time.

Afterword

White gloves. This is the first concern Kingscourt and Friedrich have when they return to Palestine twenty years after their first visit there in Herzl's *Altneuland*. In the meantime the country has completely transformed and is now a thriving and modern Jewish state that boasts an opera house, the highest sign of civilized refinement in Herzl's bourgeois imagination.

Sarah glanced at the paper. "At the national theater tonight there is a biblical drama called *Moses*."
"A noble theme," remarked David.
"But too serious. There's *Shabbatai Zevi* at the opera. And at some of the popular theaters there are Yiddish farces. They are amusing, but not in very good taste. I should recommend the opera."
"Won't it be too late to get tickets?" asked Kingscourt. ...
"I have had a box ever since the opera house was built" [David said and] began to draw on a pair of white gloves.
Gloves! White gloves! Neither Kingscourt nor Friedrich had any. In all the twenty years on their quiet Pacific island, they had no use for such fripperies. But now they were back in civilized society, and in the desperate predicament of accompanying ladies to the theater. One must behave like a civilized human being. Kingscourt asked whether they would pass a glove shop on their way to the opera.[1]

Herzl would have been tickled to know that, almost 120 years after his premature death in 1904, the Israeli Opera had commissioned a work based on his life, that tearful audiences gave that opera, *Theodor*, a standing ovation night after night, and that performances of the show were extended due to popular demand. Bracketed between the literary melodrama of *Altneuland* and the operatic melodrama about its writer's

---

[1] Herzl, *Altneuland*, book 2, ch. 5.

Afterword 191

life stretches a century in which Herzl's vision has materialized, although not as he imagined it.

Culturally speaking, the Jewish state Herzl had in mind was a copy of his Austria-Hungary, down to – well – white gloves. Only it wasn't particularly Jewish. Herzl's New Society was a reflection of his secular middle-class sensibilities and lacked denominational character, save for superficial exotica such as a Sanhedrin (a Jewish parliament or House of Lords based on ancient lore). The Jewish state that actually developed in the Eastern Mediterranean was a different creature, a highly original community that was far removed from Herzl's vision. If it was bourgeois, it tried to suppress those tendencies in the name of a passionate socialist nationalism.

The difference between vision and reality had nothing to do with the early death of Herzl, but with the Zionists who made his dream come true. One of the tragedies of Herzl's life was that the audience he initially had in mind, middle-class Jews like himself, who were frustrated by the glass ceiling imposed by antisemitism, were not interested in his message. They were too comfortable and too close to their goal to start everything from scratch in some half-savage country in the Middle East – German Jews moved to Palestine in the 1930s only after their life in Germany became unbearable.

The prophetic-looking Herzl was more popular with the impoverished and more traditional Jews of Eastern Europe. And since they had little to lose, some of them made the difficult trek to Palestine "to build and be built by it," in the words of one of their pioneering songs. And if they found Herzl's message appealing, they had a different state in mind, a Jewish state that was deeply informed by their traditional upbringing even as they rejected it. This was the secret to their success and, with the benefit of hindsight, the reason why their solution to the Jewish Problem actually worked.

It was a principle that came up again and again in all of the cultural realms Zionists innovated: in the language they reanimated and the accent they gave it; in the communal space they shaped and the houses they built; in the hard bodies they formed and the defiant spirit they adopted; in the festivals they renewed and those they made from scratch; in the art they created and in the music they wrote. Unlike Herzl's European copy, each of those realms was deeply informed by Jewish religion, by Jewish customs and practices, by Jewish history, and by Jewish mythology. They were all transformed by Zionists and received

192   *Afterword*

different interpretations, different shapes, different meanings. The initial value of those innovations resided in this very process, whereby an old civilization begat a new shape. Instead of looking for a pair of white gloves, the Zionists who built the Jewish state sewed a different garment altogether. It was an inspired dialectical move, a negation of the Jewish Diaspora and the creation of a new Jewish community that nevertheless incorporated much of the old, rejected culture into it.

But if the move was successful, the properties of the new Zionist compound it created were unstable and had the potential to break in problematic ways. One was away from Judaism, the other was back to it. Neither was envisioned by the early Zionists, who were aware of the tension between New and Jew but based their revolution on maintaining it.[2]

It is hard not to turn, once again, to "The Sermon," a short story by Haim Hazaz that questioned the relationship between Zionism and Judaism and offered a startling take on it.[3] "I'm not one to say what Zionism is," says Yudke, a shy Zionist settler, who asks to speak before a committee of his peers and goes on to give them an agitated lecture, continuing:

I'm not the man for it, even though I've racked my brain and thought about it for a long time. But that's not important. ... One thing is clear. Zionism is not a continuation; it is not medicine for an ailment. That's nonsense! It is uprooting and destruction, it's the opposite of what has been, it's the end. ... It ... is more than assimilationism, more even than communism. ... Zionism, with a small group at its head, is the nucleus of a different people. ... Please note that: not new or restored, but different. And if anyone doesn't agree, well, I'm very sorry, but either they're mistaken or they're deluding themselves. ... I believe that this land of Israel is no longer Jewish. ... Yes, it's a different Judaism, if you choose to fool yourselves and keep that name, but certainly not the same as survived for two thousand years, not at all the same.

Yudke is a self-fashioned pioneer, but his pride in the Zionist revolution and his contribution to it are tempered by his knowledge that

---

[2] For a book-length study on this tension see Yaacov Yadgar, *To Be a Jewish State: Zionism as the New Judaism*, New York University Press, 2024.

[3] Robert Alter, ed., *Modern Hebrew Literature*, trans. Ben Halpern, Behrman House, 1975, pp. 271-287.

Afterword 193

they have come at the expense of diasporic Jewish culture. Like all revolutionaries Zionists thought of their old world as a husk to be discarded, and they defined themselves against it in negative terms, even if it informed them. "This community is not continuing anything," Yudke tells his listeners, who are at first confused and annoyed by his diatribe but gradually become absorbed in his arguments.

It is different, something entirely specific, almost not Jewish, practically not Jewish at all ... We are ashamed to be called by the ordinary, customary Jewish names, but we are proud to name ourselves, say, Artzieli or Avnieli. Haimovitch, you will agree, that's a Jewish name, entirely too Jewish, but Avnieli – that's something else again, the devil knows what, but it has a strange sound, not Jewish at all, and so proud!

The Canaanites were one example of the split between an Israeli here and a Jewish there.

"The Sermon" ends inconclusively. It turns out that Yudke's lecture was only an introduction to something else he had in mind but never got to say. "And now to the main thing, to what I'm really after. I ask just a few more minutes of your patience ... " he says, but trails off and the story ends. It's a clever structure that reflects the unfinished state of Zionism itself, which was only a few decades old when the story was published in 1942. But the points it makes about the nature of Zionism, about its relationship to its Jewish past, about the character of its Jewish present, and, more importantly, about the prospects of its Jewish future are compelling and have been borne out by time since then. I'll illustrate it with a personal anecdote. At the end of a lecture I gave about Israeli cinema to the local Jewish community of Cambridge, I was invited by one of the members of the audience to join the community for Sabbath services at the synagogue the next day. "But why would I come?" I replied without thinking: "I am Israeli."

The second – and opposite – direction has existed in Israel since the 1967 war, which released the Jewish ghosts of Zionism, ghosts that had been held in check until then by the balance between New and Jew. A lot has been written about it. An early and, as it turned out, prophetic account of it is a collection of essays Amos Oz published in 1982, *In the Land of Israel*. In the first essay Oz recounts a visit he made to the Jerusalem neighborhood where he grew up, which in the intervening years had been settled by orthodox Jewish families, who had turned

194 *Afterword*

the place into a "lively Jewish shtetl" teeming with yeshiva students, Hasidic Jews, and scores of Yiddish-speaking children.[4]

It reminds Oz of a casual conversation he once had with one of his professors, who spoke about Zionism as a passing episode, "a temporary burst of secularity, a historical and political fuss, that halakhic Judaism will soon overcome and swallow." When the professor said those words in the 1960s people dismissed it as a quip. "I still don't accept the prognosis," Oz writes, "but I cannot ignore it anymore. In the neighborhood where I grew up, the battle has been won. Zionism has been repelled from here, as if it had never existed. Maybe not repelled, but demoted to the status of a servant, someone who does the dirty work of removing garbage or maintaining the sewage system ... that's what Zionism is good for in these neighborhoods."[5]

And this is just hardcore orthodox Jews. Oz also visits the religious nationalists, the settlers who live among Palestinians west of the Jordan River. One of them pays him a backhanded compliment by praising the members of the Second Aliyah – the founders of Labor Zionism – who "were very Jewish, even in their apostasy."[6] Unfortunately, he adds, the immigrants who followed them, socialists who joined the Labor movement, brought along cultural goods that were alien to Judaism: "Marxism, atheism, internationalism, etc." But all of it is gone now, the settler notes with satisfaction, "disintegrated, withered, destroyed, in Israel as in the rest of the world. The end of ideology has arrived, making it clear, once again, that in the absence of absolute values materialism and indifference soon fill the void."

"Maybe you should take another look at it," he tells Oz, "and think about your value system and how it withered and died. Without a kernel of belief in the everlasting, everything is doomed to fall apart. I am no missionary," he proclaims, "and I am not asking the prodigal sons to repent, but as someone with faith, idealism, and vision," he continues, "I can tell you that a spiritual life is not possible without some kind of inner faith." That's why Israel won in 1967, Oz is told by another confident settler. "Guns don't win wars! People do! Faith triumphs! The

---

[4] Amos Oz, "The Daily Blessings of God" (ברוך השם יום יום), in *In the Land of Israel*, Am Oved, 1982, p. 8.

[5] Ibid., p. 12.

[6] Amos Oz, "An Argument about Life and Death, Part 1," in *In the Land of Israel*, p. 94.

Afterword   195

Lord is victorious!"[7] Gone are the Maccabees and Bar Kokhba, whom Zionists worked hard to bring back from the far corners of Jewish history. God is apparently back, and he is going to help the Israelis as he had helped the Israelites before them.

A more contemporary chapter in the fight Zionism has been having with its religious ghosts, or demons, has been the widespread protests in the spring of 2023 against the most religious governing coalition Israel has ever seen, with Haredi, Mizrahi, and national-religious Jewish parties, a coalition that demonstrated its fundamentalist potential in its handling of the devastating Hamas attack in the fall of that year. But this was only a political expression of a process that began long before with the changes Oz recorded. It is tempting to say that the changes disturbed the balance between New and Jew by shrinking the New and expanding the Jew, by demanding a greater place for Jewishness in Israeli national life, whatever this means. Except that Haredi, Mizrahi, and national-religious Jews are very new phenomena, who are connected to the past as much, or as little, as Zionists were. Like all religious fundamentalist movements, they are reactions to a changing and confusing world. It would be more accurate to say that they have been trying to change the Zionist New, the innovations this book described, and replace them with their own inventions.

What becomes clearer with the passage of time is that the Zionist attempt to translate or fit Judaism into a national ideology did not work as well as its founders had hoped, or not in the way they had hoped. Judaism is a very old religion with a long and remarkable creative history. Taking it on, as Zionists tried to do, was a daring, mighty experiment, for sure. But perhaps it wasn't radical enough. Perhaps Zionists should have broken with their Jewish roots more decisively to get away from the pull of their overwhelming legacy. Y. H. Brenner said something about it at the very beginning of the Zionist experiment. "I would have erased the Jewish sense of chosenness from our books eagerly and gladly, all forms of it, this very day, scratched and erased those false nationalist phrases without leaving a trace. Because empty national pride and Jewish pretensions won't solve the Jews' problem, and national slogans are good for nothing."[8]

---

[7] Oz, "The Finger of God!" in ibid., pp. 50–51.
[8] Y. H. Brenner, *This and That* (מכאן ומכאן), second book, ch. 1, Ben Yehuda Project, available at https://benyehuda.org/read/523.

196   *Afterword*

Brenner was not blind to the charms of nationalism, which crop up occasionally in his otherwise stern work. His 1920s short story "Nerves" opens on an upbeat note: "A perfumelike smell, which came from the low clumps of acacia trees, or 'mimosas,' as some called them, scented the air of the small Jewish colony in southern Palestine."[9] Toward the end of the allegory about early twentieth-century Jewish homelessness, the mood picks up again when a family of Jewish migrants finally makes it to the Haifa shore. "It was beautiful then," says the narrator, "the great sea was ravishing, and the bay in Haifa doubly so. You see, I really did believe in beauty then … in the beauty of nature … of the cosmos … of something even higher than that." However, at the end of the story he overturns this short display of sentimentalism with one of the most cutting lines in modern Hebrew literature. Back at the small family farm where he works, he looks disapprovingly at his employers, as "they talked, yawned, drank coffee, and ate herring." The revolutionaries who came to Palestine to change the course of Jewish history created a shtetl instead. Not such a bad idea, perhaps, given his earlier comment about national pride and Jewish pretensions.

[9] Y. H. Brenner, "Nerves" (עצבים), Ben Yehuda Project, available at https://benyehuda.org/read/480.

Bibliography

Agnon, S. Y. *Only Yesterday* (תמול שלשום). Schocken Books, 1971.

Aldor, Gabi. *And How Does a Camel Dance?* (איך רוקד גמל). Resling, 2011.

Alter, Robert, ed. *Modern Hebrew Literature*, trans. Ben Halpern. Behrman House, 1975, pp. 271–287.

Ariel, Z., ed. *The Book of Festivals* (ספר החג והמועד). Am Oved, 1962.

Avidar-Tchernowitz, Yemima, and Levin Kipnis. *My Kindergarten* (גן גני). Facsimile ed. Oranit Publishing, 2011.

Azaryahu, Maoz. *Caught up in its Image: A Short History of Tel Aviv* (שבויה בדימויה). Lamda/Open University, 2021.

Azaryahu, Maoz. *The Real Tel Aviv: Historical Mythography* (תל אביב העיר האמיתית). Ben-Gurion University Press, 2005.

Bar-Or, Galia. *Our Life Demands Art: Kibbutz Art Museums 1930–1960* (חיינו מחייבים אמנות, בניין תרבות כבניין חברה). Ben-Gurion University Press, 2010.

Bar-Or, Galia, and Yuval Yaski, curators. *The Kibbutz: Architecture without Precedent. The Israeli Pavilion at the 12th International Venice Biennale* (הקיבוץ: אדריכלות בלא תקדים). Exhibition catalogue. Keter, 2010.

Baroz, Nitza Baharozi, curator. *Local Judaica* (יודאיקה מקומית). Exhibition catalogue. Eretz Israel Museum, 2014.

Bartal, Yisrael. *Cossack and Bedouin: Land and People in Jewish Nationalism* (קוזק ובדווי). Am Oved, 2007.

Bartal, Yisrael, ed. *Studies in the Second Aliyah* (העלייה השניה, מחקרים). Yad Yitzhak Ben Tzvi, 1997.

Ben-Arav, Yosef. *The Hebrew Moshava in the Eretz-Israeli Landscape, 1882–1914* (1914–1882 המושבה העברית בנוף ארץ ישראל). Yad Ben-Tzvi/ Hebrew University, 1988.

Ben-Arye, Yehoshua, Yossi Ben-Artzi, and Haim Goren, eds. *Studies in Historical Geographic Settlement of the Land of Israel.* Yad Ben Tzvi, 1988.

Ben-Asher Gitler, Inbal, and Anat Geva, eds. *Israel as a Modern Architectural Experimental Lab, 1948–1978.* Intellect Books, 2019.

Ben Yisrael, Marit, and Ada Vardi, eds. *The Book of Tom* (ספר תום). Asia Publishing/Mineged, 2022.

198 *Bibliography*

Ben-Zeev, Noam. *An Israeli Tune: Report on the Sounds of a Transformed Nation* (מנגינה ישראלית). Hakibbutz Hame'uhad, 2009.

Berkowitz, Y. D. *Collected Writings* (כתבי י"ד ברקוביץ). Dvir, 1963.

Biale, David. *Eros and the Jews*. University of California Press, 1997.

Brenner, Y. H. *This and That* (מכאן ומכאן). Ben Yehuda Project, available at https://benyehuda.org/read/523.

Carmel-Hakim, Ester. *Hanna Meisel's Lifelong Mission* (שלהבת ירוקה). Yad Tabenkin, 2007.

Carmiel, Batya, curator. *Tel Aviv in Costume and Crown: Purim Celebrations in Tel Aviv, 1912–1935*. Eretz Israel Museum, 1999.

Chinsky, Sara. *Kingdom of the Meek* (מלכות ענווי ארץ). Hakibbutz Hame'uhad, 2015.

Cohen, Nurit, curator. *Schatz's Bezalel 1906–1929* (בצלאל של שץ). Exhibition catalogue. Israel Museum, 1983.

Dagon, Yoav. *Nahum Gutman's Tel Aviv* (תל אביב של נחום גוטמן). Nahum Gutman Museum, 1999.

Doner, Batya, curator. *From the Pereman Collection to the Tel Aviv Museum* (מאוסף פרמן למוזיאון תל אביב). Exhibition catalogue. Tel Aviv Museum, 2002.

Doner, Batya, curator. *Shamir: Hebrew Graphics* (שמיר, גרפיקה עברית, סטודיו האחים שמיר). Exhibition catalogue. Tel Aviv Museum, 1999.

Doner, Batya, curator. *Pomp and Circumstance: Israeli State Ceremonies, 1948–1958* (הוד והדר, טקסי הריבונות הישראלית). Exhibition catalogue. Eretz Israel Museum, 2001.

Droyan, Nitza. *The First Yemeni Immigrants 1882–1914* (חלוצי העלייה מתימן, פרקים בהתישבותם תרמ"ב-תרע"ד). Zalman Shazar, 1982.

Efrat, Zvi. *The Israeli Project: Construction and Architecture, 1948–1974* (הפרויקט הישראלי: בניה ואדריכלות 1948–1974). Tel Aviv Museum of Art, 2004.

Elboim-Dror, Rachel. *Hebrew Education in the Land of Israel, Volume 1: 1854–1914* (החינוך העברי בארץ ישראל). Yad Yitzhak Ben Tzvi, 1986.

Enis, Ruth, and Ben-Arav, Yosef. *Kibbutz Gardens and Landscape* (גנים ונוף בקיבוץ). Defense Ministry, 1994.

Epstein-Pliouchtch, Marina, and Michael Levin eds. *Richard Kauffmann and the Zionist Project* (ריכארד קאופמן והפרויקט הציוני). Hakibbutz Hame'uhad, 2016.

Estraich, G., and M. Kurtikov, eds. *The Shtetl: Image and Reality*. Routledge, 2000.

Feldman, Nira, ed. *Paintings with Light: The Photographic Aspects in the Work of E. M. Lilien*. Tel Aviv Museum, 1991.

Fishman, Joshua A., ed. *Readings in the Sociology of Jewish Languages*. Brill, 1985.

Bibliography

Fleischer, Tsippi. *Historical Development of the Hebrew Song.* 1964/2009, available at https://www.tsippifleischer.com/book/.

Fletcher, Robert S. G. *British Imperialism and the Tribal Question.* Oxford University Press, 2015.

Frank, Rafael, *Über hebräische Typen und Schriftarten.* Schriftgießerei H. Berthold, Abt. Privatdrucke, Berlin 1926 (Hebrew tr. Moshe Yarden, Tel Aviv University Press, 2003, available at https://www.cs.tau.ac.il/~stoledo/fonts/frank-scanned.pdf).

Gertz, Nurit. *Not from Here* (אל מה שנמוג) Am Oved, 1997.

Gilad, Elon. *The Secret History of Judaism* (ההיסטוריה הסודית של היהדות). Am Oved, 2023.

Gil'at, Yael. *Yemeni Art and the Creation of National Visual Culture in Israel* (צורפות בכור היתוך: אמנויות יהודי תימן והתהוותה של התרבות החזותית הלאומית בישראל, 1882–1967). Ben-Gurion University Press, 2009.

Golinkin, Mordechai. *From the Temples of Japheth to the Tents of Shem* (מהיכלי יפת אל אהלי שם). Tel Aviv, 1948.

Gordon, Ayala. *The Hebrew Illustrated Children's Book in the International Era, 1900–1925* (הספר העברי המאויר לילדים העידן הבינלאומי, 1925–1900), Nahum Gutman Museum, 2005.

Goren, Yoram. *Fields Dressed in Song* (שדות לבשו מחול). Ramat Yohanan, 1984.

Gottesman Rachel, Tamar Novick, Iddo Ginat, Dan Hasson, and Yonatan Cohen, eds. *Land. Honey. Milk: Animal Stories in Imagined Landscapes*, Israeli Pavilion, Biennale di Venezia/Park Books, 2017.

Gvati, Haim. *One Hundred Years of Settlement: The History of Jewish Settlement in the Land of Israel* (מאה שנות התיישבות). Hakibbutz Hame'uhad, 1981.

Helman, Anat. *A Coat of Many Colors: Dress Culture in the Young State of Israel.* Academic Press, 2011.

Herzl, Theodor. *Altneuland,* available at www.jewishvirtuallibrary.org/quot-altneuland-quot-theodor-herzl.

Herzl, Theodor. *The Complete Diaries of Theodor Herzl,* Herzl Press and Thomas Yoseloff, 1960, available at https://archive.org/details/TheCompleteDiariesOfTheodorHerzl_201606/TheCompleteDiariesOfTheodorHerzlEngVolume2_OCR/page/n165/mode/2up?view=theater.

Herzl, Theodor. *Herzl's Diary 1898–1902* (עניין היהודים ספרי יומן). Mossad Bialik, 1999.

Herzl, Theodor. *Der Judenstaat.* Project Gutenberg, available at www.gutenberg.org/files/25282/25282-h/25282-h.htm.

Hirshberg, Jehoash. *Music in the Jewish Community of Palestine, 1880–1948: A Social History.* Clarendon Press, 1995.

Kadman, Gurit. *A Nation Dances* (עם רוקד). Schocken, 1969.

Kark, Ruth. *The Land that Became Israel: Studies in Historical Geography*. Magness Press, 1989.

Khan, Geoffrey, ed. *Encyclopedia of Hebrew Language and Linguistics*. Brill, 2013.

Lavie, Monica, curator. *Davar Supplement for Children* (דבר לילדים,). Exhibition catalogue. Nahum Gutman Museum of Art, 2015.

Lissovsky, Nurit, and Diana Dolev, eds. *Arcadia: The Gardens of Lipa Yahalom and Dan Zur* (תבנית נוף). Bavel, 2012.

Loeffler, James. *The Most Musical Nation: Jews and Culture in the Late Russian Empire*. Yale University Press, 2010.

Luidor, Joseph. *Recklessness* (נער פחז כמים). Pardes, 2022.

Manor, Dalia. *Art in Zion: The Genesis of Modern National Art in Jewish Palestine*. Taylor & Francis, 2005.

Manor-Friedman, Tamar, ed. *The Song of the Grass: Shmuel Haruvi Paintings* (שירת העשבים). Exhibition catalogue. Israel Museum, 2006.

Mapu, Abraham. *The Shepherd Prince or The Love of Zion* (אהבת ציון). Brookside Publishing, 1922.

Marom, Nathan. *City of Concept: Planning Tel Aviv* (עיר עם קונספציה). Bavel, 2009.

Melamed, Gur. "The Kinneret (Sea of Galilee) Yemenis" (פרשת תימני כנרת). Master's thesis, Bar-Ilan University, 2005, available at www.haskama .co.il/mediation/document/yaman.pdf.

Mendelsohn, Amitai, curator. *A Prophet in his City: The Early Work of Reuven Rubin* (נביא בעירו). Exhibition catalogue. Israel Museum, 2006.

Metzkel, Yehudit, curator. *The Song of Concrete* (שירת הבטון). Exhibition catalogue. Eretz Israel Museum, 2009.

Mishori, Alik. *Lo and Behold: Zionist Icons and Visual Symbols in Israeli Culture* (שורו הביטו וראו). Am Oved, 2000.

Mishori, Alik. *In the Living Room around the Campfire: Jewish Art in Israel, 1948–1949* (מסביב למדורה בסלון). Ben-Gurion University Press, 2013.

Moria, Yael, and Sigal Barnir, curators. *Public Domain: Homage to the Gardener of Tel Aviv, Avraham Karavan* (ברשות רבים, מחווה לגנן העיר תל-אביב, אברהם קרוון). Exhibition catalogue. Tel Aviv Museum, 2003.

Mosse, George. *The Image of Man*. Oxford University Press, 1988.

Nordau, Max. *Degeneration*. tr. William Heinemann, 1898.

Oliphant, Laurence. *Haifa: Or, Life in Modern Palestine*. William Blackwood & Sons, 1886, Project Gutenberg.

Oppenheimer, Yohai. *Barriers: The Representation of the Arab in Hebrew and Israeli Fiction, 1906–2005* (מעבר לגדר). Am Oved, 2008.

Oren, Rana, and Guy Raz, eds. *Zoltan Kluger, Head Photographer 1933–1958* (זולטן קלוגר צלם ראשי 1933-1958). Eretz Israel Museum, 2008.

Oz, Amos, *In the Land of Israel* (פה ושם בארץ ישראל). Am Oved, 1982.

Bibliography

Pekelman, Henya, *Life of a Female Worker in Palestine* (חיי פועלת בארץ). Tel Aviv University Press, 2007.

Peleg, Yaron. *Orientalism and the Hebrew Imagination*. Cornell University Press, 2005.

Penslar, Derek J. *Jews and the Military: A History*. Princeton University Press, 2013.

Penslar, Derek J. *Zionism: An Emotional State*. Rutgers University Press, 2023.

Raab, Esther. *Thistles: Selected Poems of Esther Raab*, trans. Harold Schimmel. Ibis Editions, 2002.

Ravid, Baruch. *Joseph Tischler: Architect and Town Planner in Tel Aviv*. Baruch Ravid/Bauhaus Center, 2008.

Raz, Ayala. *Changing of Styles: One Hundred Years of Fashion in Eretz Israel* (חליפות העתים, מאה שנות אופנה בארץ ישראל). Yediot Aharonot, 1996.

Raz, Guy, curator. *Photographers of Palestine / Eretz Israel* (צלמי הארץ מראשית ימי הצילום ועד היום). Exhibition catalogue. Hakibbutz Hame'uhad, 2003.

Raz, Guy, curator. *A Yemenite Portrait: Jewish Orientalism in Local Photography, 1881–1948*. Eretz Israel Museum, 2012.

Reinharz, Yehuda, and Anita Shapira, eds. *Essential Papers on Zionism*. New York University Press, 1996.

Reinharz, Yehuda, Yosef Shalmon, and Gideon Shimoni, eds. *Nationalism and Jewish Politics* (לאומיות ופוליטיקה יהודית). Zalman Shazar, 1997.

Reshef, Yael. *The Early Hebrew Folksong* (הזמר העברי בראשיתו), Mossad Bialik, 2004.

Rubin, Carmela, curator. *Place, Dream: Reuven Rubin* (מקום חלום ראובן רובין). Exhibition catalogue. Tel Aviv Museum, 2007.

Rupin, Arthur. *My Life* (חיי). Am Oved, 1947.

Schutz, Hannah, ed. *Carl Schwartz and the Beginning of the Tel Aviv Museum 1933–1947* (קרל שווארץ וראשיתי של מוזיאון תל אביב). Tel Aviv Museum, 2010.

Sela, Rona, curator. *Photography in Palestine / Eretz Israel* (הצילום בפלסטין/ארץ ישראל בשנות השלושים והארבעים). Hakibbutz Hame'uhad/ Herzlia Art Museum, 2000.

Sela, Rona, curator. *Khalil Raad Photographs 1891–1948*. Nahum Gutman Museum, 2010.

Shafir, Gershon. *Land, Labor and the Origins of the Israeli Palestinian Conflict*. University of California Press, 1991 [1989].

Shaham, Nathan. *The Rosendorf Quartet* (רביעיית רוזנדורף), Am Oved, 1984.

Shahar, David. *Myth and Education* (מיתוס וחינוך). Resling, 2021.

Shachar, Nathan. "The *Eretz-Israeli* Song, 1920–1950" (השיר הארץ-ישראלי 1950–1920 היבטים מוסיקליים וסוציומוזיקליים בשנים). PhD thesis, Hebrew University, 1989.

202   *Bibliography*

Shaltiel, Shlomo, curator. *Art in the Service of Ideas: Posters of the Young Guard Movement, 1937–1967* (אמנות בשירות רעיון, כרזות השומר הצעיר). Yad Ya'ari/Ben-Gurion University Press, 1999.

Shapira, Anita. *Berl* (ברל). Am Oved, 2000.

Shavit, Yaacov, and Gideon Bigger. *The History of Tel Aviv: From Neighborhoods to City, 1909–1936* (ההיסטוריה של תל אביב). Tel Aviv University Press, 2001.

Shelleg, Assaf. *Jewish Contiguities and the Soundtrack of Israeli History.* Cambridge University Press, 2014.

Shiloh, Margalit. *The Challenge of Gender: Women in the Early Yishuv* (אתגר המגדר, נשים בעליית הראשונות). Hakibbutz Hame'uhad, 2007.

Schneidau, Herbert. *Sacred Discontent: The Bible and Western Tradition.* Louisiana State University Press, 1976.

Shoham, Hizky. *Israel Celebrates: Jewish Holidays and Civic Culture in Israel.* Brill, 2017.

Sinai, Smadar. *Women and Gender in Hashomer* (השומרות שלא שמרו). Yad Tabenkin, 2013.

Smilansky, Moshe. *Moshe Smilansky, Collected Works,* (כתבי משה סמילנסקי). Hitahdut Ha'ikarim be'Eretz Yisrael, 1935.

Snapir, Miriam, Shosh Siton, and Gila Ruso-Zimet, eds. *One Hundred Years of Kindergarten in Israel* (מאה שנות גן ילדים בארץ ישראל). Ben-Gurion University Press, 2012.

Spiegel, Nina. *Embodying Hebrew Culture: Aesthetics, Athletics, and Dance in the Jewish Community of Mandate Palestine.* Wayne State University Press, 2013.

Tartakover, David, curator. *Touring the Land* (טיול בארץ, משחקים מחנותו של מר ברלוי). Eretz Israel Museum, 1999.

Turel, Sara. *Bar Kokhba: Historical Memory and the Myth of Heroism* (בר כוכבא: הבנייתו של מיתוס). Land of Israel Museum, 2016.

Twain, Mark. *The Innocents Abroad.* Gutenberg Project. www.gutenberg .org/files/3176/3176-h/3176-h.htm.

Tzemach, Shlomo. *My Life Story* (סיפור חיי). benyehuda.org/ read/25934#fn:4.

Tzur, Muki, and Yuval Danieli, eds. *Next Year: Kibbutz New Year's Greeting Cards* (בשנה הבאה, שנות טובותי מן הקיבוץ). Yad Ya'ari/Ben-Gurion University Press/Yad Tabenkin, 2001.

Tzur, Muki, and Yuval Danieli, eds. *The Kibbutz Haggada. Israeli Pesach in the Kibbutz* (יוצאים בחודש האביב). Yad Ben Tzvi/Machon Ben-Gurion/ Yad Tabenkin/Yad Ya'ari, 2004.

Tzur, Muki, and Yuval Danieli, eds. *Mestechkin Builds Israel: Architecture in the Kibbutz* (לבנות ולהבנות בה, ספר שמואל מסטצ'קין). Hakibbutz Hame'uhad, 2008.

Bibliography

Tzur, Muki, and Sharon Rotbard, ed. *Neither in Jaffa nor in Tel Aviv: Stories, Testimonies, and Documents from the Shapira Neighborhood* (לא ביפו ולא בתל אביב). Bavel, 2010.

Vardi, Ada. *The Story of Moshe Spitzer and His Publishing House, Tarshish* (ספר שפיצר), Asia/Mineged, 2009–2015.

Walden, Joshua S., ed. *The Cambridge Companion to Jewish Music*. Cambridge University Press, 2015.

Weissblai, Gil, ed. *Elly Gross: Letters and Ornamentations* (עלי גרוס, אותיות ועיטורים: מלאכת הספר של עלי גרוס). Exhibition catalogue. National Library of Israel, 2012.

Weissblai, Gil. *The Revival of Hebrew Book Art in Weimar Germany* (קב ונקי). Carmel, 2019.

Wolf-Monsohn, Tamar. *Bikoret Ufarshanut 44: The Hebrew Song, Poetics, History, Music, Culture* (הזמר העברי: פואטיקה, היסטוריה, מוסיקה, תרבות), Bar-Ilan University Press, 2012.

Wolpe, Michael, Gideon Katz, and Tuvia Friling, eds. *Iyunim bitkumat yisrael 8*, special issue: *Music in Israel* (מוזיקה בישראל), Ben-Gurion University Press, 2014.

Wright, Jacob L. *Why the Bible Began*. Cambridge University Press, 2023.

Yadgar, Yaacov. *To Be a Jewish State: Zionism as the New Judaism*. New York University Press, 2024.

Yana'it Ben-Zvi, Rachel. *We Are Immigrating to Israel* (אנו עולים). Am Oved, 1962.

Yizhar, S. *Preliminaries* (מקדמות). Zmora-Bitan, 1992.

Zaïd, Alexander. *Diary* (לפנות בוקר, פרקי יומן). Am Oved, 1975.

Zandberg, Esther. *Land City: Local Essays* (ארץ עיר). Bavel, 2012.

Zerubavel, Evyatar. *Time Maps: Collective Memory and the Social Shape of the Past*. University of Chicago Press, 2003.

Zevulun, Ellah, and Dov Meisel, eds. *Matityahu Shellem: Kibbutz Festivals* (החג ביישוב הקיבוצי). Ramat Yohanan, 1984.

Zuckermann, Ghil'ad. *Israeli – A Beautiful Language* (ישראלית שפה יפה), in *Another Thing* (עוד דבר). Am Oved, 2008.

Archives

Felicja Blumental Music Archive, Tel Aviv.

David Assaf early Israeli history blog, *Oneg Shabbat* (עונג שבת). https://onegshabbat.blogspot.com/.

Gideon Ofrat Art Blog. https://gideonofrat.wordpress.com/.

Zemereshet early Hebrew music archive, www.zemereshet.co.il/m/song.asp?id=332.

Index

Abramovitch, Shalom Jacob [Mendele Moikher Sforim], 15, 16, 17
accent, 25
acculturation, Jewish, 15, 70, 125, 142
Admon, Yedidya, 119, 125, 172, 173
Agadati, Baruch, 94, 107
Agnon, S. Y., 39, 64, 65, 103, 144
Ahad Ha'am, 20, 21, 34, 53, 79, 127
Aharoni, Yisrael, 133
Ahuzat Bayit, 62, 64, 66
Alterman, Nathan, 31, 106, 136, 171
Altneuland (Herzl's utopian novel, 1902), 44, 61, 102, 190
assimilation, 4, 14, 79
Avidar-Tchernowitz, Yemima, 105, 100

Bar Kokhba, Shimon, 34, 71, 101, 111, 112, 113, 195
Bar-Giora, 90
Bartók and Kodály, 185
beauty pageant, 108
Bedouin, 86, 87, 90, 121
Ben-Dov, Yaacov, 46, 148, 151
Ben-Haim, Paul, 187, 188
Ben-Tzissy, Fordhaus, 182
Ben-Yehuda, Dvora, 19
Ben-Yehuda, Eliezer, 13, 18, 19, 20, 21, 27, 163
Berdichevsky, Micha Yosef, 14, 29, 128
Bergstein, Leah, 94, 120, 122
Berkowitz, Y. D., 7, 39, 40, 47, 54, 63
Bezalel School of Arts and Crafts, 130
Bialik, Haim Nahman, 9, 20, 24, 25, 99, 103, 116, 144, 156, 158, 167
Bick, Moshe, 175
Bodko, Yosef, 153
Boscovich, Alexander Uriah, 173, 176, 185, 186
Breitberg-Semel, Sara, 146

Brenner, Y. H., 15, 195, 196
British Mandate, 18, 53, 56, 57, 66
Buber, Martin, 129, 130, 138, 142

cactus (Arab. *sabar*), 38, 52, 54
"Camel Song,", 172
Canaanism, Canaanites, 139, 140
citrus, 53
Cohen, Yardena, 94
colonialism, colonialists, 5
colonization project (Zionist), 33, 34, 50
Cossacks, 87
cult of labor, 76, 86
cultural engineering, 1, 51, 122

Dabke, 96, 121
Dan the Guard (opera), 181
Danziger, Yitzhak, 140, 139, 141
Degania, 43, 45, 47, 48, 49
Dizengoff, Meir, 61

Ehrlich, Abel, 176
Eisenberg (Harari), Yehudit, 22
Elad, Pinchas, 119
Eloul [Skorohod], Kosso, 141
encyclopedia of Jewish music, 176
Engel, Joel, 163
Epstein, Yitzhak, 5, 36
Even-Zohar, Itamar, 33, 41
Ezrahi, Yariv, 176

Feierberg, Mordechai Ze'ev, 15
Female Workers' Farm, 81
folklore, Jewish and Zionist integration, 54, 134, 184
forest, 55, 57, 58, 59, 60
forestry, 57, 58, 59
Frank-Ruhl (Hebrew font), 156
Frishman, David, 17, 22

Index
205

garden city, 62, 68
Geddes, Patrick, 66, 68
gender, 2, 6, 91, 92
Gil'at, Yael, 137
Gnessin, Mikhail, 181
Golinkin, Mordechai, 171, 180, 181
Gordon, A. D., 75
Gordon, Y. L., 71
Greenberg, Uri Zvi, 29, 30, 31
Gregorian (chants), 188
Gross, Elly, 157
Gur-Aryeh, Me'ir, 143, 144
Gutman, Nahum, 63, 135, 136, 146, 148, 155

Hagana (Zionist paramilitary force prior to 1948), 44
Haggadah, 114
Hanukkah, 104
Harshav, Benjamin, 17
Haruvi, Shmuel, 159
Hashomer, 86, 87, 89, 90, 91
Hasidism, 75
Haskala, 8, 9, 11, 14, 16, 17, 70, 71, 79
"Hatikvah", 162, 163
"Hava Nagila", 170
Hazaz, Haim, 192
Herzl, Theodor, 4
Herzlia Gymnasium, 21, 24, 65, 105
Hibbat Zion movement, 163
Hirshberg, Jehoash, 174
Hora (dance), 94, 96, 97, 184
"Hurry, Brothers" (חושו אחים, song), 168

Idelsohn, Abraham Zvi, 164, 165, 166, 170, 181, 183, 187
immigration model, Zionist, 33, 41
Institute for Jewish Music, 166
Ir-Shay, Pesach [István Irsai], 154, 155, 156
Israëls, Jozef, 128

Jephtah (opera), 181
Jewish National Fund (JNF), 57, 148
Jewish Problem, 2, 17, 130, 191
Jöde, Fritz, 178

Kabbalah, 75
Kadman, Gurit, 97
Karni, Yehuda, 164, 172, 186

Katznelson, Berl, 52, 89
Kinneret (Sea of Galilee) Yemenis, 84
Kipnis, Levin, 100, 105, 119
Klausner, Joseph, 17, 27, 89
Kluger, Zoltan, 67, 76, 78, 82, 149, 150, 151, 154
Kvutzat Kinneret, 43

Ladino, 9
Lag Ba'omer, 100, 101, 102, 111, 112, 123
Lamdan, Yitzhak, 31
Language Committee, 20
Language Defense Brigade, 24
language war, 20, 23, 105
Lavry, Marc, 175
Lerski, Helmar, 151, 152, 155
Lilien, Ephraim Moses, 129, 130
Love of Zion, 11, 12, 13, 35
Luidor, Yosef, 34, 42, 69, 73

Ma Vlast (composition by Smetana), 162
Maccabee, Judah [Judas], 34, 101, 105, 111
Maccabiah, 71
Maidens' Farm, 81
Manor, Dalia, 137
Mapu, Abraham, 11, 13, 35
Matmon-Cohen, Yehuda Leib. *See* Metmann, Yehuda Leib
Mediterraneanism, 187
Meisel, Hannah, 80, 81
Melnikov, Abraham, 141
melos, 163, 176
Men of the Trees in Palestine (British ecological organization), 59
Mendele Moikher Sforim, 15 *See also* Abramovitch, Shalom Jacob
Mendelssohn, Moses, 9, 10, 14
Merchavia (seminal cooperative farm), 44, 45
Metmann [Matmon-Cohen], Fania, 21
Metmann [Matmon-Cohen], Yehuda Leib, 21
militarism, 101
moshavot (Jewish agricultural villages; sing. *moshava*), 36, 39, 40, 42, 49, 53, 54, 56, 72, 78, 97

206

Index

Motherland songs, 163, 179
muscular Judaism, 60, 79, 164

Nardi, Nahum, 167, 174
Narodniks, 168
Navon, Aryeh, 148
negation of exile, 24
Neve Tzedek, 62
New Hebraism, 1, 68, 93, 94
Nikova, Rina, 93, 94
Nimrod (statue), 140, 139
Nordau, Max, 60, 71, 75, 79, 90, 101,
    103, 111

Oliphant, Laurence, 37, 38
Omer (festival), 94, 111, 117, 119,
    120, 121, 122, 123
Oppenheimer, Franz, 44
oratorios, 180, 182
Orenstein, Margalit, 92, 93, 94, 95
"Our Barns Are Full of Grain" (מלאו
    אסמינו בר, song), 176
Oz, Amos, 193, 194, 195

Palestine Opera, 180
Palestinians, 52, 54, 59, 93, 94, 136,
    149, 159, 172, 186, 194
passion play, 115, 116
Passover, 113
pastoral concept, 11, 35, 60, 113, 122
Pinnes, Yechiel, 168
Pioneers (opera), 181
Puhachevska (Puhachevsky), Nehama,
    18
Purim, 106

Raab, Esther, 30, 31
Raad, Khalil, 149
Raban, Ze'ev, 135
Rabbinic Hebrew, 10
Rabinowitz, Yaacov, 31
Ramat Yohanan, Kibbutz, 94, 123
Ravina, Menashe, 172, 178
Rishon Letzion, 18, 22
Rosendorf Quartet, The, 161, 162,
    183
Rosh Pina, 40
Rothschild, Baron Edmond de, 53
Rubin, Reuven, 133, 137

Rubinowitz-Hare'uveni, Ephraim, 157
Ruschkewitz, Peretz [Fritz], 144, 146

Sambursky, Daniel, 171, 174
Schatz, Boris, 60, 130, 131, 133, 136,
    138, 144, 153, 157
Schloss, Rut, 148
Schocken, Salman, 143, 144
Scholem, Gershom, 28, 31
Sejera, 80, 90
Semitic language (Hebrew), 27
"The Sermon,", 192
Seter, Mordechai, 188, 189
Shaham, Nathan, 161
Shaked, Gershon, 31
Shalita, Yisrael, 176, 177, 179
Shamir [Sheftelowitz] brothers, 153, 154
Sharet, Yehuda, 115, 177
Shavu'ot (Pentecost), 117
Shearing Festival, 120
Shelleg, Assaf, 183, 184, 188
Shellem, Matityahu, 101, 120, 121,
    122, 173, 175
Shenhar, Itzhak, 125
shibutz, 11
Shlonsky, Abraham, 31
Shlonsky, Verdina, 184
Shochat, Manya, 90, 92
Shoham, Hizky, 117, 123, 124
Siedmann-Freud, Tom, 144
Smetana, Bedřich, 162, 183
Smilansky, Moshe, 29, 72, 74, 81
Smolenskin, Peretz, 14, 17
Sokolow, Nahum, 128
Sons of Arabia, The, 29
Sparta, 89
Spiegel, Nina, 97
St. Barbe Baker, Richard, 59
Stutschewsky, Joachim, 162, 176

Tagger, Siona, 138
Technion, 23, 44, 118
Tel Aviv, 62
Tel Hai, 92
Templers, 37, 40, 56
Theodor (opera), 190
Travels of Benjamin the Third, 16, 25
Tu Bishvat, 100, 101, 111, 123, 125
Tumarkin, Yigal, 142

Index

207

Twain, Mark, 52
Tzemach, Shlomo, 13, 18

Ussishkin, Menachem, 27

Wagner, Richard, 164, 166, 183, 187
Water Festival, 120
"We Shall Build our Land" (נבנה ארצנו, song), 175
Weinberg, Jacob, 181

Yana'it Ben-Zvi, Rachel, 90, 112
Yelin, David, 20, 27
Yelin, Ita, 20

Yemeni, 83, 93, 94, 109, 134, 166, 187
Yizhar, S., 34
Yocheved bat Miriam, 31
Youth of Abraham (opera), 181

Zaïd, Alexander, 78, 89, 91, 92, 112
Zaïd, Zipora, 80, 90, 91, 92
Zamir, Emanuel, 179
Zefira, Bracha, 166, 166, 167
Zehavi, David, 119, 174, 176
Zerubavel, Evyatar, 126
Zionist Congresses, 1, 17, 111, 127, 178